Postmodernism and Politics

Postmodernism
and Politics

Edited and Introduced by
Jonathan Arac

Theory and History of Literature, Volume 28

University of Minnesota Press, Minneapolis

Published by the University of Minnesota Press
2037 University Avenue Southeast, Minneapolis MN 55414.
Published simultaneously in Canada
by Fitzhenry & Whiteside Limited, Markham.
Printed in the United States of America.

Earlier versions of Chapters 1–8 formed part of a *boundary 2* symposium
(11. 1–2, 1982–83) and appear here by arrangement with the State University of New York at Binghamton, publisher of *boundary 2*.

Library of Congress Cataloging-in-Publication Data
Main entry under title:

Postmodernism and politics.

   (Theory and history of literature ; v. 28)
   Bibliography: p.
   Includes index.
   1. Criticism — Addresses, essays, lectures.
2. Politics and literature — Addresses, essays, lectures.
3. Postmodernism — Addresses, essays, lectures.
4. Marxist criticism — Addresses, essays, lectures.
I. Arac, Jonathan, 1945–   II. Series.
PN98.P64P67 1986   801'.95'0904   85-28835
ISBN 0-8166-1467-9
ISBN 0-8166-1468-7 (pbk.)

The University of Minnesota is an
equal-opportunity educator and employer.

Contents

Theory and History of Literature
Edited by Wlad Godzich and Jochen Schulte-Sasse

Acknowledgments

First thanks are due to W. V. Spanos, who made possible an earlier, larger version of this project as a special double issue of *boundary 2* (11.1–2, 1982–83). The State University of New York at Binghamton generously allowed this new use of material in which they hold copyright. I am deeply grateful to those whose excellent essays in *boundary 2* could not be used here, as focus was narrowed chronologically, geographically, and linguistically: Joseph A. Buttigieg, Judith Kegan Gardiner, Michael Holquist, Abdul R. JanMohamed, Ned Lukacher, Jeffrey Mehlman, and Doris Sommer. I appreciate their support of this transformed collection. Thanks also to those whose contributions are included here; our work together over several years and layers of revision has been continuously rewarding.

Introduction
Jonathan Arac

In the two decades since it first consciously began to define itself, postmodern criticism has chosen to be worldy. Not that it is urbane; this is not a world in which one can or should too easily be at home. Yet the struggle against received forms of reading, writing, and public discourse has not been mundane either. Philosophy, and its difficulties, served a necessary function in countering the technicist emphases of New Criticism and structuralism alike, as well as in marking the difference between a simple quest for relevance and a movement that was willing to wield the weapons of criticism in all their cultural elaboration. Then, in the seventies, postmodernism experienced an exhilarating but unsettling confluence with poststructuralism, the critique of method, the philosophic cure, that sprung up athwart structuralism.

Now that the sixties have faded emphatically into a past, the radical social and political activities, the urgency of questioning that formed the atmosphere from which postmodernism condensed, no longer define our immediate world. They must not be repressed, however; we must solicit the uncanny without becoming somnambulists. This need locates the dialogue between postmodern criticism and the Anglo-American renewal of Marxism that is itself a product of the sixties. The problems of "Western Marxism" are well known from discussions by Perry Anderson and Russell Jacoby, and Edward Said has pertinently exposed the dangers of "traveling theory." Nonetheless, this new Marxism and postmodernism share the conviction that literature and theory and criticism are not only contemplative, not mere superstructure, but active; they share commitments to human life in history. In short, they share the world.

It would be foolish, however, to suggest that this beginning heralds the dawn of a new day. Irving Howe recently looked back to the founding of *Dissent* in 1954 and ruefully explained its premise: "We were saying . . . that socialism in America had to be seen mostly as an intellectual problem before it could even hope to become a viable movement" (*Margin of Hope* 236). At about the same time as Howe's explanation, *Diacritics* published an interview with Fredric Jameson, in which his own current theoretical concerns and the project of *Social Text* are similarily summarized: "No real systemic change in this country will be possible without the minimal first step of the achievement of a social democratic movement [but] that first step will not be possible without two other preconditions . . . the creation of a Marxist intelligentsia, and that of a Marxist culture" (73). The congruence of analysis is striking, and the endurance of the problem is dismaying.

The bar between culture and politics in the United States that seems to be marked here has stood at least since the first great American novel appeared. Hawthorne set "The Prison Door" as the title of his first chapter. It stands between the "official," political life of "The Custom House" and the passionate, artistic representation of "The Scarlet Letter," and it blocks the passage from one to the other. Of these two unequal parts that together make up *The Scarlet Letter,* each may be read as the source of the other, yet each is unconscious of the other. The marks that trace their relations remain to be produced through our reading, beyond which lies a task of historical interpretation to revise our sense of politics in the American life of letters.

Postmodernism. *boundary 2* and the Wider Debate

The preceding remarks introduced a special issue of *boundary 2: a journal of postmodern literature*, from which the essays in this volume have been selected. The history of *boundary 2* therefore forms a first context for understanding them. When it was founded in the early 1970s, *boundary 2* projected a clear sense of the "postmodern"; as a university-based intervention in the world of literature, it stood against the classics of modernism as they had been interpreted and institutionalized by the New Criticism. A Sartrean, existential concern for the engagements of worldly life opposed New Critical emphasis on "impersonality" in its many forms, whether distance through myth, hardness through image, or lucidity through point of view. The journal's roots in phenomenology reached back from Sartre to Heidegger, toward a sense of temporality against New Critical modernist spatialization; and beyond Heidegger to Kierkegaard, who offered an understanding of irony quite different from that which was popularized by Robert Penn Warren and Cleanth Brooks. This renewed sense of irony enabled *boundary 2* critics to elaborate postmodern interpretations of Eliot, Joyce, Yeats, Conrad, and other modernist classics. The "postmodern" thus proved not straightforwardly chronological. It partook of a more complex hermeneutical temporality, which proved confusing to some observers (Berman 351, n. 24 and Jameson, "Politics of Theory," 55–56, n. 1) as the journal uncovered an ever-receding history of postmodernism through unsettling received New-Critical interpretations over the whole of Western literature. The best current statement of the journal's point of view is W. V. Spanos, "Postmodern Literature and Its Occasion."

A further complication in the position of *boundary 2* emerged over time in its relation to issues of political and social life. Although conceived from the beginning as oppositional, its concerns might at first have seemed those of a "personal" individualism, which, however full-bodied in comparison to New Criticism, would remain no more than an alternative aestheticism. Already by the middle of the 1940s, however, Sartre had visibly begun his own turn to politics, and Lucien Goldmann had offered the suggestion that Heidegger's existential phenomenology took its point of departure from the critique of "reification" by Georg Lukács in *History and Class Consciousness* (1923), to which *Being and Time* (1927) offered an ontological rather than historical analysis. Since, moreover, *boundary 2* had been founded in part as an attempt to prolong the energies of the 1960s, both its situation and its intellectual genealogy pointed toward what in fact occurred: postmodernism and politics came together in the journal's agenda. Yet Lukács's insistence on "totality" seemed suspiciously like that of the New Critics on the "tradition" or on the work as "icon." In confluence with contemporary revisions of Heidegger in France, the politics of *boundary 2* proved "deconstructive" like Derrida; like Foucault more concerned with the fields of "micropolitics." This acknowledgment of the micropolitical has allowed *boundary 2* to take seriously its location as an academic journal, rather than yearning nostalgically for the days of the independent man of letters and looking only with disabling self-contempt at the current place of literary intellectuals.

The postmodernism of *boundary 2* is only one of many varieties; these essays are part of a larger debate that has been going on around the notion. The discussion has been most notable for its international and interdisciplinary extent, running from architecture through the visual arts and music, through literature and history, to the social and natural sciences, while bringing in contributions from several European cultures beyond the anglophone world (see Hassan, "Postface 1982"). Yet almost no women have figured in the debate, even though many analysts include current feminism among the features of postmodernity. Nancy Fraser's important feminist critique of Habermas ("What's Critical") stands nearly alone (see also Kristeva), although Craig Owens and Andrew Ross have effectively situated feminist work by women in relation to postmodernism. A sampling of significant positions in the overall debate would include those of the English historian Perry Anderson, who was long editor of *New Left Review;* the Harvard sociologist Daniel Bell, whose collaboration with Irving Kristol on *The Public Interest* led to his characterization as a "neoconservative"; the German social philosopher Jürgen Habermas, who is often treated as the heir of Frankfurt-school critical theory; Fredric Jameson, who revitalized American Marxist cultural studies while Professor of French at Yale amid the controversy over deconstruction; Jean-François Lyotard, a French philosopher and former independent socialist activist, long involved with the critique of Stalinism; Richard Rorty, whose renewal of American pragmatism led him out of Princeton's philosophy department and into the pages of general literary and cultural journals.

Using even this limited group as a field for comparison, it becomes obvious how little the debate has reached clarity. To begin with, the debate is motivated by evaluative differences. The first significant literary discussions of the "postmodern" some quarter-century ago by Irving Howe and Harry Levin established a clear negative stance: the postmodern was a weak successor to the vigorous glory of literary modernism, brought about because mass society had eroded the artist's vital distance. During the sixties, a more complex attention to new modes of mass media in work by Leslie Fiedler, Susan Sontag, Richard Poirier, and above all Ihab Hassan (see "POSTmodernISM") helped to establish the context within which *boundary 2* appeared. In recent years, however, the initial hostility, exacerbated by a sense of beleaguerment, has fueled new antipostmodern projects like that of Hilton Kramer's *New Criterion*. So it remains even now typically the case that to "have a position" on postmodernism means not just to offer an analysis of its genesis and contours but to let the world know whether you are for it or against it, and in fairly bald terms. Thus Anderson, Bell, and Habermas all treat postmodernism as something that we could be spared if only people would trade excessive rhetoric for sensible analysis (at just these moments, however, their own rhetoric swells); Lyotard and Rorty, on the other hand, urge us to adopt postmodern positions. Jameson argues that postmodernism necessarily includes both positive and negative aspects, but that the notion helps us to make sense of our times and therefore should be used; to all who oppose the postmodern, however, this can seem no more than disguised advocacy.

It remains wholly unsettled whether the relation of the "postmodern" to the "modern" is more a break or a continuity. Anderson finds "modern" and "postmodern" alike terms that mask more important facts about the times they purport to describe; Bell finds the postmodern acting out principles that were already dangerous within modernism; and Lyotard finds in the postmodern a sublime potentiality that is realized in the modern, unsettling our usual conception of sequence. Habermas, Jameson, and Rorty agree in finding a significant break between the modern and the postmodern, but there is no consensus as to where the break falls. Jameson, perhaps because he is a professional student of literature, roughly identifies the modern with the first half of the twentieth century and the postmodern with what has come later. Habermas, perhaps because professionally a student of social philosophy, identifies the modern with the still-unfulfilled project of the eighteenth-century Enlightenment, while the postmodern remains a threatening shadow rather than something that has quite occurred. Rorty, perhaps because his defining professional engagement was with the analytic epistemological tradition, locates the modern with Descartes and finds the major contours of the postmodern already visible in Hegel.

In their methods of analysis, these figures fall into yet further combinations. Habermas, Lyotard, and Rorty all employ versions of "thin" or "philosophical" history to establish their points; in contrast, Anderson, Bell, and Jameson, even though also writing relatively brief treatments, draw upon a much wider range of empirical materials. On the other hand, Bell joins Lyotard and Rorty in de-emphasizing "totalizing" modes of description and explanation. Among these three, however, further splits appear.

Against attempts to ground Value in Humanity, Nature, or Reason, Rorty insists on the local contingencies of values, approaching a position like that of current literary theory on "interpretive communities." Yet Rorty still relies on the integrity of his local units. He therefore warns "the intellectual" not to become separated from "the social needs of his community" ("Habermas and Lyotard" 175), learning from American intellectuals' response to the Vietnam War, which acted "to separate the intellectuals from the moral consensus of the nation" ("Postmodernist Bourgeois Liberalism" 588). Lyotard's overall position seems to agree with Rorty's; Lyotard contrasts the *"grands récits"* (perhaps best translated "tall tales") that unify human history in the name of Emancipation (the French Revolution) or Speculation (the German university) or both (Marxism) with the language games of *"petits récits"* ("white lies") that operate over smaller units both conceptually and demographically. Yet in exploring "the differend" (dispute, conflict, difference), Lyotard looks to situations where power and language intersect to victimize minorities wrongly treated as if they were members of a community from which they actually differ in ways that are "not presentable under the rules of knowledge" (14). As against Rorty, Lyotard does not trust the integrity of "communities" any more than of "totality."

In a mode that he might blush to find Lyotard characterizing as postmodern, Daniel Bell insists against both functionalists and Marxists that there is no integral entity called "society"; between the separate realms of the polity, the economy, and the culture "disjunction" prevails. Bell can therefore assert, in a statement that would seem to be so scandalous that his critics in the debate do not even comment on it, that he is "a socialist in economics, a liberal in politics, and a conservative in culture" ("Modernism and Capitalism" 206). This takes to an extreme a notion like that of the "relative autonomy" with which Althusser made possible fresh Marxist thought regarding questions of the state and of culture, and which remains crucial in the attempts by Anderson and Jameson at a "totalizing" frame of argument. Habermas, while insisting on Weber's neo-Kantian separation of rationality into separate spheres of knowledge, morality, and taste (corresponding to science, social organization, and art), tries to establish a new, if reduced, totality of "everyday life," which in order to flourish must be kept in contact with the results of all three spheres.

It might be thought that the question of art's autonomy would only be a special case of "totality," but in fact yet-different alignments emerge on this issue, which has been crucial, as we have already noted, since the beginning of the postmodernism debate. In Anderson's argument, surprisingly close to traditional Marxist "reflection" theory, the possibilities of art are determined by social conditions but art does not have the power to alter those conditions; for Lyotard, art's value depends on its maintaining itself as a separate "language game," distinct from the discourses of power. On the other side, Rorty's pragmatic anti-Kantianism grants, and encourages, that art and criticism may intervene in speculation and debate on issues that would traditionally have been reserved for natural or moral philosophy; Bell, however, is distressed at the incursion achieved by cultural values into the separate realms of politics and, especially, economics. Habermas and Jameson stand as if explicitly opposed to each other. For Habermas, the postmodern is the threat, carried on from surrealism, to deautonomize art, freeing its energies for use in all of life, but he claims that this is based on a misunderstanding, for: "When the containers of an autonomously developed cultural space are shattered, the contents get dispersed. Nothing remains from a desublimated meaning or a destructured form" ("Modernity" 11). Jameson argues that capitalist reification has already destroyed any cultural autonomy, but that cultural modes and practices are now spread throughout the fabric of social life by a process of "acculturation" ("Periodizing the 60s" 201). What remains, therefore, are opportunities for cultural production and criticism much more significant than those that had existed under earlier conditions. The struggle over what Gramsci called "hegemony" (see Williams, "Base and Superstructure" and Buttigieg) in everyday life becomes a significantly political activity once there is no longer a decisive separation of the cultural sphere. The example of Latin American liberation theology powerfully exemplifies the political potential of cultural issues.

I shall return to this question whether a change in the place of art has occurred and if so with what consequences for the power of culture, but first it is necessary to address an embarrassing fact that this survey of some exemplary positions in the postmodernism debate has rendered painfully plain. A great deal of the controversy in this debate depends on misunderstandings, not at all surprising across so wide a range of disciplinary and national traditions, which obstruct significant direct engagement with the arguments, motives, and implications of the various positions. (In "Mapping the Postmodern," Huyssen offers the most specific discriminations of American, French, and German emphases.) I shall first examine several such misunderstandings in one of the most important essays in the debate, and I shall then turn to one of the most important issues associated with the debate as it has been conducted within the profession of literary study in the United States.

Postmodernism. An Exemplary Essay: Habermas on Modernity

Jürgen Habermas's "Modernity versus Postmodernity" brought the discussion of postmodernism into its current phase. Originally an address upon receiving the Theodor W. Adorno Prize from the city of Frankfurt in 1980, it was subsequently delivered at New York University, translated as the lead article with a notable response by Andreas Huyssen in *New German Critique,* and republished as the first essay in the excellent interdisciplinary reader on postmodernism *The Anti-Aesthetic* (under the title "Modernity—An Incomplete Project"). It provoked responses in the French journal *Critique* by Lyotard and Rorty. Lyotard's reply has appeared in English both in a collection edited by Ihab Hassan and as a supplement to his earlier *The Postmodern Condition.* Rorty's response to Habermas and Lyotard has been published in English both by *Praxis International* and in *Habermas and Modernity,* which includes Habermas's response to the controversy ("Questions and Counterquestions"). The significance of "Modernity versus Postmodernity" is manifold. It attempts to reassert a reasoned commitment to the Enlightenment while speaking under the auspices of Adorno, who in *Dialectic of Enlightenment* found contemporary totalitarianism prepared for by the Enlightenment ideal of dominating nature. It participates in Habermas's "reconstruction of historical materialism," which draws upon all the intellectual resources of the twentieth century in order to redeem the nineteenth-century Marxist science of society. (Thus Habermas is the last major figure in Martin Jay's massive *Marxism and Totality.*) Habermas's essay thus stands for a left-wing progressive view of world history, underwritten by his extraordinary erudition and seriousness and projected in his thousand-page *Theory of Communicative Action.* Yet in making his case, Habermas rapidly dismisses competing political and theoretical positions with an inaccuracy, a failure of understanding, that is shocking in one whose best work so depends on probingly sympathetic critique of others, and whose long-standing ethical norm has been the transcendence of "systematically distorted communication."

Habermas honors Daniel Bell as the "most brilliant of the American neoconservatives," and he rightly recognizes Bell's concern with the "dissolution" of the Protestant ethic that had long dominated American values and with the aftermath of that dissolution, the "adversary culture" of "modernism" that now seems to reign, despite the exhaustion of its own original impulses, "dominant but dead," transformed into postmodernism. Habermas goes on to charge that in Bell's analysis, "Neoconservatism shifts onto cultural modernism the uncomfortable burdens of a more or less successful capitalist modernization of the economy and society." (This echoes a point from Raymond Williams, cited by Richard Wolheim [35] and Gerald Graff [95 n.] and echoed by Marshall Berman [122–23 and 357, n. 21] and Michael Rogin [152].) Habermas then summarizes Bell's prescription: "What new norm will put a brake on the levelling caused by the social welfare state, so that the virtues of individual competition can again dominate? Bell sees a religious revival as the only solution'' (6–7). I know no treatment of Habermas that challenges these claims; (although Habermas himself has moderated them, without acknowledging the change [''Neoconservative Culture Criticism'' 82]) we all are grateful for the rhetorical vigor that sweeps away the threat of neoconservatism. Yet these claims do no justice to Bell's arguments, however frustrating we may sometimes find his loose, repetitive, and not wholly consistent exposition.

Bell's major work addressed by Habermas is *The Cultural Contradictions of Capitalism* (1976), successor to *The Coming of Post-Industrial Society* (1973). In keeping with Bell's emphasis on the ''disjunction'' of society, economy, and culture, the later book emphasizes the cultural as the earlier had the economic. Yet Bell understands that his different realms interact with each other, with effects that include both reinforcement and hindrance. Let me try to sketch Bell's argument as clearly as possible while still acknowledging its blurrinesses. Some five centuries ago, ''modernity'' produced two new figures, the ''bourgeois entrepreneur'' and the ''independent artist'' (freed by the market from patronage) (16). Similar in their origins, these two figures diverged: ''radical in economics, the bourgeoisie became conservative in morals and cultural taste'' (17), that is to say, developed the Protestant-ethic character structure. During the ''early development of capitalism,'' the radical ''unrestrained economic impulse'' was held back by this character structure, but in later capitalist development ''the Protestant Ethic was undermined not by [cultural] modernism but by capitalism itself'': ''The greatest single engine in the destruction of the Protestant Ethic was the invention of the installment plan'' (21). Bell summarizes: ''The breakup of the traditional bourgeois value system, in fact, was brought about by the bourgeois economic system—by the free market, to be precise. This is the source of the contradiction of capitalism in American life'' (55). Thus he finds that ''the erosion of traditional American values took place on two levels'': in the ''realm of culture and ideas,'' to be sure, ''but a more fundamental transformation was occurring in the social structure itself: the change in the motivations and rewards of the economic system'' (74).

More recently, Bell summarized this topic:

> Bourgeois capitalism, as the sociological form of the modern economy, and avant-garde modernism, as the victorious feature of the culture, had common roots in their repudiation of the past, in their dynamism, in the search for novelty and sanction of change. Yet, inevitably, the different axial principles of these realms (the techno-economic realm segmenting a person into ''roles,'' the culture emphasizing the achievement of the whole person) brought the bourgeois economic system into sharp conflict with the modernist culture. . . . Thus are discerned contradictions in the fundamental structures of modern society [that is, *between* realms]. Within the realms, other contradictions have developed. . . . From the 1920s modern corporate capitalism, being geared to mass production and

consumption, has promoted a hedonism that has undercut the Protestant Ethic which was the initial motivation or legitimation for individuals in bourgeois society. (*Winding Passage* xv)

Bell does not blame modernism for the damage done by capitalism; instead he analyzes the "cultural contradiction of capitalism" as precisely its own power to undermine the human context on which its success had depended. As one who is a "socialist in economics," Bell has no reason to reject social welfare or to require "individual competition" once more to dominate. He does not believe that the political liberties he values depend on capitalism, and his notion of the "public household" seeks "to detach political liberalism from bourgeois society," for they are only "associated by origin, but not actually interdependent" (*Cultural Contradictions* 26). It is true that he looks to a religious revival, but this is part of being a "conservative culture," not in economics or politics. In the realm of culture "modernism has been the seducer" (19) by undoing "the hold of restraint" and urging "the acceptance of impulse" (18). To be a cultural conservative for Bell cannot mean merely preferring Mann to Barth, Beethoven to Boulez, or Shakespeare to Woody Allen, because in his historical scheme all these figures have worked along the axial principle of the self. No less than Fredric Jameson or Perry Anderson, Bell if taken seriously would have us trying to imagine a new art that responds not to the self, rather to communal norms known in the past as religion but that we must invent anew for our future. (I regret Bell takes no interest in the unselving energies of such a postmodern work as *Gravity's Rainbow*, which follows Slothrop from the uniquely determining perversion of his Pavlovian youth along an anti-Oedipal path until he finally becomes "a crossroads, a living intersection" [625], renewing one of Longinus's tropes for sublime mobility of identity.) In the meantime, however, Bell adapts Gramsci's analysis of hegemony ("Modernism and Capitalism" 216) to suggest that after many centuries in which bourgeois principles dominated culture, especially in religion and education, there is now a "radical disjunction" between cultural and social values, and that "such disjunctions . . . historically have paved the way for more direct social revolutions" (53). That is to say, precisely because it is now commodified as postmodernism and no longer at its former distance, the antihegemonic force of modernism can now more effectively undo capitalism.

Just as Habermas wished at the beginning of his essay to sweep away American "neoconservatism," which I have tried to suggest is hardly the best way of categorizing Bell, so he also at the end turned against what he considers the self-contradictory "Anti-modernism" based on "modernistic attitudes" of the French "young conservatives" from "Georges Bataille via Michel Foucault to Jacques Derrida" (14). (Habermas develops this topic in "The French Path to Postmodernity.") I shall discuss this issue at greater length in my next section, in relation to the questions surrounding "representation." It is interesting to note, however, that this interpretation by Habermas has not gone uncontested, for there are many, among them Fraser and Jay ("Habermas and Modernism"), to whom it remains important to emphasize the radical potential within poststructuralism. Nonetheless, there are so many who echo Habermas, ranging from Jameson ("Postmodernism" 57) and Berman (34–35) and the British sociologist Anthony Giddens (224–25) to Rorty, that it is worth devoting a little more attention to the problem. The fundamental objection offered to Foucault (and with little change to Derrida, but often by different critics) is that his work saps the basis for social action. For one who has so chided our nostalgic wish for grounding as Rorty has, it is remarkable that this becomes the basis for his criticism of Foucault: "Foucault affects to write from a point of view light-years away from the problems of contemporary society. His own efforts at social reform (e.g. of prisons) seem to have no connection with his exhibition of the way in which the 'humane' approach to penal reform tied in with the needs of the modern state" ("Habermas and Lyotard" 171–72). Rorty has forgotten here that the purpose of Foucault's prison work was not humane reform (that is to say, providing a new representation of prisoners by which they could be better known) but to facilitate prisoners' attempts at representing themselves. Moreover, Rorty does not consider that in defining the project of *Discipline and Punish* as "writing the history of the present" (31), Foucault allied himself with Nietzschean genealogy. This genealogical practice transforms history from a judgment on the past in the name of a present truth to a "counter-memory" that combats our current modes of truth and justice, helping us to understand and change the present by placing it in a new relation to the past ("Nietzsche, Genealogy, History" 160, 163–64; cf. Megill 243–44). Instead, Rorty cites "writing the history of the present" as evidence of a "remoteness" that arrogates "the eye of a future historian." Rorty therefore concludes that "there is no 'we' to be found in Foucault's writings," but surely a pragmatist can acknowledge that making a "we" is up to us as well as to the author we read. Foucault often claimed that his works were offered as tools; we join him then by using them, and enough of us have done so over the last decade that it should by this time be clear: those who claim that his work depresses are only saying that they have no use for it (although it has evidently energized them at least to rejection; only putative "others" are wholly paralyzed by its torpedo charms).

For the reader at home in the Anglo-American traditions of literary study, probably the strangest moment in Habermas's essay comes in his discussion of the need to maintain an autonomous sphere of art, while also allowing everyday life access to that sphere:

> Albrecht Wellmer has drawn my attention to one way that an aesthetic experience which is not framed around the experts' critical judgments of taste can have its significance altered: as soon as such an experience is

used to illuminate the life-historical situation and is related to life problems, it enters into a language game which is no longer that of the aesthetic critic. The aesthetic experience then not only renews the interpretation of our needs in whose light we perceive the world. It permeates as well our cognitive significations and our normative expectations and changes the manner in which all these moments refer to one another. (13)

What is strange is not the set of connections made, but the idea that without Albrecht Wellmer's inspired suggestion, Habermas would never have thought of the relations between art and life that are the basis of Wordsworth's and Coleridge's poetics, of Emerson's writing, of Arnold's criticism, of Lawrence's "art for *my* sake," of Lionel Trilling's teaching career, and Leavis's belief that close literary analysis was "the discovery and animation of central human values" and therefore in our world "involved you in an assault on a whole system of social and cultural and academic values" (Williams, "Cambridge English" 185).

Perhaps no one formed in the American literary academy can really understand what the meaning of art's autonomy has been in philosophic aesthetics (one reason for Richard Rorty's importance is his ability to speak for literature to philosophy). Addressing "The Crisis in Culture" as long ago as 1960, Hannah Arendt observed, "The great works of art are no less misused when they serve purposes of self-education or self-cultivation than when they serve any other purposes; it may be as useful and legitimate to look at a picture in order to perfect one's knowledge of a given period as it is useful and legitimate to use a painting in order to hide a hole in the wall" (203). Yet in those same years, Lionel Trilling taught *Heart of Darkness* and *Death in Venice* explicitly as "background" for his course in modern literature. Following the analysis but not the evaluation of Peter Bürger's brilliant *Theory of the Avant-Garde,* Habermas locates the programmatic, antimodernist "negation of culture" among the surrealists, as one of their "two mistakes" (10–11). Trilling, however, found the essential note of all modern literature the "disenchantment of our culture with culture itself," its "hostility to civilization" ("Teaching Modern Literature" 3).

The power of modern literature, for Trilling, is its uniquely "personal" appeal, its capacity to shake our beliefs about all aspects of our life that have been settled by society, tradition, or habit, and his essay "On the Teaching of Modern Literature" becomes what it describes. Moving from Trilling's own "personal experience" (3) as a teacher, the essay ironically strips away the pieties of literary study by charting the diminishment effected upon both our literary masterpieces and our selves by their academic institutionalization: "More and more, as the universities liberalize themselves and turn their beneficent imperialistic gaze upon what is called Life Itself, the feeling grows among our educated classes that little can be experienced unless it is validated by some established intellectual discipline, with the result that experience loses much of its personal immediacy for us and becomes part of an accredited societal activity" (10). Habermas would condemn Trilling's view as antimodernism for its distrust of liberal rationalization, and Bell would condemn it as modernism for its prime emphasis on experience (he draws the notion of "adversary culture" from the preface to the book in which this essay appears). Foucault might have found some interesting resonances in the critique of a "beneficent imperialistic gaze." (Trilling's colleague, collaborator, and student Steven Marcus was instrumental in making Foucault's work known, and as "post-modern" [39], in the United States.)

Postmodernism. An Exemplary Issue: Representation

I cannot resolve the misunderstandings that I have been exposing, but I think that the debate over postmodernism will benefit from this preliminary attempt at clarifying some problems in one of its most important statements. By the same token, I wish to offer a preliminary inquiry into one of the most vexed areas in contemporary theory, that of representation. Here I shall advance a hypothesis of my own about some relations of modern and postmodern.

It would be fruitless to detail all the critics and theorists who have helped to establish "the so-called critique of representation" as a major "form of what must be called postmodernism generally" (Jameson, "Periodizing the 60s" 194). This discussion ranges over the history of philosophy, bearing particularly on epistemology; the theory of history, whether as concept, practice of writing, or course of actions; debates over politics, whether Marxist attacks on liberalism or libertarian attacks on Marxism; and the history and future of literature, as the question of "realism" and the larger issue of "narrative" overall. Jacques Derrida ironically notes the consensus among critics that postmodern theorists, especially the French figures associated with poststructuralism, hold one simple view: "representation is bad" ("Sending" 304); figures as diverse as the DDR Marxist Robert Weimann (in much the richest engagement), the American neorealist Gerald Graff, the English semiotic materialists Rosalind Coward and John Ellis, and the late deconstructive Romanist Eugenio Donato, among many others, can all agree. I disagree, and I am happy to find myself accompanied by Hal Foster, Craig Owens, and Gregory Ulmer in their contributions to *The Anti-Aesthetic*, as well as by Fredric Jameson and Edward Said in much of their recent work. Nonetheless, it remains worth trying to spell out the contours of the problem (on which see also Spariosu), in the hope of changing the consensus.

A residual modernist problematic obstructs our understanding on issues of representation. This problematic contrasts an antirepresentational antihumanism against humanist defenders of representation—across so wide and distinguished a spectrum as that from E. H. Gombrich to Erich Auerbach to Georg Lukács. But current advanced theory crosses these lines: it is antihumanist, but it acknowledges—critically—our enmeshment in representation. This change may be related to changes in dominant modes of cultural practice, from easel paintings and novels to films and electronic media, and these in turn to the transformation from national to global modes of social and economic relations.

The received belief that "advanced" theorists are "against" representation has two damaging consequences. On the one hand it seems to require us to discard the concerns and results of much postmodern inquiry if we are to pursue the play of representations in the world, where the power of representation is something sought, indeed passionately struggled for, by groups that consider themselves dominated by alien and alienating representations (e.g., see Said, "Permission to Narrate"). On the other hand, however, it encourages an ultraleft-ist avant-gardism which assumes that any critic seriously willing to work with "representation" and its inevitably associated notions of "narrative" and "history," must be dismissed as a reactionary hierarchalist. Both of these positions deprive us of valuable critical resources; both tend to paralyze our critical enter-prise into internecine warfare—the further spinning of "theory" without any concrete engagement.

I cannot present the details of how this particular belief has become established within the American academy. I shall only try to demonstrate that much crucial postmodern theory is not against representation and to sketch the recent history of the confused transition from modern to postmodern views on representation. I shall not try to define representation; we know well enough the different things we mean by it. People do it all the time, and the crucial issue is by what means, to what purpose, with what effect—pragmatic questions rather than the essentialist fuss whether we have finally found something that will not prove after all just to be representation again. I will venture to represent the history of representation in a particular narrative, which follows.

The tangled historicity of "representation" offers no convenient place to start. Plato, Aristotle, and Descartes are particularly instructive because they mark the major line of Western metaphysics, yet each strives to reject his predecessor. Plato wished to banish the poets for their practice of mimesis, but to Aristotle mimesis guaranteed the value of poetry, Descartes helped overthrow both Aris-totelian physics and Platonic epistemology; knowledge itself became a matter of representation—the tradition Rorty has swerved from in *Philosophy and the Mirror of Nature*.

For the modernist case against representation, Virginia Woolf is exemplary. *To the Lighthouse* holds an especially privileged place in discussions of represen-tation because of the analysis Erich Auerbach devoted to it in the final chapter of *Mimesis*. There he found that Woolf challenged the very premises of order on which the Western representational tradition had depended, even as at the same time she culminated that tradition through her work's unremitting attention to the most mundane of everyday details, rendered with the richest existential seriousness. If Woolf's overall practice, then, stands as part of the modernist case against representation, that case is rendered significantly visible at memorable moments of the novel. The philosophical impasse of Mr. Ramsay—his inability to move from Q in the alphabet of thought on to R—humorously images that of the whole tradition in which he stands (part of the tangled heritage of Descartes) through the anecdotal figure of fat David Hume, stuck in a bog, and depending on the help of a woman of the people, who requires of him that he say the Lord's Prayer.

Lily Briscoe's painting has clear analogies to Woolf's own project of writing. In a remarkable moment, Woolf follows the consciousness of Mrs. Ramsay as she dissolves into a "wedge-shaped core of darkness" (95), but that moment has been prefigured in Lily's pictorial treatment. Mr. Bankes asks Lily, "What did she wish to indicate by the triangular purple shape, 'just there'?'':

> It was Mrs. Ramsay reading to James, she said. She knew his objection—
> that no one could tell it for a human shape. But she had made no attempt
> at likeness, she said. . . . If there, in that corner, it was bright, here, in
> this, she felt the need of darkness. . . . Mr. Bankes was interested.
> Mother and child, then—objects of universal veneration, and in this case
> the mother was famous for her beauty—might be reduced, he pondered,
> to a purple shadow without irreverence.
> But the picture was not of them, she said. (81)

This sequence exemplifies what the modernist philosopher Ortega y Gasset was calling the "dehumanization of art," yet Woolf also exposes women's "humanity" as no more than objectification in man's gaze, even of "veneration" (same root as Venus and venereal).

My own language here, when I write of rendering and prefiguring and exemplifying, exploits the resources of representation in order to discuss what I claim is antirepresentational. But to take a stand against representation is not in fact to escape it; by and large modernist polemic does not succeed, and confusion has come from taking its claims for results.

Another crucial aspect of the modernist case against representation involves Marxist politics. Georg Lukács was both the most important Marxist literary theorist of our century and also closely involved with the institutional dimensions of revolutionary culture; from the 1920s through the 1960s he defended the tradition of critical realism, always associated with representation. Since Lukács was identified with representation, with realism, with humanism, and also with Stalinism (if for no other reason than his survival in Moscow during the purge trials), antirepresentationalism became not only a defense of modernism, but also a declaration of anti-Stalinism. Popular-front aesthetics in the United States provided a similar target against which the *Partisan Review* critics could stand for modernism and against Stalinism. I do not think representation is Stalinist (for all its complexities, the case of Solzhenitsyn clearly shows the techniques of realist representation used to criticize Stalinism, as Lukács was quick to observe), but we cannot understand antirepresentationalism in our time without understanding this linkage. From the point of view I am developing here, even so notable an advocate of postmodernism as Lyotard echoes the modernist position when he deplores claims for "realism" as "desire for a return of terror, for the realization of the fantasy to seize reality" and urges instead, "Let us wage war on totality" ("What Is Postmodernism?" 81; see also Lacoue-Labarthe).

The major recent anti-Lukácsian Marxist theorist—Althusser—also rested immense weight upon the term "representation" (revealing residual Stalinism?). For Althusser ideology "represents the imaginary relationship of individuals to their real conditions of existence" ("Ideology" 162), and by the psychoanalytic premises that support this view, even in communist society ideology will persist, and therefore also representation. In *Reading Capital*, a German term for representation, *Darstellung* (29), names the "structural causality" (188) that operates through overdetermination and that Marx showed but never named as such. To produce this absent concept, and in language like that of Derrida's contemporaneous essays, Althusser looks to those moments when Marx represents the capitalist system as "mechanism, a machinery, a machine, a construction" (192). And this is *Darstellung:*

> the very existence of this machinery in its effects: the mode of existence
> of the stage direction (*mise en scène*) [= *Darstellung*] of the theater which
> is simultaneously its own stage, its own script, its own actors, the theater
> whose spectators can, on occasion, be spectators only because they are
> first of all forced to be its actors, caught by the constraints of a script and
> parts whose authors they cannot be, since it is in essence *an authorless
> theater*. (193)

The language of such an anti-*auteur* theory points toward a third aspect of the modernist case against representation, which involves the context of mass culture. For plot was the basis of Aristotelian mimesis, and plot has also been understood as the backbone of mass-cultural appeal, so that high culture retreated from plot, and neoplatonic arguments against plot's seductive power have been renewed. Indeed, in my elementary class on literary theory, students confronted with Aristotle's one-hundred-word summary of the action of the *Odyssey*—a decisive moment in the history of Western thinking about literature, a demonstration of the analytic power to achieve over a thousandfold reduction, the capacity to perform what the *Ion* suggests neither Socrates nor anyone else in his culture could accomplish—and asked to try a similar exercise on some work that they know and admire, regularly complain that in its plot, the admired work is indistinguishable from something they value so little as a Harlequin romance. Postmodern inquiry has renewed the attempts of Bertolt Brecht and Walter Benjamin to achieve a positive use of mass culture, but modernist hostility to mass culture has ranged from the economic determinism of the Frankfurt-school belief that its place in "the culture industry" necessarily dooms a work to cooperate with the system of domination (a view still fiercely asserted by Wolin), to the formalist conviction, which flourished in *Screen* in the 1970s, that particular signifying practices in themselves are politically reactionary (if realist) or progressive.

The immediate horizon for current debate about representation is "French theory" from the 1960s. It is worth recalling that this moment of theoretical explosion was closely linked with the prestige of China, just at the moment of the Cultural Revolution. Althusser draws significantly on the then recently discovered text of Mao "On Contradiction"; and current events in China clearly bear also on Derrida's speculations about the ideographic, and on Foucault's beginning *The Order of Things* with a fantasy from Borges about a Chinese encyclopedia. My focus now, however, is restricted to a particular institutionalization that this body of work has undergone in America: the view that as a whole it is against representation, and that in particular Derrida is. Such a view dominates the very series in which this volume is appearing. In *The Structural Allegory*, John Fekete refers to Derrida's "rejection of representation" and specifies that Derrida's "attack on representation" strives to undermine the "structure of representation" because that is the "epistemological foundation" of structuralism (235). Jochen Schulte-Sasse, coeditor of the series, in introducing Peter Bürger's *Theory of the Avant-Garde*, claims that Derrida "subjects to thorough critique the notion of representation" as a part of his attack against "epistemological closures." Schulte-Sasse finds Derrida guilty of employing "the same suspect strategies of exclusion" as does the metaphysics he is deconstructing, a "clear and neat oppositional structure (xxi, xxv).

I find several problems here. It colonizes Derrida all too easily within institutional Anglo-Saxon philosophy to consider him an epistemologist, even an anti-epistemologist; as might be expected of a Heideggerian, he is far more an ontologist than an epistemologist. Rorty, whose work influences those I have been citing, himself knows better in his direct discussions of Derrida, but this mistake (facilitated by the predominance of the term "representation" in Rorty's critique of foundational epistemology and the term's undeniable prominence in Derrida's work) is part of what has endeared his work to the literary academy. Even more important, however, is that Derrida simply does not attack representation; even where he may be quoted to this effect, he has more to say on the matter.

Derrida's *Speech and Phenomena* argues that what Husserl thought could be treated as "immediate" is instead always already mediated by representation. The inescapability of representation is Derrida's deconstructive point against the metaphysical fantasy of pure presence. Derrida defined the "prime intention" and "ultimate scope" of the book as "affirming *Perception does not exist* or that what is called perception is not primordial, that somehow everything 'begins' by re-presentation" (45 n.) The key term "trace" enters the book in order to elucidate the "re" of representation as part of the most fundamental structure of repetition that is "more 'primordial' than what is phenomenologically primordial" (67).

In *Of Grammatology* it is Rousseau (not Derrida) whose praise of the assembled people is "always a critique of representation" (296). On the other hand, in unraveling the strange graphic of supplementarity, Derrida is perfectly clear that he is following the thread of representation. The design that traces the relation of forces between the two movements of the text, Derrida writes, "seems to us to be represented in the handling of the concept of the supplement" (163). This claim inaugurates his reading, and at its end Derrida hauntingly concatenates the "entire series of supplementary significations" that he has teased out from Rousseau: "the North, winter, death, imagination, representation, the arousal of desires" (309).

Speech and Phenomena features Derrida's claim that *"Phenomenological reduction is a scene, a theater stage"* (86). His whole early essay on Freud operates by staging, as a *mise en scène*, a *Darstellung*, a representation, two series of metaphors in Freud, both of which Freud represents in terms of further instruments of representation: "Psychical *content* will be *represented* by a text whose essence is irreducibly graphic. The *structure* of the psychical *apparatus* will be *represented* by a writing machine" (199). The layered repetitions of representation here may evoke the passage from Husserl that Derrida quotes epigraphically and then again at the end of *Speech and Phenomena*: "A name on being mentioned reminds us of the Dresden gallery . . . we wander through the rooms and stop in front of a painting by Teniers which represents a gallery of paintings. Let us further suppose that the paintings of this gallery would represent in their turn paintings, which, on their part, exhibit readable inscriptions and so forth" (1, 104). Derrida's conclusion in the Freud essay echoes his reading of Husserl, while archly underwriting Freud's pansexualism: "Everything begins with reproduction" (211). Here again the connection to issues of technical reproducibility in mass culture is clear.

From the two essays on Artaud that Schulte-Sasse makes his prime examples of Derrida's inadequacies, I can offer only two representative citations. Derrida asks whether Artaud would have "refused the name *representation* for the theater of cruelty?" He answers:

No, provided that we clarify the difficult and equivocal meaning of this notion. Here we would have to be able to play upon all the German words that we indistinctly translate with the unique word representation. The stage, certainly, *will no longer represent*, since it will not operate as an addition, as the sensory illustration of a text already written, thought, or lived outside the stage. . . . The stage will no longer operate as the repetition of a *present*, will no longer re-present a present that would exist elsewhere and prior to it. . . . It will not even offer the representation of a present, if present signifies that which is maintained in *front* of me.

Cruel representation must permeate me. And nonrepresentation is, thus, original representation, if representation signifies also, the unfolding of a volume, a multidimensional milieu, an experience which produces its own space. *Spacing* . . . ("Theater of Cruelty" 237)

And here Derrida goes on to the play of trace and differance that introduces a self-disarticulating distance into what had been credited as immediacy.

I have cited this passage to show that Derrida does not *simply* place Artaud against representation. I cite the next passage to establish that Derrida does not *simply* take any side with regard to representation. Derrida's practice resembles that of novelists. The dream of metaphysics, blind to mortality, sees a world of enchanted giants. Representation, however, is the windmill in which the quest always gets tangled up. The history of metaphysics, our reality, is both the dream and its disabuse, and to gain any glimpse of a different horizon, we must stage this as a process, not state it as a position.

Here, then, Derrida summarizes his first essay on Artaud:

One entire side of his discourse destroys a tradition which lives *within* difference, alienation, and negativity without seeing their origin and necessity. To reawaken this tradition, Artaud . . . recalls it to its own motifs: self-presence, unity . . . etc. In this sense, Artaud . . . fulfills the most profound and permanent ambition of western metaphysics. But through another twist of his text . . . Artaud affirms the . . . law of difference. . . . This duplicity of Artaud's text . . . has unceasingly obligated us to pass over to the other side of the limit, thereby to demonstrate the closure of the presence within which he had to enclose himself. . . . [T]o an inexpert scrutiny, we could appear to be criticizing Artaud's metaphysics from the standpoint of metaphysics itself, when we are actually delimiting . . . a necessary dependency of all destructive discourses: they must inhabit the structures they demolish. ("La parole" 194)

Or as Derrida made the same point in *Speech and Phenomena*: "What we are describing as primordial representation can be provisionally designated with this term only within the closure whose limits we are seeking to transgress by setting down and demonstrating various contradictory or untenable propositions within it, attempting thereby to institute a kind of insecurity and open it up to the outside. This can only be done from a certain inside" (57).

No less than Althusser and Derrida, Michel Foucault devoted crucial work to representation. *The Order of Things* constantly focuses on representation, from its opening pages on Velázquez, but at the same time the book argues for radical historical discontinuity. Representation, therefore, cannot be the same across time. From the Cartesian, classical point of view, there is a problem in the relation of the modern human sciences to representation. For even though the human sciences understand "*man*" precisely as "that living being who . . . constitutes representations by which he lives, and on the basis of which he possesses that strange capacity of being able to represent to himself precisely that life" (352), the human sciences look to "unconscious mechanisms" (356) rather than to the clearly illuminated conscious space of classical representation. Against this classical objection, Foucault emphasizes that "representation is not consciousness," and "this bringing to light of elements or structures that are never present to consciousness" does not "enable . . . the human sciences to escape the law of representation" (361). There exists, then, a resemblance *but without filiation* between the human sciences and classical philosophy, which produces a recurrent anachronistic effect: "Every time one tries to use the human sciences to philosophize . . . one finds oneself imitating the philosophical posture of the eighteenth century" (363–64). This is Foucault's riposte to Lévi-Strauss's Rousseauism, the vestigial homologue to Derrida's many pages on Lévi-Strauss and Rousseau.

Foucault poses a telling formulation of the dilemma of Derrida's that we have encountered—the Samsonic position of the "destructive" intellectual, inhabiting the edifice he is pulling down—but he construes it as part of our historical moment rather than as an inherent necessity of thought or discourse:

> The human sciences, when dealing with what is representation (in either conscious or unconscious form), find themselves treating as their object what is in fact their condition of possibility. They are always animated, therefore, by a . . . transcendental mobility. They never cease to exercise a critical examination of themselves. They proceed from that which is given to representation to that which renders representation possible, but which is still representation. So [they are] constantly demystifying themselves . . . unveiling . . . the non-conscious. (363–64)

For Foucault at this point in his career, no less than for Derrida, there is nothing to do within the enclosure except glimpse the change that will transform everything—in this case the end of "*man*" and a return to the "power of discourse" (310). Foucault's later work, of course, did much to give that formulation specificity and has helped to make possible the deep concern with the mechanisms of representational power that mobilizes so interesting a current project as the new interdisciplinary journal from Berkeley, *Representations*.

I conclude this section with Heidegger's essay "The Age of the World-View" both because Derrida discusses it in a recent essay precisely on representation ("Sending") and because it allows us to consider anew the historical dimensions of the issue. "The Age of the World-View" supports Lucien Goldmann's thesis that Heidegger tries to account ontologically for the features of modern life that Lukács defined through the Marxist problematic of reification. Heidegger begins with the dual constitution of subject and object through Descartes's analysis of knowledge as representation, and he then defines "the basic process of modern times" as "the conquest of the world as picture" (353)—which involves politics and technology.

Heidegger goes beyond Lukács's focus in *History and Class Consciousness* on the characteristically nineteenth-century mode of newspaper journalism; Heidegger cites new mass media, "the unlimited power of representing foreign and remote worlds, made present through the turn of a hand, through the radio" (354). Heidegger neither glories in this new political technology of global representation, nor simply stands against it. With astonishing relevance to current debates over education in the United States, this most conservative of modern thinkers, who more than anyone else in the twentieth century remade our intellectual life through engagement with ancient Greece, warns that in the face of our historical situation, the "flight to tradition" offers only a mixture of "humility and arrogance," a "blindness and self-deception" that will not enable us to deal with our current needs (354).

Heidegger also cuts closer to where many of us live. For in defining the new forms of knowledge in our time, he emphasizes its "institutionalization" in a new "business character." The new dealer in knowledge "does business at meetings and gets information at congresses. He contracts to work for publishers, who [thereby] now help to determine what books must be written." Moreover, part of the new structure Heidegger isolates is something that many of us may value because we believe it challenges the usual business of our departmental structures, namely "the greatest possible ability to . . . switch research," a "regulated mobility of transference and integration of activities with respect to whatever tasks happen to be of paramount importance" (347–48). This is a chilling warning, set in a lecture from Germany in 1938. Does it have the same force now? Postmodern thinking about the responsibility of intellectuals has had to acknowledge that most critics and artists alike are now institutionally located within the university, another loss of the distance that modernists found a guarantee of independence. This essay of Heidegger's helps clarify the interdependence of representation not only with history and narrative, but also with professionalism and questions of intellectuals as the "new class" (see Gouldner; and Konrád and Szelényi). On all these matters, it is no longer possible *simply* to take sides. By analyzing some of the confusions that have attended recent talk about representation, I hope to have helped make possible more lucid political analyses of the postmodern situation.

Politics: Our Current Debates in Theory and History

Political lucidity requires some sense of what we mean by politics at all, and there has been no easy understanding here, either conceptually or historically. More than twenty years ago Peter Sedgwick charged that the "sociocultural" emphasis of such British "New Left" figures as Stuart Hall, E. P. Thompson, and Raymond Williams was "subversive of political activism" (138). In recent statements that appeared within a few months of each other, Edward Said and

Fredric Jameson offer perspectives that show how wide the range of uncertainty can be even among figures, both on the left, who urge that we renew our practices of narrative representation. As part of the "separation of fields" that weakens American intellectual and academic life, Said points out "literary Marxists who write for literary Marxists, who are in a cloistral seclusion from the world of real politics." As a consequence, "both 'literature' and 'Marxism' are thereby confirmed in their apolitical content and methodology: literary criticism is still 'only' literary criticism, Marxism only Marxism, and politics is mainly what the literary critic talks about longingly and hopelessly" ("Opponents, Audiences" 149). (David Bromwich similarly characterizes "left-wing literary people" as those "who in a better world would be doing political work" [35].) Said might also be challenging Foucault's claim that the role of the "universal intellectual" from Voltaire to Sartre has been exhausted and replaced by that of the "specific intellectual," working to change the practices of truth within particular disciplines ("Truth and Power" 126–33).

As if directly responding to these observations, Jameson insisted, "As far as 'the political' is concerned, any single-slot, single-function definition of it is worse than misleading, it is paralyzing," for the following reasons:

> We are, after all, fragmented beings, living in a host of separate reality-compartments simultaneously; in *each one of those* a certain kind of politics is possible, and if we have enough energy, it would be desirable to conduct all those forms of political activity simultaneously. So the 'metaphysical' question: what is politics . . . is worthwhile only when it leads to enumeration of all the possible options, and not when it lures you into following the mirage of the single great strategic idea. (75)

Since, however, the limitations of discourse necessitate "that we talk about each of these forms of political intervention separately," we must beware of the "supreme misunderstanding," that is, "the misconception that when one modestly outlines a certain form of political activity—such as that which intellectuals in the university can engage in—this 'program' is meant to suggest that this is the *only* kind of politics one should do" (Interview 75).

Perhaps Jameson here neglects an aspect of "relative autonomy": the "political" does exist as a realm of state and law. For example, we can speak literally of a "politics of reproduction" because of the battles over the legality of abortion; a "politics of sexuality" because laws forbid certain practices or fail to ensure equal protection to those who engage in them; a "politics of gender" because women have turned to courts and legislatures in attempting to gain equal access to jobs and equal pay within them. One reason the personal has become the political is because of the agitation for public remedies in areas long considered private, including a professor's expectation that a secretary will make coffee, or that a student will tolerate an unwelcome pat. Jameson does not in fact exclude these concerns, but his conceptualization tends to elide their political specificity.

Jameson's understanding of "reification" (like Bell's "axial principle" of role-segmentation in economics) recognizes the actual fragmentation of intellectual and political life, while his commitment to "totality" (like Bell's axial principle" of the "whole person" in culture) insists that these parts be understood in relation to a global context. Many developments in twentieth-century Marxism help to elucidate his position. Gramsci's analysis of "hegemony" lays the basis for understanding the cultural sphere (especially education and religion) as not merely a reflection of social and economic relations but instead a means by which those relations may be enforced, amplified, or contested. The Frankfurt-school critique of the "culture industry" gave new insight into culture as a means of domination, and if modified by the ideas of Brecht and Benjamin on "refunctioning," suggested the possibility of the mass media as an arena for political contests (see Kipnis). Althusser's conception of "ideological state apparatuses" helps to make clear how even if politics may ultimately mean smashing the state, or taking over the state, or forming a new state, nonetheless activity in the area of culture may be understood in relation to those ultimates.

In Said's terms, then, it is probable that a Marxist "reading" of a "canonical" work is in and of itself no more significant a political challenge than a deconstructive reading, an archetypal reading, or any other "approach"; all alike contribute to legitimating the academic literary institution as autonomous. If, however, Marxist literary critics make part of their argument a challenge to the idea of "literary criticism" itself, demonstrating and challenging the social uses which such an idea has served, we move toward the political (although Evan Watkins raises cogent doubts). The crucial contemporary agenda is elaborating the relations that join the nexus of classroom, discipline, and profession to such political areas as those of gender, race, and class, as well as nation.

The current movement from "literary" to "cultural" studies, from "literary criticism" to "criticism," shows this direction, as was ironically, sadly, but accurately understood by Harry Levin as early as 1960. He observed then of the separation of the sphere of high culture, "The thought that a man of letters should consider himself a practitioner of the fine arts, or that he should be designated professionally as an artist, is a legacy from Flaubert's generation which is not likely to outlast Joyce's by long" (291). Like Habermas now, Levin then valued the process of separation understood by both as part of the Enlightenment's heritage (271), but Levin saw it as already past: "Instead of a tension between the uncomprehending majority and the saving remnant . . . there has been a *détente*, a relaxation, and a collaboration for mutual profit. . . . But this is a subject notoriously better appreciated by professors of sociology and experts on mass communication than it is by old-fashioned scholars and modernist critics" (293). Postmodern critics, new-fashioned scholars, can carry on a significant political activity by relating the concerns once enclosed within "literature" to a broader cultural sphere that is itself related to, although not identical with, the larger concerns of the state and economy.

At best, however, the idea of "cultural politics" must remain vexed. The history of cultural opposition movements in the United States helps to specify some of this discomfort. The 1930s is our usual point of reference, but already then there was a previous history. Malcolm Cowley's work for the *New Republic* in the thirties was closely sympathetic to the conjunction of cultural and political radicalism, coming close to fellow traveling with communism. He had already lived through both Greenwich Village bohemianism and aesthetic expatriation, as he described in *Exile's Return*, published in 1934, the year *Partisan Review* was founded as an organ of the John Reed Club. That memoir both illuminates Daniel Bell's arguments about the erosion of the "Protestant Ethic" and shows that concerns about the "co-optation" of the avant-garde are no longer novel.

In discussing the "ideas" characteristic of Greenwich Village's bohemian ways of living around 1920, Cowley emphasizes that "from the standpoint of the business-Christian ethic then represented by the *Saturday Evening Post*," they were "corrupt." For "this older ethic . . . was a *production* ethic"; its "great virtues" included "industry, foresight, thrift, and personal initiative." Against this, however, there emerged "a new ethic that encouraged people to buy, a *consumption* ethic":

> Many of the Greenwich Village ideas proved useful in the altered situation. Thus, *self-expression* and *paganism* encouraged demand for all sorts of products—modern furniture, beach pajamas, cosmetics, colored bathrooms with toilet paper to match. *Living for the moment* meant buying an automobile, radio or house, using it now and paying for it tomorrow. *Female equality* was capable of doubling the consumption of products—cigarettes, for example—that had formerly been used by men alone. Even *changing place* would help to stimulate business in the country from which the artist was being expatriated. The exiles of art were also trade missionaries: involuntarily they increased the foreign demand for fountain pens, silk stockings, grapefruit and portable typewriters. (61–62)

The socially serious 1930s, then, found the preceding generation, which we link with modernism at its height, already liable to the charges that critics urge against postmodernism. Located halfway between, echoing Cowley's language of 1934 and prefiguring that of Charles Newman in 1984, Harry Levin wrote in 1960 of postmodernism: "This is reproduction, not production; we are mainly consumers rather than producers of art. We are readers of reprints and connoisseurs of high fidelity, even as we are gourmets by virtue of the expense account and the credit card. For our wide diffusion of culture is geared to the standardizations of our economy, and is peculiarly susceptible to inflationary trends. . . . The independence of our practitioners, when they are not domesticated by institutions of learning, is compromised more insidiously by the circumstances that make art a business'' (279). Taken further, such analysis leads to the important contemporary topic of intellectuals as a "new class," a group fully interested in social struggles, rather than independent of them (see Gouldner; and Konrád and Szelényi).

Independence is difficult to analyze. At one extreme, independence is merely isolation, irrelevance. Independence is valuable only as a relation to that from which, or perhaps by means of which, one is independent, but this opens a further danger of purely reactive independence. For the most influential American cultural intellectuals to emerge from the thirties, these problems were posed not only in terms of the dominant institutions of life in the United States, but most particularly in terms of "Stalinism." They live in history, by their own repeated choice, as the "anti-Stalinist" intellectuals, and this chosen negative independence continually acted to restrict their positive independence. Nathan Glazer offers an analysis, which I find chilling, of how this particular small group "bec[a]me *the* American intellectuals." Although in the thirties their "politics" had usually not even involved voting, let alone the give and take of "who gets what," but instead "positions on . . . great historical issues," when the postwar years brought to sudden dominance a concern with the relations between the United States and the Soviet Union, "the one thing they knew became important." Their unique knowledge was "that the Soviet Union represented a radical threat to freedom, and that variations in its leadership and policies scarcely affected in any significant way the unyielding nature of this threat," and they knew this not even directly from the USSR but because their American "experiences . . . had taught them how different Communists, and Communism, were" (34–35). Their independence from Stalinism came only at the price of their integration into the Cold War, as their independent literary views prepared them for authority in the postwar institutionalization of modernism.

If "the two M's" of "Marxism in politics and Modernism in art" were the foci that guided the course of the refounded *Partisan Review* from 1937 according to William Barrett's memoir (11), Irving Howe's retrospect found instead a fundamental split between "radicalism" and modernism as a distinctive American experience of this period ("New York Intellectuals" 218). In using modernism to criticize the "liberal imagination" from the later thirties into the seventies, Lionel Trilling was combating what he considered "the liberal intellectual middle-class acceptance of Stalinist doctrine in all aspects of life" ("Some Notes" 240). (Trilling held this view despite what seems to a later generation the overwhelming evidence to the contrary, such as the debacle of the Wallace campaign in 1948 and the failure of anything like a renewal of the popular front in the Waldorf conference of 1949, the expulsion of communists from the labor unions and their prohibition from the newly founded Americans for Democratic Action—all this even before McCarthyism.) To Howe, Trilling's critique "eased a turning away from all politics" (*Margin of Hope* 231), yet the point for Trilling had been precisely that it was Stalinists who were not really political. For by refusing to consider any facts that "refuted" their central dogma ("that the Soviet Union had resolved all social and political contradictions and was well on the way toward realizing the highest possibilities of human life") Stalinists revealed a "disgust" with the substance of real politics: "contingency, vigilance, and effort," which in a remarkable idealization Trilling associated with "such energies of the human spirit as are marked by spontaneity, complexity, and variety" (Art, Will, and Necessity" 140–41).

Trilling admitted that for himself and his associates, "Stalinist" was purely a "pejorative designation" that they used against others: "No one, of course, called himself a Stalinist" ("Art, Will, and Necessity" 140). (In fact documents cited for other purposes by Howe and Coser [171] and Klehr [171, 415] incidentally reveal that "Stalinist" was sometimes used as a self-designation.) Working with such a definition of "Stalinism," which depended neither on what people call themselves nor on their actions but rather on the cast of temperament they display, Trilling could not grant that a novel he admired for its bright, comic spirit, *The Unpossessed* (1934) by his friend Tess Slesinger, might be a Communist satire on halfhearted intellectual leftists, even though he acknowledged that after she left New York for Hollywood she "g[a]ve her assent" to "the Party" ("Novel of the Thirties" 19). (He himself in 1934 had with others only just left "the Stalinist intellectual camp" [Howe and Coser 299–300] after involvement in a planned collaborative book on Marxism and American life [Klehr 79–80; 427, n. 25]. The editors of this project, Newton Arvin, Granville Hicks, and Bernard Smith, were all close to the Communist party, and a few years later Smith's *Forces in American Criticism* [1939] provoked the first version of Trilling's manifesto, "Reality in America," called "Parrington, Mr. Smith, and Reality.") Yet Slesinger's novel does not portray the Communist party as the "rather comical remote abstraction" (19) Trilling claimed; on the contrary, the party is sought but remains rigorously offstage, a source of value in the absence of which only silly velleities are possible. Trilling here may have failed in his own appreciation for the complex variety of views. So too his opposition to "Stalinist" principles of art led him to exclude from serious consideration certain modes of writing, to downgrade realism, and in the effect of his own authority become to a younger generation "the mirror image of Zhdanov" (Aronowitz 248), independent only in relation to his chosen opponent.

We lack the history of American intellectuals from the thirties through the sixties that will allow us fully to make sense out of these crossings back and forth, yet they continue to haunt our current situation. It is in principle well known that Habermas's extreme sensitivity to the political dangers of what he reckons antimodernism can be understood in relation to the history of Germany in the twentieth century, for in the two decades before the Nazis came to power, the German academy was full of antimodernist polemic, transmitted from the intellectual concerns of teachers to the agitational concerns of students (Ringer

252). It is less generally known that at the time of the Moscow purge trials, Delmore Schwartz cried out, "If there were no such thing as an objective world, the Stalinists would have their way. But I think there is such a world. If subjective idealism were correct, the Stalinists would be in the right, and we would be lost" (Abel 63). Yet once known, this moment is obviously relevant to current concerns over the "arbitrariness" of meaning or reference, as in the work of Gerald Graff.

It is important that American academics involved in the study of current "theory" be aware of such contexts, here as well as abroad, yet even this is not enough. For Habermas's sensitivity to antimodernism forgets that in the 1920s, it was the modernizing wing in the academy that set in motion the rhetoric of "crisis"; this rhetoric was seized by the antimodernists for their own purposes, which they made prevail (Ringer 351). Those who join Schwartz in embracing the rock of reality against the Stalinists forget that Stalinism saw *its* opponents as idealists, subjectivists who ignored the plain lessons of objective truth (Rorty has valuably criticized the "silly relativism" ["Texts and Lumps"] of those who believe epistemology necessary to underwrite choice). Trilling's definition of Stalinism forgets that the German academic mandarins of the 1920s were "apolitical" in considering that the "details of everyday politics were ethically as well as intellectually beneath the notice of the cultivated man" (Ringer 121), in their "dream of a total escape from interest politics," and in their yearning to "transcend the political mechanism in terms of some idealistic absolute" (446). That is, they correspond to what Trilling called Stalinist but were in historical fact precursors of fascism. Coming from this German experience, Adorno and others of the Frankfurt school found in the American "culture industry" signs of incipient fascism, seizing on some of the same elements ("the amiable fumblings of the 'little man'") that to Howe and Coser defined the residue of the Stalinist popular front (366). Theories of "totalitarianism" appealed to the 1950s by promising to resolve these inconsistencies, eliminating the differences between Nazis and Communists, but it is now generally conceded that in offering a typology of deviation such theories overlooked too much history.

The lesson of history is that we must know both our history and our difference from our history. In 1937, when William Phillips and Philip Rahv of *Partisan Review* proclaimed that the existing contradiction between Marxism and American traditions required a "Europeanization" of American culture if Marxism were to flourish here (Gilbert 147), who would have imagined that the heritage of the "New York intellectuals" would so firmly oppose the recent excitement over "European theory"? When a young lifetime later in 1974, Warren Susman echoed in a new key Henry James's litany of American absences, "Why have we . . no Luxemburg, no Gramsci, no Lukács, no Gorz, no Althusser?" (84), who would have imagined the "arresting historical change" Perry Anderson proclaimed in 1984: for Marxist theory, "today the *predominant* centres of intellectual production . . . lie in the English-speaking world" (*Historical Materialism* 24).

Postmodernism and Politics

The chapters in this book stem from, contribute to, and interrogate this postmodern Marxist intellectual activity, relating it to political questions that are focused on the discipline and institutions of literary and cultural study, but also reaching out in the awareness and the wish that these questions function more as preliminaries than as final goals. It is important that such work is here undertaken collaboratively, for Habermas can agree with the Foucault of "What Is an Author?" on the "depersonalization" that has become an intellectual necessity in our time, after the end of "great philosophy" with Hegel and of "great philosophers" with Heidegger. In terms that echo Edward Said on Erich Auerbach ("Secular Criticism"), Habermas notes the passing of "personal testimony" and "individual erudition" as adequate, or available, grounds for the work we need ("Does Philosophy Still Have a Purpose?" 1–3).

Although they do not represent a single point of view, the chapters take a place in the contexts I have been developing. Althusserian issues are crucial to Pratt and Higgins; Foucault forms an important point of reference for Bové and Robbins; Derrida is implicated in the arguments of Polan, Parker, and Nägele; and Bové, Nägele, and West work with aspects of the Frankfurt school's heritage. Moreover, the debate on "representation" links the chapters, The constitution of the individual "subject" at the intersection of psychological and social forces of representation explicitly figures in the chapters by Pratt, Nägele, Higgins, and Robbins; the status of the "image" is explored by Polan, Parker, and Robbins in the different realms of cinema, poetry, and still photography; the formation and transmission of politically crucial knowledge preoccupies the remaining two essays, social knowledge in Bové's, moral knowledge in West's. In commenting briefly on each chapter in turn, I shall also suggest that as a whole they force us to think freshly about a very wide range of the privileged objects of inquiry that have grown up in the academic study of the humanities, such objects as the "discipline" of literary study, the "reader" of a work, the "viewer" of a film, the artist, the philosopher, the critic, the leading intellectual, and finally the very notion of "experience" itself.

Paul Bové has worked with *boundary 2* from its founding, and, according to Vincent Leitch, the dissertation Bové did with W. V. Spanos, subsequently revised into *Destructive Poetics*, was the first completed in America to be recognizably "deconstructive" (71–72). Bové's sketch of the beginnings of postmodern literary criticism, therefore, holds considerable historical interest, as does his own turn away from those beginnings. Persuaded that this earlier work continued to support the disciplinary enclosure of literary study, Bové's chapter, "The

Ineluctability of Difference," turns to Stanley Aronowitz's *The Crisis in Historical Materialism* for speculation about intellectual practice that might escape our disciplines. For new social and political movements such as feminism, antinuclearism, and the struggles by peoples of color cut across the usual boundaries that segregate politics from economics, or literature from other modes of cultural activity, and an appropriate intellectual response to these movements, whether critical, participatory, or otherwise, requires new maps of knowledge.

In "Interpretive Strategies/Strategic Interpretations," not only does Mary Louise Pratt criticize the ideology of American reader-response criticism by showing how it reinforces the existing institutions of academic study, she also develops suggestions by Terry Eagleton toward a model of the literary process that specifies the production of meaning as a social activity. In her discussions of Gerald Prince on the "narratee," Jonathan Culler on "literary competence," and Stanley Fish on "interpretive communities," she understands such activity as an area of difference and struggle, not of consensus. This is especially important because of the close relations between Fish's notion and the highly influential work of Richard Rorty, for Rorty is only sporadically alive to the kinds of issues Pratt emphasizes. She could agree with him that for "moral and political" analysis, "a person just *is* . . . a network of beliefs, desires, and emotions with nothing behind it," and that "most moral dilemmas" reflect "the fact that most of us identify with a number of different communities and are equally reluctant to marginalize ourselves in relation to any of them" ("Postmodernist Bourgeois" 585–87). However, the lines of argument Pratt develops could not agree that "we should be more willing than we are to celebrate bourgeois capitalist society as the best polity actualized so far, while regretting that it is irrelevant to most of the problems of most of the population of the planet" ("Method, Social Science" 210, n. 16). For so long as bourgeois capital dominates workers over much of the planet, so long as the defense of bourgeois capitalist society requires threatening the whole planet with nuclear destruction, and so long as that society continues to subordinate women, however good it may be, it is hardly irrelevant to the problems of the overwhelming majority who do not enjoy its benefits. "Postmodernist bourgeois liberalism" does not hold the privilege of enclosure within a single community.

Dana Polan's chapter on cinema and the ideology of spectacle engages directly the concerns with mass culture that have been so important in defining postmodernism. He shows that mass modes achieve no easy liberation from the problems of high culture, and he therefore avoids idealizing the "popular." At the same time, however, he wishes to expose certain formulations transferred from the traditional discourse of high culture into the current and growing institutionalization of film studies. The unquestioned emphasis on the visual, which underlies the received binary analysis of film theories into "realist" and "formative," carries into new territory the prestige of the aesthetic. Even deconstructive attention to "an experience of play that goes beyond a binding into the logic of narrative and representation'' may be recuperated by spectacle. The questions with which Polan leaves us lie on the advanced edge of contemporary cinema: what kind of practice will help us to think critically, both about the medium itself and about the world in which we and the medium exist?

The controversies over Ezra Pound have been immense, as has been the importance of his work both for modernism (for example, his impact on Yeats and Eliot) and for postmodernism (for example, in his relations with William Carlos Williams and Charles Olson). In "Ezra Pound and the 'Economy' of Anti-Semitism," Andrew Parker draws on deconstructive rhetorical analysis in a most challenging way. Above all, Parker challenges any dismissal of deconstruction as ahistorical, antipolitical, and, in its devotion to fragmentation, anti-intellectual because it shatters any possible objects of knowledge. Parker's deconstructive reading brings together Pound's poetic theory and economic theory, which the major line of Pound's reception has wished to separate, and it shows the coherence of these areas with the grounds for his anti-Semitism. Parker challenges by these means the construction of the idealized independence of the "Artist," which we have already noted as a prime component in the ideology of modernism, and in its place he reveals "Ezra," a historically exemplary "man of letters."

Rainer Nägele's "The Scene of the Other: Theodor W. Adorno's Negative Dialectic in the Context of Poststructuralism" addresses some of the same issues as are at stake in Habermas's "Modernism versus Postmodernism," but Nägele combines greater sympathy for poststructuralism than Habermas has with much greater knowledge of it. This context allows Nägele to illuminate the historical fate of Nietzsche and Heidegger in Germany. The exploitation of their names by the Nazis has made it almost intolerable for contemporary German leftists to believe that their ideas may contribute to a new radicalism, but just this was happening in France in the 1960s. Living in the United States, Nägele has more freedom to explore this problem than if he were working immediately within German culture and history, while he also can remark on certain resistances no less prevalent in the United States than abroad. The procedure of Nägele's chapter offers a striking conjunction of methods. It draws on the principle of "constellation," which Adorno developed from Benjamin, in order to establish relations finer and more complex than simply those of likeness or difference, while at the same time it reads the tropes of philosophic discourse with an energy like Derrida's. One effect is to transform the figure of the "philosopher," who remains a thinker of impassioned seriousness, but no longer free from the contingencies of either language or history.

John Higgins's chapter considers Raymond Williams and the problem of ideology. Born in Wales, not New York, Raymond Williams is a contemporary of Daniel Bell and Irving Howe. Like them, he early found the communism of the 1930s "an impasse" (*Politics and Letters* 52) and later suffered painful exchanges with the new radicalism of the late sixties and its aftermath. Yet his work has inspired rather than obstructed the conjunction of postmodernism and politics to which this volume is devoted. The shocks that defined the British New Left after 1956—de-Stalinization, Suez, Hungary (a time memorably captured in Doris Lessing's *The Golden Notebook*)—did not lead Williams to a "post-Marxism" as the shaking loose of the sixties did so many French intellectuals and as later developments have done in America (see Balbus and Poster). If Marxism in the 1930s gave Williams no resources with which to hold his own against conventional scholarship in a Cambridge English tutorial, by the time he was again willing to identify himself as a Marxist in the 1970s, he had developed critical resources for understanding the politics of culture that went beyond anything else in the anglophone world. While moving out from the exclusive literary canon of Eliot and Leavis to study a wider range of writing, and a wider range of media from theater to television to communications in general, Williams maintained and developed a sympathetic concern for the democratic and radical potential of such work. Moreover, his studies of the conceptual and institutional apparatus of culture (leading recently to a remarkable retrospect on modernism in "Beyond Cambridge English" 220) have powerfully complemented the "genealogical" research of Foucault. John Higgins cuts into this exemplary career as it intersects the heated debate over Althusser's theory of ideology, which still fuels current American work such as Parker's "Futures for Marxism."

Cornel West is a divinity-school professor, politically active through the Afro-American church. His analyses of how the Jesse Jackson campaign bears on the future of the American left have appeared in such diverse journals as *Christianity and Crisis, Le monde diplomatique, Social Text,* and *Democratic Left.* It shows the permeability of disciplinary bounds that West should interest himself in "Ethics and Action in Fredric Jameson's Marxist Hermeneutics," and it suggests also that Jameson has gone beyond being just a "Marxist literary critic." Jameson's recent essays on the sixties and on postmodernism have made clear that the apparatus of interpretation constructed in *The Political Unconscious,* and used there for historical literary study, is meant for use in understanding our own times and in moving toward a new future. West fears that Jameson's style, elliptic, eclectic, combining casual allusion to knotty points in dialectical theory with references to current movies and music, may fail as a mobilizing force by its enclosure within a characteristically American utopianism, yet Jameson's wager on such a postmodern style deserves to be taken seriously. (Compare the difficulties faced by Stanley Aronowitz, whose *Working-Class Hero* [1983] seeks to address American labor by avoiding any trace of the speculative discourse of his *Crisis in Historical Materialism.* But can one really mount a new strategy in the old language?) West in any case goes on to the fullest exploration that has yet appeared of another aspect of Jameson's work that bears on its potential for political mobilization, his insistence that a Nietzschean amoralism is required to avoid repeating the sentimentalities of the sixties.

West's clarifications of ethical theory from Kant through Hegel, Marx, and Nietzsche relate directly to the issue posed by Bruce Robbins in "Feeling Global:

John Berger and Experience,'' namely the continuing power of humanist figures of thought. After the challenges poststructuralism has posed, is there not something that remains, which may be very different from the *Erlebnis* of German *Lebensphilosophie* or the "experience" which seemed so self-evident to Leavis, and yet which it is still worthwhile to call, explore, and even rely on as "experience"? As a writer of fiction and documentary, analyst of the visual arts, collaborator in moviemaking, yet who also lives in a peasant community, John Berger offers ideal ground to explore this problem and its dangers of sentimentality. For Trilling, the great danger of the current institutionalization of learning was its threat to the real individuality of "experience." He noted the shift from Matthew Arnold's exigent question (echoed from Goethe) "Is it true? Is it true for me?" to what he considered the rather slacker "Is it true for us?" (Preface, xvi). Benjamin, however, in lamenting the decline of "experience" that had made storytelling no longer possible, argued for the collective sharing that was essential to the notion. Through close analysis of some moments in Berger, and engagement with arguments from British Althusserians, Roland Barthes, and Susan Sontag, Robbins comes out with a perspective much more like Benjamin's than Trilling's, and in a vein that Jochen Schulte-Sasse is now exploring (xliv).

The great impasse against which Trilling's generation and their inheritors struggled could be put this way: rejecting the false experience of Stalinism in the thirties seemed only to yield the false experience of conformity in the fifties. In certain respects we are better positioned. Let us grant that they eradicated from American culture the dangers of Stalinism; now that it is gone, we are again free to explore possibilities on the left. The debates over new developments in theory have allowed fresh perspectives on many of the shibboleths in American cultural-political discourse and given a philosophic vigor not often seen in this country before. Mass culture is our element, neither a sudden and welcome liberation from a worn-out high culture, nor the threat to corrupt all that we most treasure. Since we come late enough not to confuse ourselves with the modernists, we can accept our condition as postmodern. No doubt this was not the name one might have independently chosen; as we have seen, it was originally a pejorative from those who attributed to others a belatedness that was also their own. Finding ourselves, as if from birth, in the academy, we can work there without the shame of ivory-tower isolation or the euphoria of being at the nerve center of a brave new world. We will not transform American life today, or tomorrow, but what we do to change our academic habits and disciplines, the questions we dare to ask or allow our students to pursue, these are political and make a difference, too, for the academy itself is in the world.

WORKS CITED

Abel, Lionel. *The Intellectual Follies*. New York: Norton, 1984.

Adorno, Theodor W., and Max Horkheimer. "The Culture Industry." In *Dialectic of Enlightenment* (1947), translated by John Cumming. New York: Seabury, 1972, 120–67.

Althusser, Louis. "Ideology and Ideological State Apparatuses" (1970). Translated by Ben Brewster. In *Lenin and Philosophy*. New York and London: Monthly Review Press, 1971, 127–86.
———. *Reading Capital* (1965). Translated by Ben Brewster. New York: Pantheon, 1970.
Anderson, Perry. *Considerations on Western Marxism*. London: NLB, 1976.
———. "Modernity and Revolution." In *New Left Review*, no. 144 (1984): 96–113.
———. *In the Tracks of Historical Materialism*. Chicago: Univ. of Chicago Press, 1984.
The Anti-Aesthetic: Essays on Postmodern Culture. Edited by Hal Foster. Port Townsend, Wash.: Bay Press, 1983.
Arendt, Hannah. "The Crisis in Culture: Its Social and Political Significance" (1960). In *Between Past and Future* (1961). Cleveland and New York: World, 1963, 197–226.
Aronowitz, Stanley. *The Crisis in Historical Materialism*. New York: Praeger, 1981.
Auerbach, Erich. *Mimesis* (1946). Translated by Willard Trask. Princeton: Princeton Univ. Press, 1953.
Balbus, Isaac D. *Marxism and Domination*. Princeton: Princeton Univ. Press, 1982.
Barrett, William. *The Truants*. New York: Doubleday, 1982.
Bell, Daniel. *The Cultural Contradictions of Capitalism*. New York: Basic, 1976.
———. "Modernism and Capitalism." In *Partisan Review* 46 (1978): 206–26. Repr. as introduction to 1978 paperback edition of *The Cultural Contradictions of Capitalism*.
———. *The Winding Passage*. New York: Basic, 1980.
Benjamin, Walter. "The Author as Producer" (1934). Translated by Anna Bostock. In *Understanding Brecht*. London: NLB, 1977, 85–103.
———. *Illuminations* (1968). Translated by Harry Zohn. New York: Schocken, 1969.
———. "The Storyteller" (1936). In *Illuminations*, 83–109.
———. "The Work of Art in the Age of Mechanical Reproduction" (1936). In *Illuminations*, 217–51.
Berman, Marshall. *All That Is Solid Melts into Air: The Experience of Modernity*. New York: Simon & Schuster, 1982.
Bromwich, David. "Literary Radicalism in America." In *Dissent* 32 (1985): 35–44.
Bürger, Peter. *Theory of the Avant-Garde* (2d ed., 1980). Translated by Michael Shaw. Minneapolis: Univ. of Minnesota Press, 1984.
Buttigieg, Joseph A. "The Exemplary Worldliness of Antonio Gramsci's Literary Criticism." In *boundary 2* 11.1–2 (1982–83): 21–39.
Coward, Rosalind, and John Ellis. *Language and Materialism*. London: Routledge, 1977.
Cowley, Malcolm. *Exile's Return* (1934). New York: Viking, 1956.
Derrida, Jacques. "Freud and the Scene of Writing" (1966). In *Writing and Difference*, 196–231.
———. *Of Grammatology* (1967). Translated by Gayatri Chakravorty Spivak. Baltimore: Johns Hopkins Univ. Press, 1976.
———. "La parole soufflée" (1965). In *Writing and Difference*, 169–95.
———. "Sending: On Representation." Translated by Peter Caws and Mary Ann Caws. In *Social Research* 49 (1982): 294–326.
———. *Speech and Phenomena* (1967).Translated by David B. Allison. Evanston, Ill.: Northwestern Univ. Press, 1973,
———. *Writing and Difference* (1967). Translated by Alan Bass. Chicago: Univ. of Chicago Press, 1978.
Donato, Eugenio. "The Museum's Furnace." In *Textual Strategies*, Josué V. Harari. Ithaca, N.Y.: Cornell Univ. Press, 1979, 213–38.
Fekete, John. "Modernity in the Literary Institution." In *The Structural Allegory*, edited by John Fekete. Minneapolis: Univ. of Minnesota Press, 1984, 228–47.
Foster, Hal. "Postmodernism: A Preface." In *The Anti-Aesthetic*, ix–xvi.
Foucault, Michel. *Discipline and Punish* (1975). Translated by Alan Sheridan. New York: Pantheon, 1978.
———. "Nietzsche, Genealogy, History" (1971). In *Language, Counter-Memory, Practice*, edited

by Donald F. Bouchard and translated by Donald F. Bouchard and Sherry Simon. Ithaca, N.Y.: Cornell Univ. Press, 1977, 139–64.

———. *The Order of Things* (1966). No translator named. New York: Random House, 1973.

———. "Truth and Power" (1977). Translated by Colin Gordon. In *Power/Knowledge*. New York: Pantheon, 1980, 109–33.

Fraser, Nancy. "Michel Foucault—a Young Conservative?" In *Ethics*, forthcoming.

———. "What's Critical about Critical Theory? The Case of Habermas and Gender." In *New German Critique*, no. 35 (1985): 97–131.

Giddens, Anthony. "From Marx to Nietzsche? Neo-Conservatism, Foucault, and Problems in Contemporary Political Theory." In *Profiles and Critiques in Social Theory*. Berkeley and Los Angeles: Univ. of California Press, 1982, 215–30.

Gilbert, James Burkhart. *Writers and Partisans*. New York: Wiley, 1968.

Glazer, Nathan. "New York Intellectuals—Up from Revolution." In *New York Times Book Review*, 26 February 1984, 1, 34–35.

Goldmann, Lucien. *Lukács and Heidegger* (1973). Translated by William Q. Boelhower. London: Routledge and Kegan Paul, 1977.

Gouldner, Alvin W. *The Future of the Intellectuals and the Rise of the New Class*. New York: Continuum, 1979.

Graff, Gerald. *Literature Against Itself*. Chicago: Univ. of Chicago Press, 1979.

Habermas and Modernity. Edited by Richard J. Bernstein. Cambridge, Mass.: MIT Press, 1985.

Habermas, Jürgen. "Does Philosophy Still Have a Purpose?" (1971). In *Philosophical-Political Profiles*, translated by Frederick G. Lawrence. Cambridge, Mass.: MIT Press, 1983, 1–19.

———. "The French Path to Postmodernity: Bataille between Eroticism and General Economics." Translated by Frederick Lawrence. In *New German Critique*, no. 33 (1984): 79–102.

———. "Modernity—An Incomplete Project" (1980). Translated by Seyla Ben-Habib. In *The Anti-Aesthetic*, 3–15.

———. "Neoconservative Culture Criticism in the United States and West Germany: An Intellectual Movement in Two Political Cultures" (1983). Translated by Russell A. Berman. In *Habermas and Modernity*, 78–94.

———. "Questions and Counterquestions" (1984). Translated by James Bohman. In *Habermas and Modernity*, 192–216.

Hassan, Ihab. "Postface 1982: Toward a Concept of Postmodernism." In *The Dismemberment of Orpheus: Toward a Postmodern Literature* (1971). 2d ed. Madison: Univ. of Wisconsin Press, 1982, 259–71.

———. "POSTmodernISM" (1971). In *Paracriticisms*. Urbana: Univ. of Illinois Press, 1975, 39–59.

Hassan, Ihab, and Sally Hassan, editors. *Innovation/Renovation*. Madison: Univ. of Wisconsin Press, 1983.

Heidegger, Martin. "The Age of the World View." Translated by Marjorie Grene. In *boundary 2* 4.2 (1976): 341–55.

Howe, Irving. *The Decline of the New*. New York: Harcourt, 1970.

———. *A Margin of Hope*. New York: Harcourt, 1982.

———. "Mass Society and Postmodern Fiction" (1959). In *The Decline of the New*, 190–207.

———. "The New York Intellectuals" (1968). In *The Decline of the New*, 211–65.

Howe, Irving, and Lewis Coser. *The American Communist Party: A Critical History (1919–1957)*. Boston: Beacon Press, 1957.

Huyssen, Andreas. "The Search for Tradition: Avant-Garde and Postmodernism in the 1970s." In *New German Critique*, no. 26 (1982): 23–40.

———. "Mapping the Postmodern." In *New German Critique*, no. 33 (1984): 5–52.

Jacoby, Russell. *Dialectic of Defeat: Contours of Western Marxism*. Cambridge: Cambridge Univ. Press, 1981.

Jameson, Fredric. Interview. In *Diacritics* 12.3 (1982): 72–91.
———. "Periodizing the 60s." In *The 60s without Apology*, edited Sohnya Sayres et al. Minneapolis: Univ. of Minnesota Press, 1984, 178–209.
———. "The Politics of Theory: Ideological Positions in the Postmodernism Debate." In *New German Critique*, no. 33 (1984): 53–65.
———. "Postmodernism, or The Cultural Logic of Late Capitalism." In *New Left Review*, no. 146 (1984): 53–92.
Jay, Martin. *Marxism and Totality*. Berkeley and Los Angeles: Univ. of California Press, 1984.
———. "Habermas and Modernism" (1984). In *Habermas and Modernity*, 125–39.
Kipnis, Laura. "'Refunctioning' Reconsidered: Toward a Left Popular Culture." In *High Theory, Low Culture*, ed. Colin MacCabe. Manchester: Univ. of Manchester Press, forthcoming.
Klehr, Harvey. *The Heyday of American Communism*. New York: Basic Books, 1984.
Konrád, George, and Ivan Szelényi. *The Intellectuals on the Road to Class Power*. Translated by Andrew Arato and Richard E. Allen. Brighton: Harvest Press, 1979.
Kristeva, Julia. "Postmodernism?" In *Romanticism, Modernism, Postmodernism*. Edited by Harry R. Garvin. Lewisburg, Penn.: Bucknell Univ. Press, 1980, 136–41.
Lacoue-Labarthe, Philippe. "Talks." Translated by Christopher Fynsk. In *Diacritics* 14.3 (1984): 24–37.
Leitch, Vincent. *Deconstructive Criticism*. New York: Columbia Univ. Press, 1982.
Levin, Harry. "What Was Modernism?" (1960). In *Refractions*. New York: Oxford Univ. Press, 1966, 271–95.
Lukács, Georg. *History and Class Consciousness: Studies in Marxist Dialectics* (1923). Translated by Rodney Livingstone. Cambridge: MIT Press, 1971.
———. *Solzhenitsyn* (1970). Translated by William David Graf. Cambridge: MIT Press, 1971.
Lyotard, Jean-François. "Answering the Question: What Is Postmodernism?" (1982). Translated by Régis Durand. In *The Postmodern Condition*, 71–82.
———. "The Differend, the Referent, and the Proper Name." Translated by Georges Van Den Abbeele. In *Diacritics* 14.3 (1984): 4–14.
———. *The Postmodern Condition* (1979). Translated by Geoff Bennington and Brian Massumi. Minneapolis: Univ. of Minnesota Press, 1984.
Marcus, Steven. Review of Michel Foucault, *Madness and Civilization*. In *New York Review of Books* 7.8 (1966): 36–39.
Megill, Allan. *Prophets of Extremity: Nietzsche, Heidegger, Foucault, Derrida*. Berkeley and Los Angeles: Univ. of California Press, 1985.
Newman, Charles. "The Post-Modern Aura: The Act of Fiction in an Age of Inflation." In *Salmagundi*, nos. 63–64 (1984): 3–199.
Owens, Craig. "The Discourse of Others: Feminists and Postmodernism." In *The Anti-Aesthetic*, 57–82.
Parker, Andrew. "Futures for Marxism: An Appreciation of Althusser." In *Diacritics*, forthcoming.
Poster, Mark. *Foucault, Marxism and History*. Cambridge: Polity Press, 1984.
Pynchon, Thomas. *Gravity's Rainbow*. New York: Viking Press, 1973,
Ringer, Fritz. *The Decline of the German Mandarins: The German Academic Community 1890–1933*. Cambridge, Mass.: Harvard Univ. Press, 1969.
Rogin, Michael. "Pa Bell." In *Salmagundi*, no. 57 (1982): 145–58.
Rorty, Richard. "Habermas and Lyotard on Postmodernity." (1984). In *Habermas and Modernity*, 161–75.
———. "Method, Social Science, Social Hope" (1981). In *Consequences of Pragmatism*. Minneapolis: Univ. of Minnesota Press, 1982, 191–210.
———. *Philosophy and the Mirror of Nature*. Princeton, N.J.: Princeton Univ. Press, 1979.
———. "Postmodernist Bourgeois Liberalism." in *Journal of Philosophy* 80 (1983): 583–89.
———. "Texts and Lumps." in *New Literary History* 17 (1985), forthcoming.

Ross, Andrew T. I. "Viennese Waltzes." in *Enclitic* 8.1–2 (1984): 71–82.

Said, Edward W. "Audiences. Opponents, Constituencies, and Community" (1982). In *The Anti-Aesthetic*, 135–59.

———. "Introduction: Secular Criticism." In *The World, the Text, and the Critic*, 1–30.

———. "Permission to Narrate." In *London Review of Books* 6.3 (1984): 13–17.

———. "Traveling Theory." In *The World, the Text, and the Critic*, 226–47.

———. *The World, the Text, and the Critic*. Cambridge, Mass.: Harvard Univ. Press, 1983.

Schulte-Sasse, Jochen. "Foreword: Theory of Modernism versus Theory of Avant-Garde." In Bürger, *Theory of the Avant-Garde,* vii–xlvii.

Sedgwick, Peter. "The Two New Lefts" (1964). In *The Left in Britain, 1956–1968*, ed. David Widgery. Harmondsworth: Penguin, 1976, 131–53.

Spanos, W. V. "Postmodern Literature and Its Occasion." In *Repetitions: Essays on the Postmodern Occasion*. Baton Rouge: Louisiana State Univ. Press, forthcoming.

Spariosu, Mihai, ed. *Mimesis in Contemporary Theory: An Interdisciplinary Approach*. Philadelphia and Amsterdam: John Benjamins, 1984.

Susman, Warren I. "Socialism and Americanism" (1974). In *Culture as History*. New York: Pantheon, 1984, 75–85.

Trilling, Lionel. "Appendix: Some Notes for an Autobiographical Lecture" (1971). In *The Last Decade*, 226–41.

———. "Art, Will, and Necessity" (1973). In *The Last Decade,*129–47.

———. *Beyond Culture*. New York: Viking, 1965.

———. *The Last Decade*. New York: Harcourt, 1979.

———. *The Liberal Imagination*. New York: Viking, 1950.

———. "A Novel of the Thirties" (1966). In *The Last Decade*, 3–24.

———. "Parrington, Mr. Smith, and Reality." *Partisan Review* 7 (1940): 24–40.

———. Preface. In *Beyond Culture* ix–xviii.

———. "Reality in America." In *The Liberal Imagination*, 3–21.

———. "On the Teaching of Modern Literature" (1961). In *Beyond Culture*, 3–30.

Ulmer, Gregory L. "The Object of Post-Criticism." In *The Anti-Aesthetic*, 83–110.

Watkins, Evan. "Cultural Criticism and Literary Intellectuals." In *Works and Days* 3.1 (1985): 11–31.

Weimann, Robert. "Text and History: Epilogue, 1984." In *Structure and Society in Literary History: Studies in the Theory and History of Historical Criticism* (1976). Expanded edition. Baltimore: Johns Hopkins Univ. Press, 1984, 267–323.

Williams, Raymond. "Base and Superstructure in Marxist Cultural Theory" (1973). In *Problems in Materialism and Culture*. London: NLB, 1980, 31–49.

———. "Beyond Cambridge English." In *Writing in Society*, 212–26.

———. "Cambridge English, Past and Present." In *Writing in Society*, 177–91.

———. *Politics and Letters*. London: NLB, 1979.

———. *Writing in Society*. London: Verso, 1984.

Wolin, Richard. "Modernism versus Postmodernism." In *Telos*, no. 62 (1984–85): 9–29.

Wollheim, Richard. "Trouble in Freedonia." In *New York Review of Books* 23.11 (1976): 35–38.

Woolf, Virginia. *To the Lighthouse*. New York: Harcourt, Brace & World, 1927.

Postmodernism and Politics

Chapter 1
The Ineluctability of Difference: Scientific Pluralism and the Critical Intelligence
Paul A. Bové

I

The idea that there is a postmodern literature different from and often opposed to modernism gradually gained acceptance by scholars, critics, and teachers through the 1960s and 1970s with the result that the term itself and the variety of often-conflicting concepts it designates have become awkwardly legitimate. A detailed genealogy of this process of legitimation which described the inter- sections of discourses and practices from literature, art, and political philosophy would itself tell a great deal about how the institutions for producing and circulat- ing cultural representations work in our society and also how certain parts of the intellectual elite understand our society and its recent past. Of course, a genealogy of recent reconceptions of other representations such as "Romanti- cism" could tell us many of the same things, but perhaps in not quite such an important or fruitful way; for theorists and critics of the postmodern study and describe the present moment and so enact the present while conceiving it. Exam- ining the ways and means by which representations of the postmodern proliferate may well provide a privileged insight into the workings of our cultural apparatus. It may suggest not only how we represent our culture to ourselves, but also how we might develop alternative figures for this task that could more closely approx- imate our developing perceptions of the complexity of our social and historical existence.

There are, of course, many different senses to the term "postmodern," so that an initial "discrimination of postmodernisms" is in order. But since space permits neither such a complete discrimination nor such a genealogy, all I can hope to suggest are some of the defining and limiting characteristics of theorizing about the postmodern in literary criticism as well as some additional directions for further study.

Attempts to constitute the postmodern have provided the academy with some of the most excitingly inventive speculative analysis and critical writing of recent years. They have added a new dimension to the critical lexicon, employed and expanded innovative methods, and helped redefine our conceptions of the modern canon. One need only invoke William Spanos's "phenomenological destructions," Joseph Riddel's "deconstructions," Ihab Hassan's "paracriticisms," and Alan Wilde's studies of irony to perceive the richness and power of critical speculation on the postmodern and the way it has affected the landscape of literary study.[1] There are as many differences as similarities among these critics and their works so it would be foolish to suggest any underlying harmony of assumptions or intent. Yet, on the very broadest level, they all conceive the postmodern and their own critical practices as alternatives both to the established values and beliefs of our mass culture and to the habitual linguistic forms of critical practice which legitimate those values. In other words, put simply, in their highly various ways, these theoreticians and practitioners of the postmodern stand in opposition to the institution in which they labor and the culture which that institution, even in its current reduced state, continues to support. The postmodern appears in the work of these critics as something suppressed by modernity or as a new mode of "value-production" more suited to our world than the strategies and tactics of previous literary forms or conceptions of language. Spanos argues, for example, that postmodernism counters the aesthetic disinterest of modernism's spatialized forms by returning to the temporality of Being. Alan Wilde suggests in *The Horizons of Assent* that the postmodern, especially in American fiction, is a generative, mythmaking response to the shallow egotism of late modernism and its anomie. And Riddel's insight into the metaphoricity of language allows him to dissolve hardened critical patterns and to open textuality to the play of difference.

At times, critics of the postmodern reach beyond the traditional limits of "literary criticism" and enter directly into the intellectual debates on the social order and cultural life. For example, Spanos and Wilde both attempt to relegitimate a realm of social value in literature and criticism by developing phenomenological models of consciousness and language that "reflect" the nature and achievement of postmodern writing. Such models also require from critics and audiences an ideological commitment to the "worldliness" of art and criticism as well as to the priority of time and becoming.

These few comments on postmodern criticism suggest, even if they do not demonstrate, that constituting the postmodern as in opposition, or, at least, as an alternative to the "modern" or "metaphysical" is itself an oppositional act intended to be counterhegemonic. That is to say, it desires to break up and displace the modernist legacy, for that failed ensemble of social and linguistic relations acts hegemonically to mask social difference and the possibility of achieving even tentative but stable human values in postmodern consumer culture. That the original impulse of theorizing the postmodern is oppositional is a fact perhaps not fully explored even by its strongest representatives. Spanos has developed most keenly the antipathetic stance of his criticism, attempting explicitly to make over literary history and the purpose of criticism. His antagonistic, often violently counteractive position suggests further questions about theorizing the postmodern as an oppositional practice.

The most important of these questions is quite simple: can theorizing the postmodern be a successful oppositional practice if it remains within the limits of "lit. crit."—even as they have been broadened by these critics to include philosophy, art, and linguistics? Or to put the same question differently: is the "literary critic" the appropriate intellectual figure for carrying out such a project? Recent changes in the relation of the literary profession to society as well as the results of various nonliterary investigations into society, language, and power suggest that these questions can only be answered negatively as long as "lit. crit." refuses to take seriously the effects of the social world on the aesthetic and visionary figuration which it values, defends, and studies. Furthermore, the critic must recall that the critical act is a social act and attempt to understand and theorize the role the critic plays in culture in relation to matters of power, interest, and knowledge in our increasingly information-based media-culture. Of course many critics have attempted to develop theories and analyses that keep in sight the social-historical nature of literary production.[2] But for the most part, critics of the postmodern have not treated literature as one element in a historical culture. Rather, instead of analyzing the postmodern as a cultural configuration of social practices and discourses, they have tended to treat literature abstractly, as an "object," in its own right, of *literary* critical investigation. At times, at its best, as in the works of those critics previously mentioned, this analysis points beyond literature as a "discrete" phenomenon and exceeds the limits of "lit. crit." to touch on ontology, painting, and language theory. But these extensions suggest the need for others. Why not attempt, for example, to constitute the postmodern in the context of feminism, ecology, "interest-group politics," or cybernetics? Should not "literary critics" recognize that the therapeutic discourses of an interventionist social order may be as "postmodern" as the forms of John Barth's fiction or Robert Creeley's poetry? Indeed, that the latter cannot be satisfactorily analyzed outside the historical social order constituted by the discourses of the former?

Of course these objections to literary criticism are old ones. They can be countered on at least two levels: no critic can realistically hope to "master" the range of material needed for such contextualized cultural studies; and, literature is a social institution, but a "semi-autonomous" one with its own internal system of rules and traditions that can be studied and understood largely independently of other socially powerful discourses. To the second of these objections one might answer that it is incumbent on anyone holding such a belief to demonstrate that these rules and traditions are generated internally, independently of any other actions in the social world. It would be necessary to show that the reconstruction of these rules on something like a competence model is not ideology but the critical science about which scholars from Northrop Frye to Jonathan Culler have fantasized. They would have to show, in other words, that there is an "inside" to literary history that is independent of the "outside" history of other material practices. Or, alternatively, they would have to admit that what they produced was a static ideological model representing present interests. As to the first objection, it is simply not true that one cannot work in more than one discourse. In fact such a restrictive belief is the result of the specialized education that fragments knowledge and the intellectual labor process. Although Antonio Gramsci may be right to say that writing the history of a party is a way of writing the history of a nation, the first cannot be written as the second in the abstract, without a precise sense of how a party intervenes in society, how social needs impinge on the party, and how the party directs action and thought in response to the real needs of the people.[3]

Both objections to the necessary recognition of the social dimensions and intersections of literature merely echo the traditional division of labor that is a hallmark of the hegemony that postmodern critics hope to counter. Until and unless critics alter that division of labor by associating literary with sociohistorical studies or by carrying out group research projects to minimize the individualistic ethos of critical production, they cannot provide successful opposition to the ruling hegemony; they will too often simply replicate it. The advanced practice of critics like Wilde, Riddel, and Spanos in defining the postmodern has begun to break down this division of labor; their researches, although different, are also complementary. Moreover, their work has serious political implications primarily in its "deconstructions" of texts and false assumptions about language: thus not only do they reveal the "roots" of our representations in inescapable yet hidden linguistic processes, but they also undermine them and attempt to present alternatives. Unfriendly critics who argue that these works are abstract/ nihilist games produced by a dying bourgeois institution fail to understand adequately the very material effect that changing discourses can have on the ruling representations of even our media-centric mass culture. A more serious question is: what can be done to extend the oppositional intentions of this critical work?

It seems that a turn away from the individualistic focus on "authors" is in order along with a turn toward a more group-based research and criticism. Daniel O'Hara has elaborately demonstrated the maddening failures of individualistic strategies for visionary projection and revision throughout modern and postmodern literature and criticism.[4] Other communally based projects must be developed. Scholars must treat "authors" not only as inscribed within a great tradition—in whose techniques a writer becomes competent—but also as within a set of discourses that constitute the social world to which a writer comes. No matter how interesting, immanental studies of the internal achievements or failures of an *oeuvre* place a mistaken emphasis on "genius" or some "universal human nature" and do not take the opportunity to move from the *oeuvre* into the historical world of social discourse of which it is a (dependent) part.

Postmodern criticism cannot be oppositional if it remains within the disciplinary division of intellectual labor, no matter how hard it tries to broaden or undermine its own discipline. To theorize the oppositional effectively, a self-conscious attempt to be individually counterhegemonic is not enough. Postmodern critics must develop a detailed, scholarly comprehension of their own location within the field of discourse and cultural practice. A counterhegemonic or oppositional criticism has certain minimal requirements: a historically specific research project oriented by autonomous developments elsewhere in culture and guided by a political program that avoids, as far as possible, the suppression of memory and the division of labor that are the hallmarks of the academy's general subservience to the hegemony. In other words, radical critical intellectuals must understand the historical specificity of the cultural practices of their own period with an eye to bringing their own practice and discourse in line with other oppositional forces in a society struggling against hegemonic manipulation and state violence. Postmodern critical intelligence can complete the legitimation of its oppositional ideology only if it becomes part of the public sphere by placing itself within the context of other oppositional forces and theorizes the counterhegemonic in light of their local struggles. Such a repositioning of critical intelligence would allow it to do what it alone can best do: change the relationship of the power-knowledge apparatus to the hegemonic culture that exploits and deploys it. Only by moving in some similar direction can critics of the postmodern complete their transformation into postmodern critics.

But how can this transformation be completed? And what might a postmodern critic look like? These are questions the answers to which cannot be predetermined. The work of Jean-François Lyotard is intimately connected with the general question of postmodernism, yet in *The Postmodern Condition* his writing is hard to differentiate from that of any historian of ideas. It seems clear that "high" intellectuals are reluctant or unwilling to abandon the recognizable forms of their cultural traditions, even when theorizing what they agree is a new form of culture. Of course in studying the postmodern—as we have known to be true of the modern at least since C. S. Peirce and Walter Benjamin—critics must be concerned with popular and mass culture, and they must bring to bear on this increasingly wide range of cultural production and consumption entirely new forms of critical power. But until and unless these critics consciously position themselves within the structures they hope to identify and work upon, they cannot respond adequately to the pressures that the cultural and political present imposes on them. Critics are not "navel gazing" when they study their own history as part of their intellectual and political function.

There is still much resistance, especially among so-called humanistic literary critics, to the demand that critical intellectuals do an inventory, as Gramsci would have it, of the forces that form and determine them and their institutions. Resistance from figures like W. Jackson Bate can only misdirect the critical project of determining the role criticism and its related institutions should be playing in this postmodern Western world—especially as it impinges, and often violently, upon non-Western peoples and traditions.

Stanley Aronowitz can help us understand the nature of the task facing the postmodern critic. He has outlined in detail the changing social forces of our society and has studied the challenges they pose to the continuing intellectual usefulness of some of the major assumptions underlying important oppositional discourses. Examining Aronowitz's recent work provides not only a sharp outline of the problems and opportunities facing the radical critic, but also a strong theory of how best to deal with them to achieve counterhegemonic effects.

II

Stanley Aronowitz is not a literary critic. After years of union organizing and political activism, he is now a professor of sociology and editor of *Social Text*. His major book, *The Crisis in Historical Materialism*, is divided into two parts: the first, the long title essay, and the second, an assemblage of previously published shorter essays on a variety of topics such as political economy, narcissism, film, and historiography.[5] More than impressive, the range of Aronowitz's research is an essential aspect of radical intellectual oppositional practice.

The Crisis in Historical Materialism begins as a self-critique that outlines how the paradigms of historical materialism no longer describe our social order. Aronowitz is one of many radical intellectuals for whom orthodox historical materialism is in a crisis. Anthony Giddens perhaps puts the dissatisfaction with Marxist political economy most succinctly: "Human social life neither begins nor ends in production."[6] For Aronowitz this means essentially that Marxism has denied its own historicity and no longer can show that its basic principles— structured around the priority of production—"remain adequate to both past and present" (*CHM* 7). Paradoxically, this crisis arose at the moment when "Marxism became the leading theoretical premise" of history writing, economics, and sociology. Since the late sixties, Marxism has become a central university-based paradigm for intellectual investigation. "The academic recuperation of historical materialism," Aronowitz writes, "attested to the heuristic importance of material conceptions of social and historical structures. Yet," Aronowitz goes on, "Marxism had claimed to be a theory of revolution—a discourse of social transformation and emancipation—as much as an alternative to bourgeois social theory" (*CHM* 7). In "The Crisis in Historical Materialism," Aronowitz describes the theoretical and historical events that have cumulatively escaped Marxism's paradigms and concludes that Marxism can no longer satisfy radical needs and desires for cultural change and social harmony. These needs have taken new and different forms of expression and, as Aronowitz sees it, their heterogeneity provides radical intellectuals the opportunity to reconceptualize their role in a fragmented society. Perhaps more important, he suggests that radical intellectuals should call into question the previously ruling idea that there is or should be a master discourse of liberation and social change. Indeed, Aronowitz's book is most importantly a theoretically and historically specific defense of the idea that, in our postmodern world, no single ruling discourse of social life or autonomy is possible or desirable. It is a book about the relation of radical intellectuals to theory and it asks the question: "how do radical intellectuals theorize?"

The Crisis in Historical Materialism argues that critical theory too often models itself on a false perception of science; it refuses to recognize that our knowledge is constituted by basically discontinuous discourses and that there are multicausal explanations for social structures. It is also a critique of all theories that postulate a transhistorical Subject—such as the "proletariat"—as a privileged term in a scientistic, totalizing, and centered description of history. Aronowitz recommends a theorizing that never loses its critical purpose, that pursues an alliance with practice, that is always historically specific, and that, because it rejects the vanguard party and a role for what Foucault would call "representative intellectuals,"[7] accepts and advocates a self-managed society formed from an alliance of autonomous, sometimes competing groups. In other words, rejecting the Leninist model of the vanguard party and following one aspect of Gramsci's thought, Aronowitz advocates a "theory of the historic bloc [as] a more adequate formulation of the politics of the present period" (*CHM* 127).

Blocs replace class-based parties for both historical and theoretical reasons. Aronowitz finds in Adam Przeworski's structuralist analysis a historically specific theory of class formation which calls into question the idea of a transhistorical Subject and its class-based party politics.[8] Przeworski argues that as long as capital evolves, "classes are bound to form as the result of struggles (rather than the other way around)" (*CHM* 73). The proletariat or any other class exists only insofar as it is constituted as the result of a struggle "about class" (*CHM* 73). Struggles that form classes are struggles against domination and for autonomy; the politics appropriate to such struggles is a politics of association that, if necessary, alters its alliances as the forms of capitalism evolve.

Just as it is central to his revisionist thinking about class, his attack on scientism is crucial to Aronowitz's revisions of intellectual practice. Following Paul Feyerabend and Thomas Kuhn,[9] Aronowitz argues that the cultural dominance of modern science must be explained in sociohistorical, not epistemological, terms. Foreshadowing the point he develops in "History as Disruption," Aronowitz writes that modern enlightenment science can no longer be "regarded as a continuous process of theory formation according to the dictates of reason" (*CHM* 57). As Aronowitz sees it, Feyerabend analytically clarifies the ambiguous language of science itself to reveal that the philosophical and popular belief in an internally consistent developing "progress" in science is inescapably ideological. Aronowitz correctly points out that analytic philosophy cannot explain or change this and that society needs an ideology-critique of science. He finds the beginning of such a critique in Larry Laudan's recent work, which, although within analytic philosophy, suggests that the idea that science and knowledge "progress" is an ideological belief that does not reflect the way science works.[10]

Aronowitz's interest in these theories of science lies basically in his attempt to demonstrate the historical limits of Marxist discourse. His claims for the historical nature of scientific knowledge are not new or extreme among radical intellectuals. But the works of these theorists contribute to the crisis in historical materialism. Aronowitz writes that "the new philosophy of science, despite its reluctance to push further to a critique of society itself, has opened the way for the self-critique of Marxism as a kind of scientific ideology" (*CHM* 57).

Aronowitz traces these scientistic errors in Marxist theory and practice from Lenin and Lukács to recent practitioners of "Lenin's theory of monopoly capitalism, dependency theory, and capital-logic theory" (*CHM* 144). Lukács, Aronowitz claims, develops his theory of mediation as an equivalent of Lenin's conception of the party as the voluntaristic location of "scientific politics" (*CHM* 15). Mediation produces objective knowledge of social laws and structures. For both Lenin and Lukács, according to Aronowitz, "the reflection theory of knowledge" and "a correspondence theory of truth" (*CHM* 15) guarantee the scientific status of the party's politics. Mastery over nature, Lenin felt, provides a closer and closer correspondence between reality and the laws of science. And since mastery over nature is a function of the productive forces of society, production, for Lenin as for Marx, is the central practical and theoretical source of knowledge and politics.

Although Lenin always adapted his position to changing historical conditions, his theory of monopoly capitalism and imperialism aspires to the condition of scientific consistency that Aronowitz also finds in dependency theorists such as Rosa Luxemburg, André Gunder Frank, and F. H. Cardoso as well as in capital-logic theoreticians such as Harry Braverman, Paul Sweezy, Paul Baran, and Paul Mattick. Aronowitz's arguments with these three theoretical models for explaining late capitalism are not systemic; he neither attempts simply to correct the models they develop nor to offer a competing model of his own. Rather, as in the case of his objections to Lukács's theory of mediation and to Lenin's theory of the vanguard party, Aronowitz argues against the scientistic impulse behind these theories by showing that they are not identical with the totality, as they claim, and that in their attempts to assert truths in identity theory they are as coercive as the hegemony they oppose. By accepting a scientific paradigm, not only do these theorists forget the degree to which their own "scientific" models are part of capitalist ideology insofar as they share formal structures of argument and evidence with technology and modern science, but they also uncritically accept science's most powerful and insidious proposition: the development of a paradigm that will function as a field-theory of explanation.

In his critique, Aronowitz tries to displace this central tendency of Marxist analysis to form "field-theories." His objections to Lukács and to the more recent theorists of late capitalism focus on their various attempts to generate master discourses that either claim to take all culture and economy within their descriptive, explanatory, and predictive range or else reduce those phenomena they cannot subsume to marginal areas of art and emotion. Aronowitz contrasts these theoreticians to those like Althusser and Gramsci who place greater emphasis "on the centrality of ideological structures as elements of capitalist hegemony" (*CHM* 170).

Hubristic intellectuals generate master discourses and they are, in turn, betrayed by the complexity of the very history they fail to encompass.[11] Lukács's theory of mediation, for example, develops Marx's previously ignored remarks on the fetish into an explanation of the proletariat's refusal to accept its own historical role. Reification and commodification of social relations in capitalist societies make it impossible for the proletariat to recognize the underlying forms by which capital rules. As Aronowitz rightly points out, Lukács's analysis turns attention to culture as a location of capitalist domination and along with Gramsci's theory of hegemony revives "considerations of ideology and culture within Marxist theory" (*CHM* 19). Lukács remains an optimist: with the aid of the party, workers will acquire revolutionary consciousness, see the real relations of capital, and rise up in revolt. Although Lukács's theory is more satisfactory than Lenin's conception of a "labor aristocracy" bought off with the spoils of imperialist warfare, it is, for Aronowitz, nonetheless a "total field theory" that, in its implicit commitment to models of single causality and progress, fails to comprehend historically specific conditions that call for alternative discourses to describe multiple causations.

The Frankfurt school attempts to provide one such alternative; it points out the socially *regressive* nature of fascism and concludes that there is no necessity or inevitability to the constitution of the proletariat as a revolutionary class or subject. There are, of course, problems with the Frankfurt school's methodology. For example, it undermines the legitimacy of its analysis with its despairing conclusion that there is no possible opposition to the authoritarian state. As Aronowitz helps to show, in its important reversal of Lukács, the Frankfurt school ignores the oppositional impact of certain everyday modes of resistance to the state as well as certain contradictions within mass society. But, despite its own tendency to project an absolute hegemony as the fate of capitalist society, Aronowitz takes from the Frankfurt school's work hope that we may find acceptable alternatives to thinkers like Lukács who, in their attempts to build unified field theories, reproduce scientific ideologies of causality, progress, and prediction. Such ideologies are not adequate to postmodern society with the multiple foci of resistance to capital that have developed, for example, in feminism and no-growth movements, and they should be abandoned in favor of critical models of thought more like those of Max Horkheimer, Theodor Adorno, and Herbert Marcuse. I will return a bit further on to Aronowitz's objections to the despairing conclusions of critique in its "pure" form.

For Aronowitz, capital-logic theory is a recent sign of the endurance of this scientistic model in historical materialism, and in finally dismissing this theory, he summarizes his attitude toward all unicausal, scientistic explanations:

> My argument may be expressed in one final principle: the counterlogic of the erotic, play, and the constituting subject may not be reduced either to the mode of production of material life or the mode of social reproduction (family, school, or religion in their capacity as ideological apparatuses of the state). Political economy ends when theory seeks to specify the conditions of transformation. Marxism as critique consists in showing that the science of political economy is descriptive of the commodity fetish. The apogee of critical science resides in specifying the non-subsumable. (*CHM* 196)

For Aronowitz, all unified field theories are reductive because either they ignore those elements of cultural life that they cannot subsume or they marginalize them as "anomalies" to be incorporated at some future time into the paradigm. The political effect of such theories is either the coercive inclusion of the anomalous in a total order or a discriminatory exclusion that denies their reality as agents in society. "Critical science" attends to those anomalous people and movements; it confronts "theory" with them as proof of its untruth, of the nonidentity of a theory with the totality. Moreover, critical science tries to find in those "marginalized" figures traces of a reality that has escaped capital's hegemony and evidence of the theoretical and political possibility of noncapitalist social organization. In "specifying the non-subsumable," critical science locates those forms of life, action, and thought that are the necessary condition for the future transformation of society. It does not involve predicting the unknowable, that is, "the conditions of transformation." Such prophetic, prescriptive attempts are coercive and require, by definition, the deployment of a unified theory that functions, at least instrumentally, as "true." Yet theory can "specify" those nonsubsumable elements of society by describing them and theorizing their forms of resistance and association. Such specification may indeed aid in bringing about the "conditions of transformation" because it shows the untruth of all field theories and undermines their legitimacy as prescriptive, but coercive, worldviews.

Aronowitz's commitment of "critical science" to specifying the nonsubsumable elements of the counterlogic of oppositional groups and practices will not eventuate in mere empiricism. Rejecting the urge to totalize allows the intellectual to see the "*partially* realized elements of an oppositional culture within the framework of mass culture." Ernst Bloch has shown how capital conflates need and desire.[12] "The counterlogic," Aronowitz writes, "is to maintain their separation, to define desire as that which goes beyond need and is unrecuperable by the prevailing structures" (*CHM* 196). Aronowitz and Bloch are both developing Marx's insight that capital will produce its own gravediggers, but not on a class-based productionist model. Aronowitz suggests that critics and scholars should study the marginal elements of society and culture; but since capital can subvert the margins by making them fashionable, marginality should not be valorized per se as a form of subversion. Intellectuals should study the margins to describe and theorize the counterlogic of opposition to hegemony as it appears in the crevices of capital's dominance. Aronowitz clarifies how the very conditions that capital generates limit its development and so create crises: "What I am saying is that the dialectic of accumulation consists in its reliance on the conditions that produce its own limits. The study of the counterlogics to capital is long overdue. For it is here that the crisis will be discovered, not in the operation of 'objective' laws" (*CHM* 197).

In his discussion of "scientistic" elements from Lenin and Lukács to the capital-logicians, Aronowitz integrates three crucial themes: first, the changed role of the radical intellectual from descriptive scientist to critical scientist; second, the need to rethink the relationship between Nature and Society in light of feminism and psychoanalysis; and third, following Adorno's thesis, the need to develop a new dialectics which will not suppress difference or negation in the name of a formal logic of identity or an a priori concept of a transhistorical subject.[13] Since master discourses subject nature, humanity, and history to distorting models and plans for action, radical intellectuals can no longer legitimately adopt the role of the traditional intellectual who produces totalizing and representative theories if they intend their work to be part of the struggle for social self-management and cultural autonomy. This changed role for the intellectual has both a theoretical and a political consequence, although the two cannot be in any serious way divided. Theoretically, radical intellectuals must follow Adorno's critique of Hegelian identity theories and accept negation, not the "negation of negation," as the determining moment in developing a dialectics of difference. Important political consequences follow from accepting negation's role in a liberating project. To accept this role requires an antihegemonic politics of association between different, sometimes even contradictory and competing, autonomous groups—in other words, the politics of the bloc.

Aronowitz's discussion of theory shows the importance of historical specificity and difference in developing a radical theory. Adorno's "negative dialectics" provides a philosophical explanation of the compelling need to adjust scientistic models to the demands of changing social formations. In discussing the failure of historical materialism to live up to its "vision," "Adorno attempted to show that the very *categories*, the presuppositions from which Marxism springs, were misdirected" (*CHM* 25). The "necessity of philosophy" that Aronowitz tries to reestablish consists in critically clarifying the appropriateness of theoretical categories to the specific historical formations of the period to which they are applied.

Adorno's critique of Leninism not only explains the importance of critical negation and the errors of totalization but leads as well to the recognition of the importance of nature as itself a nonsubsumable category of theory. By analyzing Lenin's refusal to consider epistemological problems in *Materialism and Empirio-Criticism*, Adorno shows that this Marxist dialectic culminates in a formal logic of identity like Aristotle's. The power of negation for Adorno consists in its ability to discredit all theories of totality, which are, he holds, always theories of identity and merely based on formal logic: "'totality,'" Aronowitz quotes Adorno as saying, "'is to be opposed by convicting it of non-identity with itself'" (*CHM* 27). In a way that prefigures Habermas's work[14]—although with different results—Adorno insists on a return to the kind of questions raised by Kant and not answered by Hegelian and Marxist dialectics, which suppress difference in the negation of the negation. "The recuperation of difference," Aronowitz writes, quoting Adorno, "by a higher identical synthesis is 'a primal form of ideology'" (*CHM* 27). Adorno denies that any subject exists a priori and transhistorically; insofar as any subject exists it is formed by and in history. Adorno accepts Freud's demonstration of the insurmountable divisions in the self and, in a way that prefigures Derrida,[15] Adorno writes that "'the most enduring result of the Hegelian logic is that the individual is not flatly for himself, he is his otherness and linked with others.'" Aronowitz's comment suggests the link with poststructuralism: "non-identity is not difference *between* two things (subject/object) but exists within each" (*CHM* 27). The "difference" within the subject is, thus, never negated, suspended, or overcome. Subsumption of difference is not legitimate. Difference can only be repressed through social and discursive power. A subject fully present to itself will never emerge in history.[16]

Politically, Adorno offers a critique both of Western liberalism and of Stalinism. Both attempt to suppress and contain difference; both think it can be overcome. The present situation in Poland reveals how actually existing socialism cannot concede the nonidentity of the party and the workers' desires and needs.[17] Liberal Western society tolerates pluralism only as long as it creates no authentic opposition that cannot be contained by a system of hegemony and bureaucracy.

Aronowitz finds in Adorno's critique of Enlightenment reason and politics a critique of science that allows for a reconceptualization of nature. Science is capitalism's attempt to deny the difference of nature. Aronowitz claims that the very institution of probability theory and the introduction of the complementarity principle into physics "all show the will to totality in modern science," by incorporating uncertainty and instability into a unified, predictive system. On this model, for Aronowitz, the "rationalization of difference is reproduced in social science" in its quantifying techniques for prediction and control (*CHM* 28). Demonstrating the illegitimacy and inadequacies of totality theories and of identity logics means that both science and Marxism must change to accept nature's difference and to theorize its relationships with history in such a way that the counterlogic to capital can be described and extended.

Throughout *The Crisis in Historical Materialism*, Aronowitz complains that Marxism's enormous stress on the development of the forces of production as mastery over inner and outer nature does not allow Marxist materialism to theorize nature's resistance to mastery and its "priority" to history. Marxism's sense that human labor can produce an identity between nature and society obscures the point of departure for theorizing that very relationship: " 'The objectivity of historic life,' " Aronowitz quotes Adorno as saying, " 'is that of natural history' " (*CHM* 28). Adorno recalls that Marx himself recognizes the equally determining role of natural history on human affairs, something that Aronowitz feels Marxism has forgotten. Adorno thinks that Marx's "critical" use of a "socially Darwinian" theme is important because it testifies to Marx's acceptance of an independent natural limit upon social consciousness and historical practice: " 'Even if a society has found its natural law of motion,' " Adorno argues, " 'natural evolutionary processes can be neither skipped nor decreed out of existence' " (*CHM* 28). Adorno criticizes not only Marxism's failure to acknowledge the independence of "external" nature, but also its failure to acknowledge the autonomy of "internal" nature, of desire, which expresses itself, even if distortedly, throughout capitalism. Adorno's position "recognizes the disjunction between human desire and its object, but at the same time understands that nature gives rise to the social process and becomes part of the process as its 'unconscious' " (*CHM* 28).

Aronowitz returns to Marx to legitimate his departure from Marxism on the issue of nature's relation to the social process. "The principle of historical materialism suggests that Marx be read in order to be forgotten." The dead should bury the dead, for the job of radical intellectuals is to change, not repeat history: "to find those changes in theory needed to comprehend changes in the development of human societies and the evidence that contravenes our expectations" (*CHM* 46). On this matter, radical theorizing means rejecting basic Marxist notions such as "nature is congealed in the products of labor" or "that nature is a 'tool house' and a 'laboratory,' an object to be worked up into use-values" (*CHM* 47). Aronowitz, of course, also rejects idealistic alternatives to these figures of speech; describing nature as a pure, abstract "Other" to the social is an ahistorical idea that ontologizes nature.

But above all, Aronowitz stresses that a radically historicized sense of nature has disastrous social as well as ecological consequences. Aronowitz argues that none of Marx's "technological metaphors" can be a philosophical basis for rethinking nature's relation to society because like Lukács's historicist rejection of the immanence of nature "as part of the social problematic" (*CHM* 49), these metaphors are part of an Enlightenment ideology. Sounding his theme of the historical difference between the postmodern era and those in which the orthodoxies of Marxism developed, Aronowitz argues that "the historical conditions that necessarily prompted both Marx and Lukács to insist upon the centrality of the social dialectic have been surpassed" (*CHM* 49). Epistemological questions that challenge realist views of nature and knowledge are just part of a series of events and critiques that no longer tolerate the reduction of historical materialism to economic categories. Aronowitz suggests that Engels's "view of nature as a constant process of coming into being and passing away" is a more acceptable starting point for a historical materialist conception of nature (*CHM* 48). Among other reasons for accepting Engels's position, not least is its compatibility with some recent structuralist and poststructuralist attempts to rethink materiality itself. Noneconomic determinations of social process are material in nature. Sexual and linguistic relations contribute, for example, to the repression of women by preventing the symbolic representation of woman as anything but the "Other," as the absent "Other" of the Western imaginary. In effect, language, discourse, and desire represent noneconomic but material forces.

Louis Althusser writes that "an ideology always exists in an apparatus, and its practice or practices. This existence is material."[18] Aronowitz argues that a recognition of this broadened sense of materiality, combined with Freud's demonstration that self-knowledge is not possible, will compel a revision of Marxism that leads to acceptance of the idea of "*the substantiality* of human nature" and "of the constitution of the subject at the conjuncture of nature and history" (*CHM* 51). Following Adorno's critique of Marxism's logic of identity, Aronowitz writes that:

> Marxism's will to uniformity constitutes its very weakness. . . . It is no longer acceptable in the light of the discovery that the "mastery" of nature is not unproblematic. Therefore, production itself becomes problematic, and history can only be made consciously by recognizing nature's "needs." The rational management of society would entail recognition of what Leiss has termed "limits of satisfaction."[19] (*CHM* 60)

The "needs" of "internal" nature, made clear by psychoanalysis, have serious repercussions for social theory. In *Civilization and Its Discontents*, Freud shows that sex and desire constitute a counterlogic to socially productive labor: the

interchange between work and the erotic is one location of the subject's constitution in and of civilization.[20] Sublimation provides certain forms of socially useful
gratification, but by no means settles the struggle between nature and history;
these are incommensurable realities, but they are dialectically related. This difference between nature and history is the transhistorical mark of negation that
Adorno regards as the necessary basis for a critical dialectic, and it is what
Aronowitz makes the basis of his "scientific criticism." Aronowitz urgently
attempts to form this new criticism because he believes it will help prevent the
revolt of nature against a coercive society. Capital no longer only oppresses
society, but by its attempted domination of nature and the pysche threatens to
end it as well.

Radical theory can join other forces in preventing this apocalypse by recognizing the independence of nature and by theorizing desire as part of the counterlogic
of postmodern society. The possibility and efficacy of such theorizing is
strengthened by feminism and ecology and by the counterhegemonic speculations
of writers such as Gilles Deleuze and Félix Guattari and by Jacques Lacan's
subversion of the determining power of the Oedipal structure. The shift of capital
from production to consumption along with the development of advertising and
other aspects of the "production of signs" has released desire from some of the
more familiar and repressive forms of bourgeois reproduction. In other words,
capital catches itself in a contradiction: the use of advertising to exploit desire
to sustain consumer society has released desire itself as a "natural" force no
longer contained by the repressions that directed all energy into production.

Marxism's commitment to production and the domination of nature sometimes
prevents it from examining everyday life and the roles of language, sexuality,
and women in constituting material life.[21] But such an examination requires
going beyond historicist forms to a dialectic that will not subsume the ineluctable
differences between nature and society into an exclusively social dialectic. Althusser's theory of ideology provides a beginning to such a theory although Aronowitz
remains highly skeptical of Althusser's "humanistic" assertion of the radical
disjunction of history and nature. Also, insofar as Althusser believes that the
economic base, in the last instance, determines cultural life, he too is, from
Aronowitz's perspective, part of orthodox Marxism. Nonetheless, in spite of
these reservations, Althusser's theory of ideology —"as the lived experience of
the relation to the real of that which is prior to symbolization"—is a significant
advance because it severely limits the authority of rationalism and scientism—
despite Althusser's own invocations of "science." Like the works of Walter
Benjamin and Michel Foucault, Althusser's writings insist that "humans are
constituted by non-commensurable rationalities that are in perpetual conflict"
(CHM 69).

The political equivalents of these conflicting and incommensurable rationalities
in the postmodern period are the "new movements of liberation [which] insist

that the multiplicity of voices of liberation must remain autonomous'' (*CHM* 131). The liberation of desire as a revolutionary force requires the renunciation of all institutional forms that might embody visions of centralized power or of new hegemonies. Like Foucault, perhaps even under his influence, Aronowitz concludes that the multiple, local, autonomous struggles for liberation occurring throughout the postmodern world make all incarnations of master discourses absolutely illegitimate.[22] The role of the intellectual must, therefore, change: ''the liberation of desire requires a return to the notion of will, since it does not accept the claims of centrally-organized political parties to *represent* desire. The problem of representation is unsolvable by means of a master discourse'' (*CHM* 130). Like Foucault, Aronowitz rejects the traditional intellectual's role of producing representations of the desires of the oppressed. Such production is parallel to the forces of domination themselves, is always based on false identity theories, attempts to totalize social process, and denies radical difference. It is always a dream of a new hegemony. Despite its intentions, it represses difference. In the postmodern world, politics and social reality have so changed that struggling individuals and autonomous liberation movements will not accept the guiding role of often white, often male, middle-strata intellectuals.

One could argue that at this point Aronowitz's own argument leads to a typical and dangerous form of American pluralism. Aronowitz has considered the possibility that widely diffused oppositional groups can be subverted. As a tactic to prevent this outcome, he recommends a bloc politics, but with a stress, theoretically justified by Adorno and the theoreticians of desire, on the autonomy of groups within the bloc. Conceding that capital can recuperate almost any opposition—it has, itself, accepted the ''logic'' of decentralization ideologically and to some extent economically—Aronowitz insists that the demand for self-managed societies will force capital to take a stand: ''The demand for a self-managed society on the basis of the formation of an historic bloc that is simultaneously anti-capitalist and anti-hierarchical remains beyond the recuperative power of the prevailing order'' (*CHM* 134). Although any specific reform can lose its subversive characteristics, the relentless drive for autonomy cannot. Capital cannot tolerate concessions neither it nor the state can control. ''There can be no vision of homogeneity'' (*CHM* 135). This statement applies both to the existing hegemonic forces and to the antihegemonic, oppositional groups. There can be no unified strategy of revolution on the 1917 model because without a master discourse no image of a new hegemony can be projected and pursued. Alternatively, Aronowitz projects a utopian vision of sometimes conflicting heterogeneous desires coexisting without antagonism or hierarchy (*CHM* 135).

Having refused all legitimacy to master discourses, Aronowitz cannot produce a theoretical model to clarify his vision or to explain how to bring it about. But without such a discourse, he seems unable to explain how the society he envisions will escape the pessimistic conclusions of Freud and Nietzsche. But the essence of Aronowitz's vision, the optimism of his will, depends precisely on leaving the answer to these problems to the social struggles of everyday life waged by liberation groups and individuals.

III

The role that radical intellectuals can play in developing the moral and intellectual leadership of this utopian society depends on fulfilling the ideological potential of what Aronowitz calls "critical science" or "scientific pluralism." Initially, this critical practice must be separated from other phenomena. It is not a version of bourgeois pluralism,[23] nor does it share scientist commitments to unified field theories, unicausal models, and the commensurability of discourses. Finally, it must be separated from "pure critique," which often results in either determinism or voluntarism.

"Critical science" places limits on the voluntaristic aspirations of radical intellectuals to produce master discourses and turns theory toward the specificity of historical trends. Although critical theory does reestablish the authority of resistance to the "immutable" laws and forces of development and oppression and so politically restores the individual subject to a role in social formation, this does not simply abrogate the operation of laws in social development. Rather, it mediates them, "rendering them no more than tendencies" (*CHM* 198). Critical practice that associates itself with struggles for liberation cannot naively assume success based on desire or will or the inevitable coming of a socialist society. If such criticism is to be efficacious, it requires detailed research into the concrete and specific constitution of the historical moment in which it is placed. The "romance of interpretation," as Daniel O'Hara calls the foolish aspirations of critical thought to sublimity, is a hindrance to liberation.[24] As long as it refuses to abandon a belief in what Jonathan Arac calls the "heterocosmic autonomy of literature," it will remain acceptable to liberal pluralism.[25] Capitalist, patriarchal society has no trouble tolerating or ignoring it.

Aronowitz points out a useful alternative direction for criticism in a postmodern world, especially for a criticism that attempts both to theorize and to embody the postmodern:

> The problem is to construct a critical science whose "last instance" is the concrete, the historical specificity of social praxis while, at the same time, making the rigorous distinction between praxis as the constituting moment of history and the way in which history as already constituted takes on the appearance of the social formation's impenetrable facticity. Thus, there is a *positive* moment in all critical theory, a descriptive moment when the unfolding of capital's forms of appearance appear to possess the weight of natural law. The critical moment consists in the activity of showing how these forms are produced by classes and masses. The task is to integrate

the descriptive into the critical, making the return to the concrete the dominant moment of social theory. (*CHM* 198)

Critical description denaturalizes the appearances of capitalist society and reveals the origins of these appearances and their underlying forms in struggles for dominance and hegemony. This is a genealogical moment in the line of Nietzsche.

But if the radical intellectual adopts this critical science of tendencies in place of the attempt to develop and transmit a master discourse, the question still remains: how does this provide social leadership? For whom does the intellectual work? To whom does the intellectual *show* "how these forms are produced"? What are the social consequences of this educational gesture? How will it help bring about the nonantagonistic forms of autonomy that constitute Aronowitz's utopia?

On these matters, *The Crisis in Historical Materialism* is not completely clear. The refusal of the representative role of the intellectual could result in the dispersion and co-optation of intellectual practice. One possibility is that intellectuals might become "specific intellectuals," as Foucault suggests, engaged in the struggle of autonomous groups in their local situation. But Aronowitz is clearly concerned that such dispersed actions can be co-opted. Fragmented groups and discourses "are, by themselves, not adequate to global structures whose mode is to subvert the autonomy of the margins and the underclasses" (*CHM* 196–97). Scientific criticism can form the ideology of the autonomous groups, "leading" them into an association that will not subsume their specifiable differences. Criticism becomes the ideology of bloc politics.

The crucial role of ideological criticism has come about because social changes in advanced societies will be determined by cultural questions. Economic struggles among elements of an ever more proletarianized population will expand, but their potential for liberation can only be fully cultivated insofar as they become battles for cultural autonomy as well. A utopian vision of nondomination will guide this scientific criticism. Theoretically and ideologically, it will show to all those counterhegemonic groups that no alternative hegemony is consistent with human aspirations for liberation and equality. Politically, critical science will theorize how "building from a micropolitics of autonomous oppositional movements, whether derived from production relations or not, a new historical bloc may emerge" (*CHM* 127). Scientific criticism would theorize a bloc that is, by definition, *antihegemonic* in its politics and culture, in its ideology and the forms of everyday life. Theory must refuse doctrine if it is to assume the perspective of self-management.[26] It must describe and defend the "*permanence of difference*" against the common sense of identity in both socialism and liberalism.

Of course, Aronowitz's position faces severe criticism. Questions will be posed by both economistic and critical Marxists. Also, he will be questioned about the efficacy of his defense of the power of historical "tendencies" as opposed to "laws." Is this an adequate way around scientism and extreme voluntarism? Is it an adequate description of the strength of certain existing historical social configurations? Can this be reconciled with his acceptance of Althusser's theory of ideology? Does not his preservation of critique's positive moment—showing the real structures behind reified appearances—preserve some elements of Lukács's theory of mediation? Does the incommensurability of discourse allow for a sort of eclectic borrowing from other theories to form an ideology of the "bloc"? Does Aronowitz avoid structuralist rhetorics in order not to circumscribe the desire of autonomous groups and individuals? Indeed, it seems Aronowitz has not fully come to terms with the implications of Lacan and Althusser on the transhistorical persistence of ideology. How will this affect the utopia he envisions? Can critical science become the ideology of that society and of all its autonomous groups? Without leading the way and representing that utopia to these groups as the best of all possible worlds, how will it become their ideology? How will education avoid *leading* groups to their goals? How will criticism avoid the advocate's role of convincing others that the utopia of ineluctable difference is exactly what we all desire?

These are not caviling questions, nor do they undermine the significance of this book. Aronowitz himself writes in his "Prospectus" that he will "open up more questions than [he] can as yet hope to answer" (*CHM* 8). I certainly cannot offer a full answer to any or all of these questions. It would be useful for critics to carry on the historical research required for understanding how these questions have come to be so important to intellectuals now. We might better see what needs they express and what we might hope to gain from answering them. In other words, we could learn their political origins and consequences and so might better judge what our own actions and institutions should be.

As I have argued elsewhere,[27] there is good reason to be suspicious of all institutions that establish or depend on structures of "representative" or "leading" intellectuals and parties. The long-growing historical and theoretical dissatisfactions with the Leninist party and its Lukácsian justifications have led intellectuals to pose questions such as those Aronowitz treats and those others that arise in any reading of his work. Such questions try to find for critical intellectual work a political role that is not part of some antidemocratic ideology or apparatus.

We might sketch our problem in this way: on the one hand, critical intellectuals concerned for the values of participatory democracy and sensitive to the hope that people can control their own representations cannot accept the many self-justifying professional and pragmatic models for critical practice so common today;[28] on the other hand, Lukácsian and Althusserian models of englobement and totalization sustain Leninst practices and visions that often blunt decentralized drives of particular groups toward democratic forms of self-determination. Aronowitz's work greatly aids efforts to get beyond the double obstruction posed by professionalism and by leftist totalization. He has demonstrated how critiques of science, the analyses of various feminisms, and the development of local forms of political struggle must all be taken into account in any effort to theorize the political position of a critical intellectual.

The critical mind must address the politics of the moment, but must also avoid being bound merely to the rhetoric and concepts of the narrowly defined present. One might, for example, use the skills of literary criticism to study the discursive structures at work in the representations by American media of current struggles to eliminate apartheid in South Africa. Such a critical project might have a doubly beneficial critical and political result. It might not only elucidate dominant structures of race, economics, and ideology involved in such representations and their effects on United States policy, but might also help to develop new ways for the Western intellectual to defend what is valuable in his or her own tradition, despite the endless need to revise most and discard much of it. That is, such a political critical move—based on a refusal of totalization and the representative intellectual—could be liberating in two ways: it might help to weaken the support of a reactionary American government for a tyranny it claims to dislike, and it might strengthen the critical, self-examining tendencies that are what is worth preserving in our tradition.

This small example does not in any way answer the many far-ranging theoretical questions provoked by Aronowitz's work. My sense is that the answers are needed but that they can only be found in the process of trying to adapt critical motives to the values and projects of participatory democracy. I see no other conclusion to be drawn from Aronowitz's analysis of the politics of the bloc and of the new and important decentralizing movements of feminism and ecology. For literary critics to join in this movement of forces opposed to tyrannical totalization and representation, they must begin by offering a thorough critique of the new ethics of professionalism that some leading figures and their followers now propel into the market of critical celebrity. Critical intellectuals will have to investigate the origins and contemporary functions of those ethics in order to negate them; then perhaps the work of building more positive institutions and progressive critical practices can begin to go forward.

IV

One of the most marked changes in the elite culture of postmodern society is the decline from the late 1950s in the importance of so-called advanced literary study. There are many economic, cultural, and ideological explanations for this decline. Any literary criticism that does not take this decline and other related changes into account is simply refusing to recognize a discomforting reality. Furthermore, this situation in English studies should no longer be described in terms of a crisis-rhetoric for it is a permanent feature of our society and critics have no right or reason to assume it will pass away. Residual formations persist when societies change and "literary" criticism as an academic profession is largely a residual formation. With the exception of certain aspects of minority and women's studies and some advanced literary theory, the profession seems to have little "liberating" role to play in our society. Some debate could be staged about composition theory and teaching; perhaps it is finally beginning. But the *normal* criticism produced and published by dozens of academic journals and presses seems more and more indifferent to human desires and needs. Neither the program of "good citizenship" prescribed by Wayne Booth[29] nor Geoffrey Hartman's seductive arguments for criticism as art[30] seem very effective as antihegemonic tendencies.

What are the possibilities afforded by the specific cultural formations of postmodernism for human liberation and what role can the critical theorizing of the postmodern as antihegemonic hope to play? These are some of the questions that criticism and teaching can try to answer specifically by furthering the desire for autonomy and self-management among students and intellectuals inside the academy. If in so doing, support for other forms of struggle also emerges, then the critical project will have some concrete social effect. In any event, Aronowitz reinforces the sense that the future is uncertain. Despite the powerful, but flawed, vision of utopia he projects—which reminds us of our power to imagine alternative lives—he devastatingly exposes the residual myth of progress in our visions and strategies of liberation, and this leaves no easy place for assurance or optimism.[31]

NOTES

1. See William V. Spanos, "The Detective and the Boundary: Some Notes on the Postmodern Literary Imagination," *boundary 2* 1 (1972): 147–68, reprinted in *Existentialism 2*, ed. William V. Spanos (New York: Thomas Y. Crowell, 1976), 163–89; Ihab Hassan, *Paracriticism: Seven Speculations of the Times* (Urbana: Univ. of Illinois Press, 1975); Alan Wilde, *The Horizons of Assent* (Baltimore: Johns Hopkins Univ. Press, 1981); Joseph N. Riddel, *The Inverted Bell: Modernism and the Counterpoetics of William Carlos Williams* (Baton Rouge: Louisiana State Univ. Press, 1974). The work of all these critics goes beyond the polemical sketch I am offering here. Indeed, all their works have helped to define the space in which these issues can be raised, and they have ramifications well beyond the range of this essay.

Since I intend many of my comments as something of a self-criticism, see Paul A. Bové, *Destructive Poetics: Heidegger and Modern American Poetry* (New York: Columbia Univ. Press, 1980) in which I wrote too abstractly and ahistorically of "the radical flux, disorder, alienation, and death which characterize the Postmodern world" (x).

One other important theorist of the postmodern is Charles Altieri whose essay, "From Symbolist Form to Immanence: The Ground of Postmodern American Poetics" (*boundary 2* 1 [1973]: 605–41), is fundamental. Altieri's work has developed in different directions since the midseventies and culminated in *Quality and Act* (Amherst: Univ. of Massachusetts Press, 1982); I cannot deal with the range of his work in this essay. See my review of *Quality and Act, Contemporary Literature* 24 (1983): 379–86.

2. See, for example, Fredric Jameson, *The Political Unconscious* (Ithaca, N.Y.: Cornell Univ. Press, 1981).

3. Antonio Gramsci, "The Modern Prince," *Selections from the Prison Notebooks*, ed. and trans. Quintin Hoare and Geoffrey Nowell Smith (London: Lawrence and Wishart, 1971), 151.

4. See, for example, Daniel O'Hara, "The Romance of Interpretation: A 'Postmodern' Critical Style," *boundary 2* 8.3 (1980): 259–84.

5. Stanley Aronowitz, *The Crisis in Historical Materialism: Class, Politics and Culture in Marxist Theory* (New York: Praeger, 1981); all further references to this work appear parenthetically in my text as *CHM*. See also Stanley Aronowitz, *False Promises: The Shaping of American Working Class Consciousness* (New York: McGraw-Hill, 1973), *Food, Shelter and the American Dream* (New York: Seabury Press, 1974), and *Working-Class Hero* (New York: Pilgrim, 1983).

6. Anthony Giddens, *A Contemporary Critique of Historical Materialism* (Berkeley and Los Angeles: Univ. of California Press, 1981), 156.

7. See Michel Foucault, "Intellectuals and Power," *Language, Counter-Memory, Practice: Selected Essays and Interviews*, trans. Donald F. Bouchard and Sherry Simon, ed. Donald F. Bouchard (Ithaca, N.Y.: Cornell Univ. Press, 1977), 207.

8. Adam Przeworski, "Proletariat into Class: The Process of Class Formation from Karl Kautsky's 'Class Struggle' to Recent Controversies," *Politics and Society* 7 (1977): 343–402.

9. Paul Feyerabend, *Against Method* (London: New Left Books, 1975); Thomas Kuhn, *The Structure of Scientific Revolutions* (Chicago: Univ. of Chicago Press, 1962).

10. Larry Laudan, *Progress and Its Problems* (Berkeley: Univ. of California Press, 1978).

11. "Hubris" is not a very exact term, but it does, I think, get at the sense of arrogance and imperialism in intellectuals which is satisfied by generating master discourses. Of course, insofar as such models still constitute a measure of elite intellectual success, they are also socially a base of professional power.

12. Ernest Bloch, "Non-Synchronism and Dialectics," trans. Mark Ritter, *New German Critique*, no. 11 (1977): 22–38. This is also an important essay for Aronowitz's understanding of historiography.

13. Aronowitz's point of departure is Theodor W. Adorno's *Negative Dialectics*, trans. E. B. Ashton (New York: Seabury Press, 1973). On Adorno and poststructuralism, see the chapter by Rainer Nägele in this volume.

14. Jürgen Habermas, *Knowledge and Human Interests*, trans. Jeremy Shapiro (Boston: Beacon Press, 1971), 198–209.

15. Jacques Derrida, *Glas* (Paris: Editions Galilée, 1974).

16. See Derrida's brilliant demonstration of the nonimmanence of the self in his critique of phenomenology, *Speech and Phenomena and Other Essays*, trans. David B. Allison (Evanston, Ill.: Northwestern Univ. Press, 1973).

17. Cf. Rudolph Bahro, *The Alternative in Eastern Europe*, trans. David Fernbach (London: New Left Books, 1978). Commenting on the system of economic regulation in Eastern Europe, Bahro writes that the system is socially unsatisfactory "because the party and state apparatus programme the economy in such a way as to transform every increase in productivity into a growth in production" (451).

18. Louis Althusser, "Ideology and Ideological State Apparatuses" (1970), in *Lenin and Philosophy*, trans. Ben Brewster (London: New Left Books, 1971), 156. For an examination of literary transformation that suggests the material nature of literary discourse, see Jonathan Arac, *Commissioned Spirits: The Shaping of Social Motion in Dickens, Carlyle, Melville, and Hawthorne* (New Brunswick, N.J.: Rutgers University Press, 1979).

19. Alvin Gouldner also argues that advanced societies must find ideologically legitimate ways to restrict production, i.e., to limit the quest for satisfaction in commodities. See *The Two Marxisms* (New York: Seabury Press, 1980). This position is not simply the naive blindness of a powerful intellectual in a "post-scarcity, affluent society" with no regard for less-developed economies. It is rather a reflection of the recent recognition that ecological disaster is a worldwide product of capital and industrialization. See William Leiss, *The Limits of Satisfaction* (Toronto: Univ. of Toronto Press, 1978), 113–14.

20. Sigmund Freud, *Civilization and Its Discontents*, trans. James Strachey (New York: W. W. Norton, 1962).

21. It is not coincidental that the election of a reactionary government, the resurgence of anti-feminism, and the rise of antiecological "deregulators" all take place at the same time as, or follow shortly upon, the publication of a series of "pro-family," "common-sensical," and "anti-modernist" books, which announce themselves as radical and even Marxist but can easily be seen as defenses of repressive social forms and partisan ideologies. See, for example, Christopher Lasch, *Haven in a Heartless World: The Family Besieged* (New York: Basic Books, 1977); *The Culture of Narcissism: American Life in an Age of Diminishing Expectations* (New York: W. W. Norton, 1978); and Gerald Graff, *Literature against Itself* (Chicago: Univ. of Chicago Press, 1979). Graff and Lasch have defended their work of the seventies by suggesting that it was never meant to be conservative and has been seriously misread. Graff, for one, has certainly been sometimes unhappy with the "allies" his work has found. One must, therefore, accept the motives underlying their defense and point out additionally that their positions have indeed changed in important ways. Nonetheless, despite their intentions and after-the-fact apologies, one should also see that these texts functioned—and perhaps do still function—precisely in the manner I have suggested.

22. Foucault, "Intellectuals and Power." Aronowitz does not derive his theory of the radical intellectual from Gramsci's theory of the organic intellectual, but there are interesting relationships to be worked out.

23. For an example of this influential ideological position in literary criticism, see Wayne Booth, *Critical Understanding: The Powers and Limits of Pluralism* (Chicago: Univ. of Chicago Press, 1979).

24. See O'Hara, "The Romance of Interpretation."

25. Jonathan Arac, "The Criticism of Harold Bloom: Judgment and History," *Centrum* 6 (1978): 42.

26. On Gramsci's refusal of doctrine, see Joseph Buttigieg, "The Exemplary Worldliness of Antonio Gramsci's Criticism," *boundary 2* 11.1–2 (1982–83): 21–39.

27. Paul A. Bové, *Intellectuals in Power: A Genealogy of Critical Humanism* (New York: Columbia Univ. Press, 1986).

28. See the introduction to this volume by Jonathan Arac for an analysis of the problems with these models. See also Edward W. Said, "Response to Stanley Fish," *Critical Inquiry* 10 (1983): 371–74.

29. See Booth, *Critical Understanding*, 34; and Linda Blanken, "A Good Citizen in the Republic of Criticism," *Humanities* 2.6 (1981): 11–12.

30. Geoffrey H. Hartman, *Criticism in the Wilderness: The Study of Literature Today* (New Haven, Conn.: Yale Univ. Press, 1980).

31. I would like to thank Joseph Buttigieg, Barbara Jetton, Karl Kroeber, and Cornel West for discussing this essay with me. I owe a larger than usual debt to Jonathan Arac and Dan O'Hara who generously gave of their time to read closely earlier drafts of this essay; they made valuable comments and asked necessary questions, many of which I am not yet able to answer.

Chapter 2
Interpretive Strategies/Strategic Interpretations: On Anglo-American Reader-Response Criticism
Mary Louise Pratt

When the call for self-justification goes out, reader-response criticism often presents itself as a corrective to formalist or intrinsic criticism. This explanation, though undoubtedly true, does not seem altogether adequate. On the one hand, formalism and New Criticism are already so discredited in theoretical circles that there seems little need for another round of abuse. On the other hand, much reader-response criticism turns out to be a notational variant of that very formalism so roundly rejected. An antiformalist theoretical stance invoked to uphold a neo- or covertly formalist practice is a contradiction not altogether unfamiliar these days, and one which suggests that in addition to the dead horses being flogged, there must be some live ones running around escaping notice. Gazes must turn outward, beyond the corral.

It's true that interest in reader response was sparked by a problem in formalist theory, namely the fact that readers commonly disagree as to the aesthetic structures and properties of texts, and that this disagreement doesn't feel at all inappropriate even though it puts into question the objectivity in which formalism seeks to validate itself. Ironically, reader-response criticism seeks its validity in the fact that though disagreement is common, consensus happens too—lots of it, which undermines the affective fallacists' arguments condemning the (supposed) randomness of the "purely personal." It is the existence of degrees of consensus that reader-response critics have sought to represent through such

For helpful comments and suggestions, I would like to thank Elizabeth Traugott, Ed Cohen, Bill Todd, Renato Rosaldo, Jonathan Arac, and Herbert Lindenberger.

concepts as the superreader, informed reader, literary competence, interpretive community, and others (see below for detailed discussion of these last two). In a somewhat broader perspective, reader-response criticism can be located within a general trend in the humanities and social sciences, as Susan Suleiman observes: "The recent evolution of all these disciplines has been toward self-reflexiveness—questioning and making explicit the assumptions that ground the methods of the discipline, and concurrently the investigator's role in delimiting or even constituting the object of study."[1] Within this trend, as Suleiman points out, literary theory has been particularly influenced by the shift in linguistic theory to the notion of individual subjective competence as the object of study rather than either collectively constituted *langue* (as in Saussurian linguistics) or empirical data (as in ethno- and socio-linguistics). Of equal importance has been the rising credibility of psychology and psychoanalytic theory, which have given reader-response criticism its latest breakthrough, in the theory of the nonessential subject.[2]

American reader-response criticism has also shown a concern with pedagogy, suggesting some interaction with conditions in the academy. The rise of American New Criticism is often seen as part of a general shift in the academy from a stress on encyclopedic knowledge, to a stress on knowledge as technique or method. New Criticism is both an agent in this shift of values and a pedagocical response to it. With students who have technical knowledge and lack encyclopedic knowledge, what you have left to teach *from* is the text, and what you have left to teach are techniques. In analogous fashion, reader-response criticism and pedagogy clearly capitalize on the culture's intense focus on self-knowledge and self-observation, and on the validity now accorded to personal and intuitive knowledge. Students come to us trained, like ourselves, in observing their own responses, in talking about them, and in considering them important. Many of them (not to mention us!) have been through intensely self-reflective therapy processes, and can construct and articulate elaborate personal responses to just about anything. These then are the abilities—now socially recognized and legitimized—that we can count on to teach from during the Great Decline of literacy. And this is an improvement over formalism, if only because it is true, among other things, that readers make meaning.

Jane Tompkins contextualizes the reader-response movement even more broadly in the two dazzling essays with which she introduces and concludes her recent anthology of reader-based criticism. Examining the differing conceptions of the reader/audience and of response from the Classical period through the Renaissance, the Augustan Age, and early and late formalism, Tompkins concludes that "the development of literary theory from the Romantics onward leads in a straight line to literary formalism, effecting a total reversal of the assumptions that had been in force since the Renaissance."[3] What Tompkins is referring to, roughly, is the familiar shift from a conception of literature as a form of action and power to be used for accomplishing particular social, moral, and political goals, to the modern view that art should "do nothing" and simply be an end in itself. In the former case, the response aimed for is *results* in the form of political, social, and moral beliefs and behaviors; in the latter case, response is private experience undergone by the self in isolation. In the former case, the task of criticism is above all to monitor and influence artistic production; in the latter, the task of criticism is to specify meaning(s) after the fact. In this context, Tompkins finds that:

> What is most striking about reader-response criticism and its close relative, deconstructive criticism, is their failure to break out of the mold into which critical writing was cast by the formalist identification of criticism with explication. Interpretation reigns supreme both in teaching and in publication just as it did when New Criticism was in its heyday in the 1940s and 1950s. In the long perspective of critical history, virtually nothing has changed as a result of what seems, from close up, to be the cataclysmic shift in the locus of meaning from the text to the reader. (224–25)

With some notable exceptions, Tompkins's conclusion does seem to be borne out by the material assembled in her anthology, and also by two other recent collections, Susan Suleiman and Inge Crosman's *The Reader in the Text: Essays on Audience and Interpretation* and Stanley Fish's *Is There a Text in This Class?: The Authority of Interpretive Communities.* The appearance of these three volumes, all in the same year (1980), the continuing publication of books in the reader-response field, and the prevalence of reader-response concerns in such professional forums as *PMLA* all together form the occasion for the present essay.[4] After some further general commentary on the reader-response movement as a whole, I will give detailed consideration to three specific concepts that seem to be having considerable critical impact: Gerald Prince's concept of the narratee, Jonathan Culler's literary competence, and Stanley Fish's interpretive community. Throughout, the focus will be in part ideological.

Of the three anthologies just mentioned, Suleiman and Crosman attempt a state-of-the-art overview, while Tompkins aims for a historical perspective, documenting the trajectory of reader-oriented criticism since World War II, and Fish's book takes the form of a critical autobiography in which Fish reviews his own trajectory through the 1970s (and adds a new chapter). In all, as Tompkins says, interpretation does reign supreme, first in the sense that many of the essays are devoted to producing interpretations of particular (usually sacred) texts, and second in the sense that what theoretical work there is aims mainly toward producing theory to suit the ends of interpretive criticism. Those interested in theory will sense a limitation here, which can perhaps be characterized by this passage from Althusser:

Left to itself, a spontaneous (technical) practice produces only the "theory" it needs as a means to produce the ends assigned to it: this "theory" is never more than the reflection of this end, uncriticized, unknown, in its means of realization, that is, it is a by-product of the reflection of the technical practice's end on its means. A "theory" which does not question the end whose by-product it is remains a prisoner of this end and of the "realities" which have imposed it as an end.[5]

In Althusser's terms, what we find in these three volumes and throughout Anglo-American reader-response criticism is the technical practice of interpretive criticism at its scintillating best, and theory, for the precise reasons Althusser gives, developing only within the assigned ends of that practice. Althusser suggests that the state of affairs he describes is a necessary one, that any theorizing that is tied to specific practice can never produce adequate theory; theorizing must therefore in his view be carried on autonomously, independent of practice. I think this note of inevitability is unnecessary. It seems to me perfectly possible and perhaps even crucial to elaborate theory and practice in conjunction and I see no reason why this must inevitably produce a theory imprisoned by ends it neither acknowledges nor criticises. But it can happen, and it certainly has happened in reader-response criticism. Tompkins asks why it happened here, and the explanation she seems to settle on is institutional inertia and inflexibility: "It seems, then, that there is no escape from interpretation, not because the text is undecidable, as the deconstructionists would have it, but because the institutional context within which the critic works—a context created by the doctrines of literary formalism—dictates that interpretation is the only activity that will be recognized as doing what criticism is supposed to do" (Tompkins 225). The weakness of this explanation is that it requires us to separate the institution of criticism from the critics who participate in it, thus mystifying the former and atomizing the latter. Clearly, the institution of criticism is a power structure constituted by and through critics.

At this point, the historical analysis of Raymond Williams can perhaps add some explanatory power. In Williams's view, focus on reception has always been the distinguishing characteristic of bourgeois aesthetics, even in its formalist phases:

The replacement of the disciplines of grammar and rhetoric (which speak to the multiplicities of intention and performance) by the discipline of criticism (which speaks of effect, and only through effect to intention and performance) is a central intellectual movement of the bourgeois period. . . . From the description of a theory of perception aesthetics became, in the eighteenth and especially the nineteenth century, a new specializing form of description of the response to "art." . . .What emerged in bourgeois economics as the "consumer"—the abstract figure corresponding to the abstraction of (market and commodity) "production"—emerged in cultural theory as "aesthetics" and "the aesthetic response." All problems of the multiplicities of intention and performance could then be undercut,or bypassed, by the transfer of energy to this other pole. Art, including literature, was to be defined by its capacity to evoke this special response.[6]

In this view, it is formalism that is a notational variant of response-oriented criticism, involving a shift in emphasis from "the perception of beauty" to "the perception and contemplation of the 'making' of an object, its language, its skill of construction, its 'aesthetic properties'" (Williams 250).

What Williams's analysis suggests is that the difficulty reader-response criticism has in "breaking out of the formalist mold" is due less to institutional inertia than to a set of ideological commitments that both formalism and reader-response criticism share. If it is to achieve the real break with formalism that Tompkins and others seek, it is those commitments that reader-response criticism will have to transform, notably, I would argue, its commitments to the autonomy of art, to the mystification of art's relationship with history and with social and material life. Such a transformation will require, among other things, exploring the specifics of reception as a socially and ideologically determined process, and coming to grips with the questions of artistic *production*. The theory must be able to characterize the text as *product* as well as raw material for interpretation. It is obviously not in the slightest degree necessary for reader-response criticism to exclude questions of production from the domain of literary studies. To say that a text can be made to mean anything by readers does not *require* one to deny the text's existence as a historically determined product. Yet many reader-response critics seem bent on doing just that, even among those who believe texts can have a degree of determinate meaning. One way of making this bias explicit is to observe that if anyone were interested, the arguments used to bring down the affective fallacy could be applied with equal force against the intentional fallacy. For instance, just as textual reception can be shown not to be the private personal exercise in semantic promiscuity that it was feared to be, so it can be shown that textual production is not simply a matter of individual authors acting out inscrutable intentions, personal prejudices, and private anxieties. Just as the subject who reads a text must be seen not as an autonomous, self-consistent, essential self but as constituted by its social reality, so must the same be said for the subject who produces a literary text. It is therefore a little surprising to find quite literal defenses of the intentional fallacy surviving in the midst of reader-response theory, such as Jonathan Culler's wholesale dismissal of the question of production on the grounds that "the assumptions of writers are of difficult access and their statements about their own works are motivated by such varied factors that one is continually led astray if one tries to infer from them the conventions assumed."[7] It takes an ideological explanation such as that offered by Williams to account for this kind of asymmetry. The intentional fallacy is no longer a sufficient excuse for refusing ... historically determined human productions, any more than u... is sufficient grounds for refusing to treat literary interpretations ... human productions. Just at there are ways of talking about reception... beyond individualized "affect," so there are ways of talking about produ... that go beyond individualized "intention."

Another way of posing the same issue is to say that just as reception takes place within and is determined by interpretive communities or shared norms of interpretation, so production takes place and is determined by productive communities or norms of production. Indeed, it is safe to say that wherever there is a community interpreting art, there is a homologous or conjoined or overlapping community producing art, and there is every reason to expect that the shared community producing art, and there is every reason to expect that the shared beliefs and conventions shaping interpretation at a given moment are also bearing on production at that moment as well. Indeed, reader-response criticism exemplifies such a claim—it deals in the same self-reflexiveness and indeterminacy as the twentieth-century art with which it is so often concerned. Who would deny the mutually determining relationship between contemporary criticism and the *nouveau roman*? Here we approach the point where it becomes fruitful to talk about reception as production. Despite all the cries that readers make meaning, it is still easy to lose sight of the fact that reception of art *is* production—the production of meaning according to socially constitutive signifying practices, which is what, in a different mode, artistic production is as well. If you are going to regard interpretations as products of human subjectivities socially determined in specific ways peculiar to a specific community at a specific time, then you have, I think, to be willing to see works of art this way too. In other words, you have to be willing to *read* or *receive* or *respond to* texts as historical productions. This is not the only way they may be received, but it is one, and it is one to which current theory of aesthetic reception and response must give a place if it is to avoid serious self-contradiction.[8]

Terry Eagleton's discussion of the relation of the literary text to ideology is suggestive here. The literary text, says Eagleton, *produces* ideology (as opposed to reflecting, reproducing, representing it) the way a dramatic production produces a dramatic text, "transforming it into a unique and irreducible entity."[9] At the same time, what gets produced in either case—ideology or the dramatic text—is itself a production, with its own history and its own determinants:

> What is at issue here then is the *production of a production.* . . . The dramatic production, in other words, can never simply be the production of the text as autotelic artefact, as an exhibition of jewellery might display a necklace; it is, inevitably, a production of the text as product. . . . The production does not merely "double" the text's self-understanding but constructs an interpretation of that self-understanding, an ideology of that ideology. (Eagleton 67–68)

What is helpful about this model for reader-response criticism is how readily it extends to incorporate reception as yet another form or process of production. The text produces (operates on, transforms, interprets) ideology; the reader produces (operates on, transforms, interprets) the text. Such a formulation avoids reifying either text or reader, and captures our sense of reading as a creative, making activity rather than a simple process of re-ception, re-production, re-presentation. At the same time, it ties the reading process into a whole chain of different forms of production (in which criticism would presumably be yet another link), and thus overcomes the tendencies to isolate reading as an activity, and to overlay or distort the other productive processes that are at work. One need not, in this view, "downplay" the text in order to "do justice" to the reader:

> The text is not a mere set of abstract notations, a skeletal framework which "inspires," "cues," or intimates" the production, a threadbare score on which the production improvises. . . . Such a conception abolishes the problem by effectively abolishing the materiality of the text, dwindling it to a ghostly presence, and so reverting to the essence/existence duality which belongs also to the opposing error of fetishising the text. The text's determination of the dramatic performance is considerably more rigorous than such metaphors would suggest: in the conventional way, every line, every gesture, every item of the text must be produced on stage. (Eagleton 67)

At the same time, the reader is not pinned down altogether:

> But if the production cannot absolutely transcend its text, it can at least round on it, torture and interrogate it with a critical rigour . . . the production moves now with, now athwart the ideology of its text, in a double movement constituted at once by the aesthetic logic of its ideologically determinate productive techniques and the ideological demands which determine those aesthetic devices. (Eagleton 68)

Transposing the analogy to the text-reader relation, the argument would say, minimally, that every reading necessarily stands in definable relation to the text, though what this relation is varies. This I think is the bottom line on which all reader-response critics would agree. No doubt some would want to allow for that relation to vary more widely than Eagleton would, but I do not believe this is a problem for the model. The reason it is not a problem is that in Eagleton's model text and reading exist at different theoretical levels or as Eagleton puts it, "inhabit distinct real and theoretical spaces" (64). They are incommensurate entities, between which there is a "relationship of labour" (66). There is no way, then that they can be considered as rivals in competition for control of meaning or for primacy in the theory.

Notice how this analysis transforms that touchstone of modern criticism, the Jakobsonian six-point model of communication whereby you have an addressor, addressee, message, code, channel, and context all coexisting as "factors" more or less in tandem, at a single theoretical level. At most, code might be conceived as existing at a different theoretical level from the other five. Following Eagleton's model, you get something more like levels of production whereby out of elements of context (itself a product), subjects produce texts which other subjects in turn produce into a range of significations. Such a model has potential for correcting some of the deficiencies of the communications model, notably its tendency to view the message simply as a reflex of a preexisting, all-encompassing, uniform code to which all participants stand in the same relation. As Jacques Leenhardt puts it,

> The "code" in no way transcends the text but, on the contrary, is produced by the "message" at the moment when the latter manifests itself in social reality. Abstract notions such as "code" and "message" as well as "addresser" and "addressee," are no longer meaningful when applied to literature or any other cultural object, because it is the process of meaning alone, the process of the emergence of meaning, which in every instance gives the cultural object its specific characteristics.[10]

The kind of production model I am talking about would be able to express the perspective Leenhardt is calling for here. Moreover, by differentiating among processes and levels of production of meaning—context as production, speaker's production, hearer's production—this model can allow for the simultaneous operation of different, possibly conflicting, practices. It can therefore, as Leenhardt requires, "take into account the specific hierarchization of the processes of meaning, at every point of social reality" (Suleiman and Crosman 224). It can also, one might add, express the complex situation that obtains when speaker's production and hearer's production are widely separated chronologically and/or culturally.

I suggested earlier that reader-response criticism's acceptance of what Tompkins calls "the formalist identification of criticism with explication" was symptomatic of its ideological commitments to some basic tenets of bourgeois aesthetics, notably to a kind of consumerist view of art which calls for dehistoricizing the art object, detaching it from its context of production, and making it available for privatized leisure use. Without exaggerating the affinity between formalist and reader-based criticism, I think one can hardly be surprised to see the affective fallacy bite the dust before the intentional fallacy does. It is production and not reception that threatens the doctrine of the autonomy of art. These shared ideological commitments likewise explain why reader-response criticism has realized so little of what Tompkins sees as its potential to "repoliticize literature and literary criticism" (Tompkins xxv). Tompkins concludes that ultimately repoliticization is the net effect of accepting the relativity of interpretation and the constitutive power of interpretive systems: "When discourse is responsible for reality and not merely a reflection of it, then whose discourse prevails makes all the difference" (xxv). Tompkins sees, and obviously welcomes, the possibility of a return to the position of the Greek rhetoricians, for whom "mastery of language meant mastery of the state": "The questions that propose themselves within this critical framework therefore concern, broadly, the relations of discourse and power. What makes one set of perceptual strategies or literary conventions win out over another?" (226). Tompkins is right about this repoliticizing potential, so right that her conclusion is one most of the critics she discusses are manifestly at pains to avoid. Thus while acknowledging that all interpretations are "interested," are produced with respect to values and beliefs, few are tempted to make any declarations as to what they take their own interests, values, and beliefs to be, or those of professional criticism overall. As I shall be discussing in more detail below, questions of power relations are rarely addressed or are simply translated into the mysterious presence or absence of consensus. In general, it has been much more comfortable, as Althusser puts it, to "take recognition of the existence of an object for the knowledge of it." [11] With a few important exceptions such as the Leenhardt article cited earlier, and somewhat isolated observations by others, [12] the new awareness of the relativity of interpretation and the social constitution of reality has translated not into a repoliticization but into the complementary effort to depoliticize. Long-standing social and aesthetic categories are redeployed in the effort. For instance, the fact that interpretations are relative and variable translates into a celebration of the freedom of the interpreting subject when read through the rosy ideology of individual liberty (alias the denial of power relations). Equality and fraternity also come in to produce a vision of harmonious, nonhierarchical communities (or classrooms) where all interpretations are created equal and consensus is reached by a process of dialogue and persuasion among peers. In the psychoanalytic arm, we find depoliticising through the transfer of literary experience into the privatized realm of personal self-knowledge. Tompkins is right to point out the complete silence around the question of the goals of literary criticism and pedagogy, a silence that points unmistakably to the current acute crisis and confusion on these issues. The contrast with areas of criticism that *are* politicized is revealing here. In feminist criticism, for instance, one finds plenty of discussion and a good measure of overt consensus regarding objectives; one finds reader-based criticism and pedagogy oriented explicitly toward accomplishing those objectives (I am thinking here of books like Gilbert and Gubar's *Madwoman in the Attic*, Fetterley's *Resisting Reader*, [13] and of many MLA sessions through the 1980s oriented toward teaching us how to reread the canon). And, significantly, one finds that in such a case, separation of reception from production—the text as found object—makes no sense. The goal is for people to learn to receive literary production as politicized and to politicize their own reception thereby.

In the remainder of this chapter I propose to look in more detail at three influential theoretical constructs that have emerged from the body of reader-response criticism collected here: Gerald Prince's concept of the narratee, Jonathan Culler's concept of literary competence, and Stanley Fish's concept of the interpretive community. My overall aim is to argue that all three are best understood as theoretical constructs which, to retain Althusser's terms, are by-products of a technical practice whose end they do not question.

The Narratee

The work of Gerald Prince illustrates perhaps most straightforwardly the range of reader-response criticism that is a notational variant or even a direct extension of formalism. Prince's 1973 study of the narratee is widely regarded as a classic in the reader-response field.[14] Prince himself, however, has never disguised his commitment to formal structural analysis and the objectivity of the text. Indeed, he might well agree with Jane Tompkins's assessment that: "[Prince's] narratees, like Wayne Booth's narrators, belong to the text. Thus the focus on . . . narratees is ultimately a way of re-focusing the text; it does not endow the reader with any powers he did not already have, but leaves him in the same position he had occupied in formalist criticism, that of a flawed but reverential seeker after the truths, in this case the structures, preserved in literary art" (Tompkins xii–xiii).

Prince is best known for his earlier work on the structural analysis of what I think he would agree to call the kernel of skeleton structures of narratives—the basic chronological and causal sequence with reversal and resolution which Prince seems to regard as a universal, culture-independent form, the way the sentence is regarded in linguistics.[15] In the era of reader-response, Prince has turned his attention to those portions of narrative texts that do not seem to be part of this neutral narrative core, notably the evaluative, explanatory, and interpretive commentary which in most storytellings ends up being most of the text. Although the narrative kernel in Prince's view is predictable and stable in form, enough so to be specifiable by a formal grammar, this other material is highly variable and unpredictable in relation to the kernel. "Introduction to the Study of the Narratee" undertakes to anchor some of this nonnarrative evaluative and explanatory material in the subjectivity of a hypothetical "narratee," treating it as a kind of rhetorical overlay through which participants try to express, manipulate, or influence each other's responses during the process of transmission of the narrative core. Prince's work on the narratee and the reader remains formalist first in the sense that its cornerstone remains the decidedly formalist notion of the autonomous narrative kernel, and second in the indirect sense that it finds everything else problematic. In the end, Prince's analysis is directed toward explaining this problematic material in terms that will preserve the validity of an inquiry that treats text and fictional world as autonomous.

The concept of the narratee is most clearly delineated in the case of so-called frame narratives, which have a built-in fictional addressee, such as Camus's *La Chute* or Conrad's Marlow stories. In nonframe narratives, as Suleiman correctly observes, the narratee is the same thing as "the inscribed or encoded reader of the work" (Suleiman and Crosman 14), just as the narrator in these cases is the same as the implied author. In contrast with the usual treatment of the encoded reader as a highly abstract, loosely defined function or position or cluster of suppositions, one is struck in Prince's approach by an insistence on conceiving the narratee as a full-fledged fictional person, with a genuine discernible personality whether or not "he"[16] is actually named or referred to in the text. Thus we are told at the outset that one of the main reasons narratees "deserve to be studied" is that "the variety of narratees found in fictive narrations is phenomenal. Docile or rebellious, admirable or ridiculous, ignorant of the events related to them or having prior knowledge of them, slightly naive, as in *Tom Jones*, vague, callous as in *The Brothers Karamazov*, narratees rival narrators in their diversity" (Tompkins 8). Repeatedly we are referred to the task of constructing a "portrait" of the narratee or to the ways texts "provide us with interesting details about the narrator's personality" (Tompkins 15). These turns of phrase are not in themselves intended to be taken very seriously, but they nevertheless invoke a whole set of values of personality, individuality, and privatized selfhood that informs all of Prince's analysis, committing it immovably to the Jakobsonian communication model discussed earlier.

Initially, the main textual data Prince proposes to explain through the concept of the narratee are those in which the narrator refers to other beings or assumes the presence of other subjectivities, as in the following "signals of the narratee":

1. direct address, as in "dear reader" remarks
2. collective generalizing "we" as "that confusion in to which we are all thrown by the spectacle of the extraordinary" (12)
3. "rhetorical" questions of the type "And what was the young hero planning to do now?"
4. the collective or shared-knowledge demonstrative, as in "it was one of those hot afternoons in July."
5. negations of the type "No, it was not the loss of his horse he lamented."
6. comparisons and analogies
7. metalanguage like "Memory fails me here. . . ."

Prince analyzes such phenomena as sources of information about the narratee. For instance, negations as in 5 are analyzed as the narrator's responses to theories advanced by the narratee. The questions in 3 are seen as addressed by the narratee to the narrator. The *we* in 2 gives information about the nature of the narratee who, it is understood, "has experienced the same feelings" referred to in the *we* statement. The demonstratives likewise refer to the narratee's experiences. Comparisons provide information about "the type of universe with which he is familiar"; metacommentary reveal and overcome the narratee's prejudices and apprehensions (15).

There are obviously other ways of analyzing these data. They may be treated, for example, as characteristics of the narrator, as expressions of beliefs the narrator holds regarding the world and the hypothetical audience, or as hypotheses the narrator makes anticipating the character of the audience, or as attempts by the narrator to situate the audience. Or if you wanted a narratorless analysis, they could be treated as references made by the text to generalized cultural codes shared by the community to which narrator, narratee, and text belong. They can also be analyzed as instructions from the author to the real-world reader on how to make sense of the text. Prince opts to view them as characteristics added onto the zero-degree narratee who is always already there in the narrative without, however, suggesting either a way or a need to prefer this analysis over the other possibilities. The only objective Prince declares for his approach is that of producing a "more precise and refined typology" (11), which of course means nearly nothing, because typologies can be infinitely precise and refined.

The portrait of the narratee expands and then explodes in the end. If everything in the text is addressed to the narratee by the narrator, then everything can be read as providing information about the narratee—or about the narrator. Similarly, what is described as the basic competence of the zero-degree narratee can equally be described as that of the zero-degree narrator, or as that of the grammar presupposed by the zero-degree narrative text. At this point, narrator, text, and narratee become simply reflexes of each other. The analysis cannot help but circle back on itself: the language of the narrative text (or the narrator) defines and constitutes the narratee, but lo and behold, narratees can "determine to a certain extent the different types of narrative" (16). The "rapports and distances" between narrators and narratees "determine to a great extent the way in which certain values are praised and others are rejected in the course of a narration" (20). But with no trouble at all the direction of determination in this statement can be reversed, that is, the ways certain values and beliefs are praised and so on determine and constitute the rapports between narrators and narratees. The reversal has no impact on the explanatory power of the claims being made. This inevitable circularity is overlooked in the analysis of the narratee's role as mediator between narrator and reader: "Should certain values have to be defended or certain ambiguities clarified, this can easily be done by means of asides addressed to the narratee. Should the importance of a series of events be emphasized, should one reassure or make uneasy, justify certain actions or underscore their arbitrariness, this can always be done by addressing signals to the narratee" (21). The problem here is that since everything is a signal addressed to the narratee, nothing in particular distinguishes these operations from any others in the narrative text. How can you address an aside to someone you are already talking to head-on?

As I mentioned earlier, what remains stable in Prince's analysis is the concept of the value-free, zero-degree narrative core, a neutral structure specified by the zero-degree grammar and immune to any "personal" characteristics either the narrator or -ee might have. Values—ideology—represent variable, unstable elements, which Prince chooses to explain (make stable or determinate) by reference to the idiosyncracies of hypothetical characters. Hence, I suggest, Prince's striking insistence on conceiving of the narratee as a specific person or personality. Even the so-called zero-degree narratee is characterized not as a function or abstraction, but as a person, a cooperative, well-meaning but limited kind of guy who knows some things and not others, and has some positive and some negative characteristics; "he knows, for example, the language employed by the narrator, he is gifted with an excellent memory, he is unfamiliar with everything concerning the characters who are presented to him" (11). In this personalizing of the narratee, one cannot help but see nostalgia for the personalized spoken word. Personified narrators and narratees like Conrad's "make the narration appear more natural" (22). However out of fashion, direct statements addressed by narrator to narratee are "the most economical and effective" way of establishing "the true significance of an unexpected act or the true nature of a character" (21). This is nostalgia not for the traditional storyteller performing the ancient lore for the assembled tribe, but for a pre-mass-media, privatized ideal of communication as personal exchange between discrete and integral personalities, in which the basic shape of discourse is anchored in pregiven shared codes, while values are secured by the integrity of individual subjects themselves. Ironically, Prince seems to be operating to some extent within the very ideology called into question by some of the texts he discusses, notably Conrad and Camus.

Similar difficulties arise in a more recent essay, "Notes on the Text as Reader,"[17] where Prince examines what he calls "reading interludes," a term that refers, once again, to a range of explanatory, evaluative, interpretive, and deictic material in narrative texts. Examples of reading interludes include:

1. parenthetical explanations and translations, e.g., "You couldn't bring them any slow c.p. (colored people's) time" (Suleiman and Crosman 231)

2. specifying connotations, e.g., "The observers, those people who insist on knowing where you buy your candelabras . . ." (231)

3. specifying symbolic readings, e.g., the narrator's comment in *Sarrasine*, "Ah! it was death and life indeed!" (234)

These reading interludes are analyzed as instances of a text "performing some of the reading operations that a given reader may perform" (230), which is immediately translated into "the text reading itself." Here, then, it is the text that gets personified. The same two related difficulties arise as with the narratee. First, the data accounted for in terms of the text performing reading operations on itself could also be accounted for in other ways—for instance, as expressions characterizing the narratee, as operations performed by the narrator for the benefit of the narratee, as expressions characterizing the narrator, and so forth. No means are suggested for preferring the "text as reader" analysis over others. Secondly, as with the narratee, the new category introduced ends up disappearing into all the others. If you see reading interludes as performing operations that readers would otherwise perform for themselves, then everything in the text ends up being conceivable as a narrative interlude. Everything the text does can be viewed as work the reader might otherwise do. If the plot has a resolution, the reader does not have to hypothesize one; if it lacks a resolution, the reader does have to hypothesize one (or more). Is plot resolution therefore a reading interlude, an operation the text performs on itself? Only the questionable but unquestionable distinction between narrative core and nonnarrative "interpretive" overlay seems to limit the analysis. It is only with respect to this distinction that reading interludes can be referred to as a "fragmentary text in the text, constituting a language that is *other* in the language of the text and instituting some of the intertextual coordinates of a communicative situation" (237). It's a little hard to conceive of a text that is partly written in a language that is other than the language the text is written in, except in terms of a dominant or basic language, which in Prince's case is apparently (though implicitly) some neutral narrative discourse, probably of the type exemplified in his made-up examples like "John punched Jim; then Jim kicked John, then they threw bottles at each other . . ." (228).

The continual collapse of text-reader-narrator onto each other despite attempts to keep them apart suggests again that we should relent and start looking for an analysis of the production of meaning that does not insist on drawing these distinctions at a single theoretical level and positing a simple, linear directionality of determination among them.

Literary Competence

Since the publication of *Structuralist Poetics* (Ithaca, N.Y.: Cornell Univ. Press, 1975), Jonathan Culler has been developing the case for redirecting literary study away from the interpretation of specific texts and toward the examination of "literary competence," that is, the knowledge that enables people to interpret texts. It is an extremely attractive program, one that is proving expecially useful for working out the specifics of interpretive strategies.[18] Literary competence theory, like its linguistic analogue, is a powerful means for generalizing about the dominant status quo, a project that can hold interest for both those interested in preserving that status quo and those interested in changing it. However, to return again to Althusser, we find in Culler a theory that remains the by-product of an established technical practice and that, because it does not question the ends of that practice, can only reflect them uncritically.

Any analysis of Culler's concept of literary competence has to start by examining its analogy with linguistic competence. Culler is gratifyingly careful to refer to linguistic theory only as an analogy for literary theory, but, as always with the rhetoric of analogy, the point is still to suggest for his concept the authoritativeness and explanatory power that the linguistic model has already established for itself. The difficulties with literary-competence theory are two: on the one hand, it inherits the original weaknesses of linguistic-competence theory, and on the other, it differs from the linguistic construct in theoretically important ways that make the analogy—and the theory built on it—seriously distortive.

One symptom of the difficulties is that, while literary competence presupposes linguistic competence, Chomskyan competence theory clearly excludes a concept such as literary competence. The latter, it would argue, belongs to the domain of context-bound language use as opposed to context-free grammar. In its well-known phrasing, linguistic competence was originally described as the knowledge people have that enables them to produce and understand the sentences of their language. This knowledge was construed, aprioristically, to consist of a range of what were considered to be the most basic syntactic and semantic patterns at sentence level, those around which relatively clear judgments of grammaticality, ambiguity, truth conditionality, and literal semantic well-formedness seemed possible. It specifically excluded the knowledge that enables people to use language effectively in specific contexts for particular comunicative ends, that which later came to be known as communicative competence. It also excluded the range of phenomena that came to be known as "performance factors," the results of such mishaps as limits on memory, slips of the tongue, false starts, ignorance, limits on vocabulary, and so forth. It was these variables that the Chomskyan concept of the ideal speaker was supposed to exclude.[19] The overall objective, then, was to separate off the social and material aspects of language and delineate an autonomous, asocial, culturally neutral, nonmaterial (i.e., abstract) object of study (alias "the purely linguistic") for the discipline of linguistics. Everything subsumed under "language use" or "communicative competence" or "discourse" was seen as forming a different theoretical level where the autonomous system was deployed in various ways, and where "nonlinguistic" cultural and social factors played a role.

Objections have been voiced consistently to this division of labor, and the validity of postulating a category of the "purely linguistic" has often been questioned.[20] Though it is not always acknowledged by Chomskyans, the plausibility of that category has depended to a significant extent on its being posited not just as a theoretical abstraction, but as a fact of nature as well. Hence the importance given to the innateness hypothesis, and to linguistic universals. Hence too the great weight given to the controversial empirical claims that with or without instruction children spontaneously acquire competence by the age of four (i.e., before entering our formal school system), and that no other primate can learn true human grammars.[21] Part of what legitimizes the concept of the ideal speaker is the vision behind it of this innocent, spontaneously grammatical child. In reality, there is of course no point ever at which language exists as the innocent fact of nature that competence theory postulates. First-language acquisition may indeed take place outside formal schooling, but it is nevertheless completely indistinguishable from primary socialization. The supposed basic phonological and syntactic structures are never not laden with social meanings.[22] The fact that no such thing as the "purely linguistic" exists empirically does not necessarily invalidate the competence *model*, but it is enough to warrant doubts as to how productive it is to anchor the study of language in this particular abstraction. At the very least, it should suggest that the explanatory power and scope of these models is more severely limited than celebrants acknowledge.

Some generative grammarians, including Chomsky, now acknowledge the validity of a concept on the order of communicative competence as a complement to autonomous linguistic competence, but show little interest themselves in working out such a concept. The usual argument is that a study of communicative competence could never achieve the formal rigor to which generative grammar is committed. It is also true, however, that the concept of communicative competence poses problems for competence theory, or rather brings to the fore some bugs that had previously stayed politely under rocks. For example, the notion of an ideal speaker (alias The English Language) is perhaps minimally distortive when what is under discussion are sentence-level practices that are in fact pretty widely shared among English speakers (it helps a lot that variation and intonation have been largely ignored at this point). But as you move upward from sentence into discourse, a socially neutral concept of the ideal speaker becomes impossible to maintain. Verbal activities like cocktail-party conversation, therapeutic discourse, ritual insults, job interviews, doctor-patient dialogue, clerk-customer exchanges, scientific demonstrations, personal anecdote, military jargon, greetings, and introductions cannot be described apart from social categories and relationships.[23] Nor does it make sense at the level of discourse to try to posit an encyclopedic ideal speaker who is somehow master of the whole verbal repertory. It becomes clear that the relevant concept here is the speech community, not discrete individuals, and that what you need to talk about is not tacit knowledge, but discursive practices deployed along all lines of social differentiation.

Attempts to extend competence theory usually bump up immediately against these limitations, and often a healthy demystification of the ideal-speaker concept results. Nevertheless, it is also true that part of the appeal of the competence model for other disciplines like criticism is precisely its equation of competence with spontaneous or even innate knowledge, the suggestion that tacit or informally acquired knowledge has a kind of natural validity beyond socialization. Culler's treatment of literary competence is interestingly ambivalent on these points. Literary competence is described variously as an account of "the meanings readers give to literary works and the effects they experience" (Literary Competence," Tompkins 105), of "the underlying system which makes literary effects possible" (Tompkins 106), of "readers' judgments, intuitions, and interpretations" ("Prolegomena," Suleiman and Crosman 51), of the "special conventions that readers call upon'' to produce interpretations ("Prolegomena" 57). The argument seems to oscillate between stressing the intuitive aspect—literary knowledge as "effects," what readers "implicitly know" or "intuitively felt"— and stressing the artificiality and specialness of interpretive conventions. Culler does explicitly reverse the Chomskyan tack when he argues for the existence of literary competence on the grounds that it is *not* spontaneously acquired, that it *has* to be taught: "it is, alas, only too clear that knowledge of English and a certain experience of the world do not suffice to make someone a skilled and perceptive reader of literature. Something more is required, something teachers of literature are employed to provide. Either teachers of literature have brought off an unprecedented confidence trick or else there is knowledge and skill involved in reading literature'' (Suleiman and Crosman 52). The divergence from the linguistic analogy here is very important, for it brings into focus the prescriptive character of Culler's analysis. With linguistic competence, everyone who speaks by definition has it or they would not be able to perform. Hence the judgments and intuitions of *all* native speakers have equivalent validity as data for the linguist. When there is disagreement, it is because "performance factors" interfere, or informants speak different varieties of the language or the grammar is fuzzy on that particular point. With literary competence, however, in Culler's formulation, it is not the case that everyone who can read literary works has literary competence or they would not be able to read literary works. Rather, most people who read literary works do not know how to do so—correctly, that is, where correctly means in such a way as to arrive at "what we would ordinarily call 'understanding the poem'" (Tompkins 102), where *we* apparently means certain literature professors (*not* Norman Holland) plus other educated people who think as they do. With literary competence, then, only certain readers' intuitions, interpretations, and interpretive strategies count as manifestations of competence. As it happens, those strategies—the rule of significance, the conventions of thematic unity, of thematic contrasts, of alethic reversal, and so on—are those of mainstream intrinsic criticism. Thus, though Culler criticizes what he calls "interpretive criticism" for its theoretical impoverishment, what he is doing here is not offering an alternative criticism, but rather adding on the theoretical dimension he saw lacking. A competence is being supplied to support a particular kind of performance, or, as Althusser would put it, a "theory" is being created to meet the ends of a technical practice. What we have is less a reorientation of the discipline of literary studies than an elaborate shoring up of the dominant status quo, and of the interpretive authority of the academy: "To characterize this competence may be extremely difficult, but one can scarcely doubt its existence without rejecting the whole institutionalized teaching process, *which does seem to work*" (Suleiman and Crosman 52, emphasis mine).[24]

The prescriptive goal is not made explicit, however. Culler's objective seems rather to be to portray the status quo—what "we" do—as beyond questioning, almost as a fact of nature, just as the Chomskyan idea of competence does with grammar, or as functionalist social science does with social practices. This undertaking entails a certain amount of confusion and contradiction. For instance, Culler opposes using surveys of reader responses when it is a question of surveying just any readers: "To take surveys of the behavior of readers would serve little purpose, since one is interested not in performance itself but in the tacit knowledge or competence which underlies it" (Literary Competence" 111) (as if competence could be examined through anything but performance!). But he also argues that surveying published professional criticism is "more than adequate to ensure the breadth of an investigation into conditions of meaning" ("Prolegomena" 57). Norman Holland is criticized for failing to see that "a person is a place of intersecting roles, forces, languages, none of which belong to him alone, all of which are interpersonal" (Prolegomena" 56) and at the same time it is argued that the trouble with Holland's use of free associations is that the latter are not interpersonal enough: "A first priority, then, if one is to study reading rather than readers, is to avoid experimental situations that seek free associations and to focus rather on public interpretive processes" (57). (The real problem here seems to be that Holland's five experimental readers are undergraduates crudely constituted by "the clichés and codes of different subcultures.") The existence of an interpersonal literary competence that "readers" share is assumed, then later called into question: "Questions such as to what extent individual readers perform the same operations or how far these operations are confined to a tiny community of professional critics cannot really be answered until we are rather better at describing the operations in question" ("Prolegomena" 62). The competence/performance analogy itself falls apart when handled. According to Culler, as soon as literary competence is established as the object of literary study, textual interpretation (i.e., performance) becomes "secondary," only "indirectly involved" in the study of literature: "Whatever the benefits of interpretation to those who engage in it, within the context of poetics it becomes an ancillary activity—a way of using literary works—as opposed to the study of literature itself as an instituiton" ("Literary Competence" 106). Notice that the project of producing a theory of reading here becomes homologous with the formalist project of studying literature as an institution, a *langue*. But the real trouble here is that if you place interpretive criticism outside the domain of literary study, you eliminate it altogether, in which case there is no longer any performance for your competence theory to account for, in which case there is no competence either. Check the Chomskyan analogy: the idea was to replace the *study of performance* with the study of competence, not to replace performance or make it ancillary. The net effect of Culler's competence theory can therefore not possibly be the one he declares, namely that of "loosening interpretation's hold on critical discourse" ("Literary Competence" 107), any more than the net effect of linguistics could be to eliminate sentences. It can only be the reverse. The ultimate thrust of the account is rather to naturalize and legitimize the set of practices summed up under interpretive criticism, not to undermine them. Given this prescriptive use of competence and performance, it seems an outright contradiction, on the one hand, to bemoan "what has been lost or obscured in the practice of an interpretive criticism which treats each work as an autonomous artifact, an organic whole whose parts all contribute to a complex thematic statement" (107), and, on the other hand, to postulate "the convention of thematic unity" as the basic principle of competent reading. One is equally surprised to find interpretive criticism accused of forcing readers to move too quickly from poem to world, a mishap termed "premature foreclosure—the unseemly rush from word to world" ("Literary Competence" 117).[25]

Once a distinction is drawn between competent and incompetent reading (alias understanding and misunderstanding, alias them and us), the problem arises of finding a principled, noncircular, and seemingly nonprescriptive way of differentiating the two. While linguists back up their grammatical judgments by referring to a general consensus of speakers of English, virtually all of whom are assumed to possess grammatical competence, there is no such backup for the norms of interpretation Culler is advancing. Rather, there is a real, and potentially infinite, variety of other practices of reception, both in and outside the academy, whose occurrence (and unacceptability) Culler must somehow explain. Mainly his strategy is to invoke the integrity of the academy (can so many smart people be wrong?) or to treat the notion of "understanding a literary work" as an *a priori*, a fact of nature. For instance: "the experience of reading poetry leads to *implicit recognition* of the importance of binary oppositions as thematic devices" ("Literary Competence" 114, emphasis mine). The description of how interpretive consensus is reached is fascinating in the way it alternately invokes spontaneous intuitions and institutional authority:

> Poetry has complex effects which are difficult to explain, and the analyst finds that his best strategy is to assume that the effects he sets out to account for have been conveyed to the reader and then to postulate certain general operations which might explain these effects and analogous effects in other poems. To those who protest against such assumptions one might reply, with Empson, that the test is whether one succeeds in accounting for effects which the reader accepts when they are pointed out to him. The assumption is in no way dangerous, for the analyst "must convince the reader that he knows what he is talking about"—must make him see the appropriateness of the effects in question—and "must coax the reader into seeing that the cause he names does, in fact, produce the effect which is experienced; otherwise they will not seem to have anything to do with each other" (p. 249). If the reader is brought to accept both the effects in question and the explanation he will have helped to validate what is, in essence, a theory of reading. ("Literary Competence" 113)

I find the language of this passage quite extraordinary. On the one hand, the argument is rooted in the notion of aesthetic effects, which we are invited to think of as intuitive and universal. Should they not prove universal, however, analysts are to assume the dissenting readers have made a mistake. And suddenly we have a burst of language that sounds fine when thought of as characterizing debate among peers, but which rather chills the soul when thought of as applying in situations of hierarchy: readers must be convinced, coaxed, made to see, brought to accept both the critic's analysis of the effects and the effects themselves, regardless of whatever effects and analyses the readers themselves might have had in mind. I do not think it is unfair to see here either an authoritarian approach or a naive failure to consider the question of language and power relations, or both.

Other analyses are possible. Retaining the linguistic analogy, for instance, one could account for interpretive diversity the way linguists account for linguistic diversity, by the concept of dialect or language variation. People who use double negatives are not incompetent; they are competent in a variety of English different from that of speakers who use single negatives. In effect, as I will clarify, this is the move Stanley Fish makes in the face of interpretive disagreement. Culler does not make this move, again because he is committed to a prescriptive position. Rhetorically, the prescriptive use of competence hinges here on the ambiguous use of the term "reading." Just as "readers" in Culler's argument often means "certain readers," so "reading" does not refer intransitively (as the competence model might suggest) simply to literacy. When poetics is called a theory of reading, what is meant is a theory of reading literary works correctly, or perhaps even a theory of producing academically acceptable readings of literary works. Culler should not be forgiven this obfuscation, and, at the same time, we should recognize that he is either stepping or falling into an opening to prescriptivism that competence theory readily supplies through its commitment to describe *the* English spoken by *the* ideal speaker, and through its attempt to forge a "pure" object of study for linguistics. The moral of this story is not necessarily to abandon competence models, but at least to bring them into line with the view of the subject that Culler himself introduces, as "a place of intersecting roles, forces, languages" ("Prolegomena" 56) constituted ongoingly in social practice.

Interpretive Community

As a longtime champion of readers' rights, Stanley Fish has pretty consistently opposed normative and formalist theoretical positions. It is he who has been willing in his recent work to confront the terrifying fact that texts can be made to mean pretty much anything. Given the human capacity for interpretation, Fish concludes, there is no principled way to assign texts a determinate meaning.

And yet, he observes, remarkable degrees of consensus as to meaning of texts do occur, and people seem perfectly willing to commit themselves to specific interpretations, even people who, like Fish himself, are acutely aware of the infinite possibilities. To make sense of all this, Fish embarks on the task of working out in the reader-response arena the theory of the socially constituted subject, the social constitution of reality, the collapsing of subject and object. The result is an enormously productive clarification of how meaning-making goes on, not just in literature but in general. The consequences of Fish's vigorous attack on the concept of literal meaning have only begun to be felt in linguistic or literary circles.

Particularly given the autobiographical bent of his most recent book, *Is There a Text in This Class?*, it is fair to see Fish's theoretical work partly as a personal quest to examine, and with any luck to validate, the bases of his own critical and pedagogical practice. Few familiar with Fish's work over the years will have overlooked the conspicuous breach between his theoretical writings, with their antiformalist, antinormative stance, and his textual criticism, usually presented with polemical vigor as the self-evident last word. Although he often presents himself as trying to assuage the anxieties raised in others by Hirsch, Abrams, and others, I think it is fair to say that Fish is also trying to find some comfort for himself. Without exaggerating the personal, it would seem that the specifics of Fish's trajectory, especially the contradictions between theory and practice in which he has operated, and the related discrepancies between being a (good) Miltonist in the established sense and a (good) theoretical upstart in the boat-rocking sense, have a great deal to do with what happens in the four new essays that give his collection its title. In these essays, originally the 1979 John Crowe Ransom lectures at Kenyon College, Fish continues to work out the powerful theoretical apparatus centered on the concept of interpretive community and the social constitution of reality. What he works it out to is the rather remarkable conclusion that theory (or at least this theory) can *in principle* have no implications for the practice of criticism due, it seems, to the fact that regardless of their theoretical awareness, people somehow "can't help" (*Is There a Text* 361) believing what they believe and doing criticism however it is they do it (more on this later). For the same reason, what people actually do is of no particular consequence and no theoretical interest because it attaches to nothing outside itself. Here, obviously, is where Fish turns his back on the most important implications of the very concepts he has introduced. For what the theory of socially constituted reality says is that what people actually do and the interpretations they actually produce are attached to *everything* outside themselves, to the whole of their social and material life. This is why, you will recall, Jane Tompkins sees this theory as repoliticizing criticism: "When discourse is responsible for reality and not merely a reflection of it, whose discourse prevails makes all the difference" (Tompkins xxv). This is the implication Fish seems to want above all to avoid, and from which we can see him (along with practically everybody else on the bus) beat the great all-American retreat—into strange arguments about human nature, the omnipotence of the academy, the utter illusoriness of doubt, indecision, ambivalence, contradiction, ignorance, and all the other openings through which power is exercised or resisted, and through which changes occur.

What is being sought for criticism in Fish's new program is not something totalitarian, not power without responsibility, but something more like authority without either power or responsibility, a space to be an expert (an_____ist) without being The Boss, a space where, as Fish keeps trying to argue, it's all a game, which means that, unlike reality, when it is all over you get up and go home, mysteriously receiving a check as you leave, however. Fish would probably agree that he exemplifies his own observation (made with respect to Stephen Booth) that "at the heart of the institution of criticism is the wish to deny that its activities have any consequences" (*Is There a Text* 355). This quotation will in turn have brought to your mind the Althusser passage I have been harping on, and should have made clear that Fish too has produced a theory designed only to uphold the technical practice that gave rise to it, and which does not question the ends whose by-product it remains.

As I argued earlier, when confronting the question of how to assign validity to interpretations, Culler simply states that certain interpretations are intrinsically competent and others are not. Fish, recognizing a mystification here, asks "Says who?" and comes up with his concept of interpretive community. Interpretations, in this view, are never intrinsically valid or invalid; all are potentially valid with respect to some set of assumptions. Interpretations get validated by virtue of being assented to, accepted, and ratified by communities that hold the assumptions on which they rest. Validity, in other words, consists of consensus; consensus rests not on agreement as to the interpretation itself but on agreement as to the beliefs and assumptions on which the interpretation is based and with reference to which the interpretation is "obviously" correct. People who share the same assumptions and beliefs will spontaneously see as valid any interpretation arising from those assumptions and beliefs. They can't help it. For any interpretation that gets put forward, consensus of some kind is therefore likely, because the individuals constructing the interpretations get their beliefs and assumptions from the societies into which they project their interpretations. Completely idiosyncratic or "personal" interpretations are therefore impossible.

> Hirsch, Abrams, and the other proponents of objective interpretation . . . are afraid that in the absence of the controls afforded by a normative system of meanings, the self will simply substitute its own meanings for the meanings (usually identified with the intentions of the author) that texts bring with them, the meanings that the texts "have"; however, if the self is conceived of not as an independent entity but as a social construct whose

operations are delimited by the systems of intelligibility that inform it,
then the meanings it confers on texts are not its own but have their source
in the interpretive community (or communities) of which it is a function.
(*Is There a Text* 335)

Complete relativism, where mutually incompatible interpretations are seen as
having equal validity, is also impossible, according to Fish, because it is impossible not to hold the assumptions one holds or to believe what one believes:

> The fear that in a world of indifferently authorized norms and values the
> individual is without a basis for action is groundless because no one is
> indifferent to the norms and values that enable his consciousness. It is in
> the name of personally held (in fact they are doing the holding) norms and
> values that the individual acts and argues, and he does so with the full
> confidence that attends belief. (*Is There a Text* 319)

Interpretive consensus is thus gloriously inevitable, and produces itself spontaneously and democratically without the need for compulsion or exercise of authority:

> (There is something of the police state in Abram's vision, complete with
> posted rules and boundaries, watchdogs to enforce them, procedures for
> identifying their violators as criminals). But if the understandings of the
> people in question are informed by the same notions of what counts as a
> fact, of what is central, peripheral, and worthy of being noticed—in short,
> by the same interpretive principles—then agreement between them will be
> assured, and its source will not be a text that enforces its own perception
> but a way of perceiving that results in the emergence to those who share
> it (or those whom it shares) of the same text. (*Is There a Text* 337)

If you detect the sweet scent of utopia here, you are right. Here and throughout
the argument, the problem is not that Fish's claims are false, it is that they are
true only part of the time. For instance, the preceding quotation simply overlooks
the real existence of cases where agreement is not ensured and is in fact imposed
by the "posted rules and boundaries" of power hierarchies. The real fact that
belief systems have internal contradictions is ignored. It is true some of the time
that, as Fish says:

> (1) communication does occur, despite the absence of an independent and
> context-free system of meanings, that (2) those who participate in this
> communication do so confidently rather than provisionally (they are not
> relativists), and that (3) while their confidence has its source in a set of
> beliefs, those beliefs are not individual-specific or idiosyncratic but
> communal and conventional (they are not solipsists). (*Is There a Text* 321)

It is also true some of the time that (to paraphrase):

> (1) communication does fail, does get conflicted despite the presence of
> communal and conventional systems of meanings, that (2) those who

participate in such communication often do so provisionally and with little confidence, and that (3) their lack of confidence has its source in the absence of consensus as to beliefs.

As the passages I have been quoting suggest, the utopian rainbow seems also to tinge the portrait of the general "we" that is so often called upon in these essays. It is a we who "always already" has a sense of knowing everything it needs to make sense of the world, a full and self-consistent set of beliefs in which it has unquestioning confidence and with respect to which everything is fully and adequately meaningful (is it possible this is a socially constituted unified subject?). Fish needs such a subject, some of the time, in order to be able to talk about interpretive communities as spontaneously forming, egalitarian entities that could not be coercive if they tried because—we hear this over and over—people cannot help believing what they believe and apparently cannot be forced to believe anything else, cannot be unsure what to believe or hold contradictory beliefs, either. But many of Fish's readers will find themselves asking "Why can't they?" Although it is certainly true, some of the time, that people hold with full confidence the beliefs in whose name they act and argue, that is not necessarily true all the time for all the beliefs that might be in play in a situation. Although it is certainly true that one cannot simultaneously doubt everything, as Fish points out, it does not follow that one cannot genuinely doubt certain of the beliefs by which one is nevertheless living, acting, interpreting, and arguing. There seems to me to be a huge gap between the claim that all interpretation and understanding rest on assumptions and the claim that "we always know for certain what is true" (365). This gap is filled in Fish's discussion by the vagueness of this phrase. Does it mean "There are always certain things we believe are true" or does it mean "We always (believe we) know everything that is true"? There are quite truly worlds of difference between these two claims.

It is interesting to contrast Fish's cheery relief in the face of socially constituted reality with the bleak connotations that Pierre Maranda gives the same creature in his contribution to the Suleiman and Crosman anthology:

Literature has an audience because even though it enjoys a degree of freedom that enables it to be bolder and more exploratory than schooling, it remains essentially conservative in its endeavors: the alternatives proposed in the most outlandish novels, poems, and plays are innocuous to the established order, i.e., against the pseudodemocratic hierarchical structure of our society. . . . No revolutionary art or counterculture can alter our deeply set semantic charter. It will take more than a new Bible and World Wars to modify drastically our thresholds of acceptance or rejection. We have developed such defense mechanisms (e.g., against unemployment, recession, and other menaces to our self-confidence) that we can quickly defuse and neutralize the very broad range of challenges that, a few decades ago, would have compelled us to revamp our thought structures.[26]

Conclusions opposite to those of both Fish and Maranda are reached by Jacques Leenhardt in his "Toward a Sociology of Reading," also in the Suleiman and Crosman collection. Using data from a gigantic experimental study, Leenhardt compares readings of the same texts by readers from different social systems and positions, and concludes, among other things, that works of art can make belief systems short-circuit, revealing instabilities and possibilities for change.

Fish's initial depiction of worldviews as always stable ("the full confidence of belief") rather than stable at some points and in flux at others, plus his rejection of dialectical thinking, obliges him to beg three questions in particular. First, how within a given social group do disagreements occur? Second, how does change in the subject occur? And third, what are doubt and uncertainty? To the first of these, Fish offers two answers. One is that every interpretive disagreement is a function of people being members of different interpretive communities. But this is only a label and not an explanation. The begged questions include on what basis subjects constituted by the same society nevertheless form different interpretive communities, and how, if differences are a matter of unquestioned assumptions, dialogue can go on between interpretive communities. The other answer offered is that disagreement is possible *within* interpretive communities, and indeed it is only the stable framework of the community that makes disagreement meaningful and coherent. Here the begged question is what causes disagreement to arise at all within an interpretive community that hold the same worldview. The only example analyzed is that of the academy, and here Fish cops out by blaming disagreement on the norms of the profession whereby critics are "obliged by the conventions of the institution to dislodge" existing interpretations (350).

Given Fish's view (some of the time) of belief systems as closed and complete, neither of the preceding definitions of the interpretive community can explain in any coherent way why change comes about, either in the specific interpretations held by individuals and communities or in the interpretive assumptions by which they operate. As ever, the question of power relations is ruthlessly avoided. If everyone experiences their worldview as satisfying and complete, what motivation would members of one community have for adopting the norms of another? And what motivation would members of one community have for wanting to persuade members of another to change their mind? What would be at stake? Within a given interpretive community, what would produce change in the strategies at work, and how could such change take place without producing simply a split into two communities? And how could the common experience of simply not understanding something or not feeling qualified to judge be accounted for? Fish's analysis obliges him to mystify change; he can only acknowledge its occurrence and comment on it after the fact, as in:

> The reservation . . . that one's beliefs and therefore one's assumptions are always subject to change—has no real force, since until a change

occurs, the interpretation that seems self-evident to me will continue to seem so, no matter how many previous changes I can recall. (*Is There a Text* 361)

We always know for certain what is true . . . even though what we certainly know may change if and when our beliefs change. Until they do, however, we will argue from their perspective and for their perspective. (*Is There a Text* 365)

Again, the only instance in which a motive for change is suggested is in the academy, where the critic is institutionally obliged to generate new interpretations. The closing essay, "Demonstration vs. Persuasion: Two Models of Critical Activity," attempts to fill this gap by explaining the process of persuasion, as distinct from demonstration where "interpretations are either confirmed or disconfirmed by facts that are independently specified" (*Is There a Text* 365). But the attempt fails when persuasion ends up collapsing onto demonstration. Even the handy game analogy falls into contradiction on the point of what change and dissent are. At one point we read "one can argue with an umpire but one cannot ignore or set aside his decisions and still be said to be playing the game" (202); at a later point we find "one cannot disrupt the game because any interpretation one puts forward, no matter how 'absurd,' will already be in the game (otherwise one could not even conceive of it as an interpretation)" (357).

In the end, Hirsch, Abrams, and the rest of Fish's targets are likely to be little consoled by the recognition that all interpretive activity is constrained by social and institutional assumptions. For surely the problem for them was not that it was altogether unconstrained, but that it was not constrained enough. The fact that for specific individuals "the condition of being independent of institutional assumptions and free to originate one's own purposes and goals, could never be realized" (321) may be less than a relief when it is substituted by the possibility of infinite numbers of interpretive communities constituting their own totally incompatible realities around the same texts, confident beyond reckoning in the correctness and fullness of their beliefs. Put another way, Fish, like Walter Benn Michaels,[27] forestalls any fears that individuals will run wild and interpret promiscuously by introducing the community. But this simply shifts the threat of chaos: who is to prevent the communities from getting out of hand? The question of what constrains and constitutes interpretive communities is apparently too uncomfortable to ask. The answer, it would seem, is the shape of the rest of the community's social and material life.

The inability of Fish's analysis to account for change is closely linked to that other silence by now so familiar in reader-response criticism, the silence surrounding the goals of criticism. When Fish poses the question whether any "extrainstitutional goal" can be found for criticism (*Is There a Text* 358) and whether teachers have anything backing them up other than the "accidental" (!) fact of their classroom authority (359), his answer in effect is no. It is just that we teachers "can't help" thinking we are right and trying to get others to agree with us (365). This just seems to follow somehow from the fact that "we are always in the grip of some belief or other" (365). The mystification here comes again from the failure to recognize that interpretive communities are bound to be communities on other grounds as well, bound to have common interests besides the production of interpretations, bound to correspond to other social differentiations.

By treating signifying practices as the joyous and spontaneous deployment of unchallengeably held beliefs, Fish achieves a kind of innocence for interpretation, again much as the Chomskyan notion of competence does for language. Largely this is achieved by ignoring the fact that interpretive communities are always part of social structures. Fish recognizes at least some of the time that interpretive communities (alias circles of ideology) do not float free with spaces between them like bubbles in the air or single-family dwellings on Maple Street. He stresses the fact that there are no spaces, that they are more like cells in a honeycomb or condos in Florida. He recognizes, some of the time, that consensus is never peaceful, that interpretations are always jostling for space, thumping on each others' walls, but he seems unwilling to pursue the full consequence of this fact, namely that there is always doubt, conflict, disagreement, because interpretations are always there in multiplicity denying each other the illusion of self-containment and truth, the full confidence of belief that each would like to maintain. People and groups are constituted not by single unified belief systems, but by competing self-contradictory ones. Knowledge is interested, and interest implies conflict; to advance an interpretation is to insert it into a network of power relations. Indeed, it is fair to say that much of the "confidence" and passion people display in their beliefs is precisely conditioned by the presence of threatening alternatives.

Although Fish does not believe we are hermetically closed systems, what his theory buys for us is in the end almost exactly what Culler's literary competence ended up buying for us, a license for academic critics to proceed exactly as they have been, with "a greatly enhanced sense of the importance of [their] activities" (*Is There a Text* 368) and a gold star for being honest and calling an interpretation an interpretation instead of a fact. Although Culler comes out saying "what we are doing is correct and let us be specific about it," Fish comes out saying "what we are doing is exactly as good as anything else we might do so there is no point being specific about it." There is an air of openhearted egalitarianism about this latter position, as against the prescriptivism of Fish's bad guys, but such a theory in spite of itself winds up resting interpretive authority on nothing but pure power, turning criticism into the "supremely cynical activity" (358) that Fish does not want but apparently some of the time believes it to be.

NOTES

1. Susan Suleiman, "Varieties of Audience-Oriented Criticism," introductory essay to *The Reader in the Text: Essays on Audience and Interpretation*, ed. Susan R. Suleiman and Inge Crosman (Princeton, N.J.: Princeton Univ. Press, 1980), 4.

2. I refer here to the shift away from a romantic view of the self as consisting at bottom of an unchanging, authentic essence, a kind of "true self," to a dissolved view of the self (or subject) as a conjuncture of diverse social practices entirely produced and positioned socially, without an underlying essence.

3. Jane Tompkins, "The Reader in History: The Changing Shape of Literary Response," in *Reader-Response Criticism: From Formalism to Post-Structuralism*, ed. Jane P. Tompkins (Baltimore: Johns Hopkins Univ. Press, 1980), 224–25.

4. Suleiman and Crosman, *Reader in the Text;* Tompkins, *Reader-Response Criticism*; and Stanley Fish, *Is There a Text in This Class?: The Authority of Interpretive Communities* (Cambridge, Mass.: Harvard Univ. Press, 1980). See also Steven Mailloux, *Interpretive Conventions* (Ithaca, N.Y.: Cornell Univ. Press, 1982), and forthcoming work by Ellen Spolsky and Ellen Schauber.

5. Louis Althusser, "On the Materialist Dialectic," in *For Marx*, trans. Ben Brewster (London: Verso, 1979), 171. For cogent criticism of Althusser's isolation of theory, see Simon Clarke, Terry Lovell, Kevin McDonnell, Kevin Robins, Victor Jeleniewski Seidler, *One-Dimensional Marxism: Althusser and the Politics of Culture* (London: Allison and Busby, 1980).

6. Raymond Williams, *Marxism and Literature*, (Oxford: Oxford Univ. Press, 1977), 149–50.

7. Jonathan Culler, "Prolegomena to a Theory of Reading," in Suleiman and Crosman, 51.

8. I recognize that the notions of meaning as production and the sign as product have problems of their own. For instance, as Paolo Fabbri has suggested, it is unclear what the concept of scarcity could mean with relation to the production of meaning. This is a chunk of theory that needs much work.

9. Terry Eagleton, *Criticism and Ideology: A Study in Marxist Literary Theory* (London: Verso, 1978), 64. I am indebted throughout this section to discussions with Ed Cohen. As Eagleton himself acknowledges, there are difficulties with this analogy, and of course the argument is limited from the start by its being based on an analogy. Nevertheless, I do think that in the present context it offers a helpful thinking tool. It is interesting to note that Eagleton's own view of reading, as laid out in *Criticism and Ideology*, is based largely on the notion of consumption and lacks a good deal of the dynamism I am groping for here.

10. Jacques Leenhardt, "Toward a Sociology of Reading," in Suleiman and Crosman, 224.

11. Althusser, *For Marx*, 181.

12. See, for example, articles by Robert Crosman, Naomi Schor, Wolfgang Iser, and Louis Marin in Suleiman and Crosman.

13. Sandra M. Gilbert and Susan Gubar, *The Madwoman in the Attic: The Woman Writer and the Nineteenth-Century Literary Imagination* (New Haven, Conn.: Yale Univ. Press, 1979); Judith Fetterley, *The Resisting Reader: A Feminist Approach to American Fiction* (Bloomington: Indiana Univ. Press, 1978). Note, too, the organization of Elaine Showalter's anthology, *The New Feminist Criticism: Essays on Women, Literature, and Theory* (New York: Pantheon, 1985). The three major sections progress from women as critical readers, to the relations between critical reading and "women's cultures," to the relations between critical reading and "women's writing"—that is, from consumption to production.

14. Originally published as "Introduction à l'étude du narrataire," *Poétique* 14 (1973): 178–96. Translated and reprinted as "Introduction to the Study of the Narratee" in Tompkins, *Reader-Response Criticism*. As I discuss at the end of this section, most of the criticisms I make of this essay apply also to Prince's more recent effort, "Notes on the Text as Reader," in Suleiman and Crosman.

15. See Gerald Prince, *Grammar of Stories: An Introduction* (The Hague: Mouton, 1973).

16. I do not wish to single Prince out for his use of the male pronoun here. In fact in my own

reading of reader-response criticism the only writer to seek out sexually neutral language and give up on "the reader, *he*" is Peter Rabinowitz (see his "What's Hecuba to Us?: The Audience's Experience of Literary Borrowing," in Suleiman and Crosman). It is rather amazing that a body of criticism supposedly taking recognition of the constitutive power of language and the social construction of reality should consent to retain the myth of the "impersonal he." For nascent attention to such concerns, however, see Jonathan Culler, "Reading as a Woman," in *On Deconstruction* (Ithaca, N.Y.: Cornell Univ. Press, 1982), 43–64.

17. First appearing in Suleiman and Crosman.

18. See, for example, Mailloux, *Interpretive Conventions*, and the forthcoming book on literary competence by Ellen Spolsky and Ellen Schauber. The other theorist whose model provides tools for analyzing specifics is, of course, Wolfgang Iser.

19. I. M. Schlesinger points out that you do not need the concept of an ideal speaker at all to exclude such variables from competence. You can simply define competence in such a way as to exclude them. All of this suggests that the idealization is serving some other function. See Schlesinger's "On Linguistic Competence," in Yeshiva Bar-Hillel, ed., *Pragmatics of Natural Languages* (New York: Humanities Press, 1971), 150–72.

20. For a range of fairly recent critiques, see Michael Halliday, *Language as Social Semiotic* (Baltimore: University Park Press, 1978); Roy Harris, *The Language Makers* (Ithaca, N.Y.: Cornell Univ. Press, 1980); Rosalind Coward and John Ellis, *Language and Materialism* (London: Routledge and Kegan Paul, 1977); David Silverman and Brian Torode, *The Material Word* (London: Routledge and Kegan Paul, 1980); Gunther Kress and Robert Hodge, *Language as Ideology* (London, Routledge and Kegan Paul, 1981); Roger Fowler, Bob Hodge, Gunther Kress and Tony Trew, *Language and Control* (London: Routledge and Kegan Paul, 1979).

21. For excellent discussion and refutation of these claims, see Harris, *Language Makers*, especially the final chapters.

22. Kress and Hodge make an initial attempt to demonstrate this in *Language as Ideology*.

23. For further discussion of the consequences of this fact, see Mary L. Pratt, "The Ideology of Speech Act Theory," *Centrum* N.S. 1.1 (Spring 1981): 5–18.

24. Jonathan Arac has expressed a somewhat different view of Culler's relation to the status quo, which merits a hearing here. Arac argues (personal communication) that "Culler recognizes that there does exist a 'discipline' (to use, as he does not, Foucault's notion) of literary studies which in its power-relations produces certain skills and capacities. By his specification of its codes, norms, practices, he may seem (as Foucault does to some) to stand solid with it, but he also marks it as a target for possible contestation in a way that Holland does not, in pretending that it's not really effectively there. In my reading of Culler, I don't recall anywhere he himself glories in practicing unity, contrast, reversal, etc. His Flaubert book tries to set new terms into play."

25. *Premature foreclosure*: A common but embarrassing affliction that can ruin your text life. Especially common among people with materialist tendencies.

26. Pierre Maranda, "The Dialectic of Metaphor. An Anthropological Essay on Hermeneutics," in Suleiman and Crosman, 189.

27. Walter Benn Michaels, "The Interpreter's Self: Peirce on the Cartesian 'Subject'," in Tompkins, 185–200.

Chapter 3
"Above All Else to Make You See":
Cinema and the Ideology
of Spectacle
Dana B. Polan

The universal language has been found!
—spectator at an early Lumière film showing (ca. 1895/6)

Two scenes from films:

Early in *Give a Girl a Break* (1953), Bob Dowdy (Bob Fosse) goes for a walk with Suzie Doolittle (Debbie Reynolds), a girl he has just met and with whom, as is inevitable in a musical, he has fallen in love. Singing that their unity in love matters more than any other kind of unity—especially political and social— he begins to dance through the park, in a frenetic display of leaps, somersaults, and spins. As he moves through the obviously studio-set park, one sees across the river the United Nations building, here also obviously a set. Against a public realm of politics—on the other side of the river, elsewhere, rendered unreal by a Hollywood "magic"—Dowdy's song and dance pits the world of love, the personal, against the social. But beyond the denotated message of love *and* beyond the opposed message of world politics, there is at work in the scene another force, not really reducible to a message, not completely codifiable as a signified—a force that exceeds the denotational significations of the scene. This force is the virtuosity of performance, the sheer bravura of Dowdy/Fosse's dance. Planned for carefully by a story that has figured Dowdy as the pip-squeak who gets no one's attention, the sequence demonstrates that kind of showstopping display that works all the better because of its dramatic necessity (the little guy gets his chance, but a chance not only for him but also for us spectators who have come to see a musical). Story and show (which is here the skill of performance) come together in the ultimate sense of the film, of its project: the project of "entertainment," the world transformed into a good show. Beyond an explicit message about the world, beyond a politics, the film, its entertainment, is all the more resolutely political as an aesthetic activity: a spectacle, precisely.

In *An American in Paris* (1951), Jerry Mulligan (Gene Kelly) and Henri Borel (George Guetary), unwitting rivals for the love of the same woman, sing how "'s wonderful, 's marvelous" that they are in love. Dividing the lines of the song up between them, and dancing together in unison, the two men are virtually mirror images of each other in performance but for the fact that Gene Kelly is Gene Kelly while George Guetary is only George Guetary. The two men are identical in gesture, but then the Kelly character gets his chance: not immediately a narrative chance but a spectacle one. For a part of the song and dance, Kelly breaks out of the harmony and symmetry, and dances one of his own tap dances. Without any diegetic indication, the love-triangle plot here resolves itself to the advantage of Mulligan. Kelly/Mulligan is, after all, a better spectacle; in a film that allows Borel no chance to dance with the heroine, Lisa (Leslie Caron), we want nothing more than for Lisa/Leslie and Jerry/Gene to dance together, and in this overdetermined entertainment, to dance is to love, is to unite story and spectacle. Victims of a literal cultural imperialism (the American star/character who has been made to appear more interesting than the Frenchman)—an imperialism of the narrative but even more so of the spectacle—Borel can only cede his place to the better performance. After Kelly's famous *American in Paris* ballet, Borel appears on the scene to give up his role, as character in a narrative and as performer in a spectacle, and drive away.

In these examples (two out of many possible ones), we can read the social practice of a cinema of spectacle, its insertion as aesthetic practice into the fabric of everyday life. What we find is an "entertainment" in its virtually etymological sense—a *holding-in-place*, a *containment*, in which awareness of any realities other than the spectacular gives way to a pervading image of sense as something that simply happens, shows forth, but that cannot be told. This is the fiction of spectacle, its Imaginary. Broader than the sense in which we take fiction to mean simply a story that did not happen, fiction here is a practice by which a society engages in an "aestheticization of politics" similar in many ways to the process of aestheticization that Walter Benjamin describes in "The Work of Art in the Age of Its Mechanical Reproduction." In fiction, an aestheticizing activity works to preempt the demands of other practices, banishes them, transforms them. While this replacement of other forms of human signification and interaction by the involvements of spectacle may well include an activity of fiction at the level of diegesis (whether the characters are real or not, for example), fictionalizing is actually a larger process that substitutes the instantaneity of sight, observation, a whole complex of looking, for analysis, commentary, distanced criticism. The limit-form of such fiction, I will suggest, is the form of spectacle.

I would like to situate my comments here between (but perhaps ultimately beyond) two first visits to the cinema. I will describe the second of these visits later; the distance (not geographic, but ideological) between these two visits is the distance that a certain political cinema tries to traverse.

The first of these visits is an impressive one. On 4 July 1896—two-and-one-half months after what history reports as the first public projection of films—the Russian writer Maxim Gorki goes to the cinema for the first time. One can almost feel his thrill at this new marvel as he writes a review for the next day's newspaper: "Last night, I visited the kingdom of shadows."[1]

The kingdom of shadows. The phrase and its resonances are apt ones. Very early in the official history of the cinema, we have someone who senses the arrival of a new power in the Western world and, consciously or not, feels the need to describe that power figuratively, as if figurative language alone could replicate the appeal of this emergent art.

The kingdom of shadows is an apt description of two sides of the cinematic experience.[2] Gorki captures something of the contradictory quality of the cinema. On the one hand, a film, when projected, is physically nothing more than lights flickering on a screen—shadows, mere ephemera. And yet, those shadows, that mechanical act of projection, become caught up in another projection—the mental projection of audiences who gift this insubstantial material with a life and psychical force, and turn the emptiness of shadows into the fullness of a kingdom. It is not accidental that two social practices of the modern age—cinema and psychoanalysis—both employ the concept of *projection* to describe the process(es) by which dreams and wishes come to be represented on a screen before the dreamer or spectator. As it entered the consciousness of the twentieth century, the cinema was seen as that medium where dreaming truly became a social event.[3]

The cinema has been one of the most important kingdoms of our century. Complete with its own royalty—its constellation of stars—and its legal system of rules and prohibitions, the cinema has exhorted and received massive investments—economic (in its "golden" years, Hollywood was one of the ten largest industries in the world) as well as psychical. Any number of anecdotes stand as symptoms of these investments—some verging on the pathological, as the many cases of star worship that Edgar Morin describes in his book, *The Stars*, attest.[4] Morin quotes the testimony of moviegoers—worshipers—who experience the cinema not in terms of the standards of their own experimental reality, but in terms determined by the flickers on the screen which come to be the basis of reality. People learn to kiss, to talk, to live, according to shadows that they make, and need to make, into a kingdom.

But this may only be one side of the cinema, the side *bound*—virtually in Freud's sense of psychology as cathected energy—to a particular economy, a particular fixing of psychological/libidinal forces, to a *representation*.

When Gorki's shadows receive the (his) psychological investment to become a kingdom—a particular order of pleasure—what appears to happen is a fixing of cinematic energies to a particular end. The shadows come to *represent* because a specific way of seeing comes into play as a binding of meaning to and by certain perceptual schemata (to use Gombrich's term in *Art and Illusion*). In such cases, we see cinema according to a "restrained economy," to use a concept that Jacques Derrida opposes to the potential open-endedness of a "general economy," a radically free play of sense and nonsense, a freedom that, for Derrida, is the condition and being of signification.[5] In other words Derrida argues that any signification is potentially and finally an infinite polysemy but that a historical sedimentation, an institution of particular ways of meaning-making, closes off this potentiality. What I want to suggest is that the contradictory, sense of the phrase, "the kingdom of shadows," is a prime example of what Derrida is getting at when he refers to the act of signification as a *coherence in contradiction*, sense as sense-less. Examining how myth-criticism often founds its faith in a validity of interpretation upon a faith in the there-ness, the *presence*, of meaning (in other words, in an adequation of hermeneutic method to its object), Derrida argues that the claim of presence to a final significance within acts of signification is itself a myth, one that claims that beneath the ephemera and chaos of appearance, there is a base, a basis for meaning, a coherence that guarantees *and* determines sense.[6]

Derrida desires an overthrow of the false claims of such "coherence" and a return in its stead to a play against fixities. His championing of avant-garde activity (as in his discussion of Artaud) is precisely an attempt to support practices that refuse social(ized) definitions of signification.[7]

"The focus-knob channels the eye to the center of the screen, it controls the overflow of cinematic energies which thereby submit to discipline and become concentrated . . . in a unified equilibrium. . . . But when the knob is turned, it alters recognition, the unifying circulation—it turns information into texture. . . . When one goes from focus to out-of-focus, one passes from one order of energies to another."[8] In an extremist recognition of the contradictions of coherence, Claudine Eizykman, filmmaker and poststructuralist critic, celebrates the excessive moments, the *ostranenie*, in which a cinema (the cinema she calls N.R.I.: Narrative-Representational-Industrial) gives evidence of its fragility, of its arbitrariness. For Eizykman, the turn of the focus-knob is a subversive act that overthrows the restrained economy of accepted ways of watching film. While I hope to suggest that a position like Eizykman's (as with Derrida's) ultimately partakes of the same metaphysical philosophy as the very practices it sets out to critique, that first, biting moment to Eizykman—her recognition of the changeability, the cultural basis, of ideology and representation—is an important one. Eizykman's argument is a reminder of the arbitrary nature of the sign (even of a sign as seemingly natural as the cinematic image).

Now, this notion of coherence in contradiction, this notion of a fixing of the flux of experience within representation, may well seem itself to be in contradiction with a central premise of spectacle as social practice: that the offer of spectacle is exactly that of a breakdown of coherence, a disordering of orders (political, diegetic, whatever) for the sake of visual show. What Derrida and followers like Eizykman will value in the activity of deconstruction—the ways, for example, that it reads contradiction where previously there had seemed to be coherence—is an activity, I would suggest, that is present in spectacle as part of its lure: an experience of play that goes beyond a binding into the logic of narrative and representation.

For example, in *1941*, the individual vignettes, the character motivations, the sheer interest of story, become so many elements in a broader process whose "sense" is more than any simple addition of the pieces. To be sure, the individual narrative bits add up first to a narrative kernel, a signified: everything that happens in the film signifies that 7 December 1941 was a particularly confused and confusing night. But beyond that meaning, the narrative becomes a mere pretext for a more encompassing signification or intimation of confusion as a good show *for the spectator*. A scene where an out-of-control army tank goes crashing through vat after vat of paint with corresponding color changes might stand as a paradigm of the whole film, trading as it does narrative sense for kinetic visual display. There is in a film like *1941* a kind of leap from quantity of visual effect into a realm of different quality; the film exceeds story and becomes an explosion (literally so in the end credits) of sights and sounds.

This is to suggest that the very free play, the general economy, that Derrida and Eizykman promote can itself be a fixity, a force that binds. A general economy is still an economy. A film like *1941* may ultimately exceed the specific restraints of story, in which imagery merely exists as a conduit for narrative meaning, but it is not, for all its excess, necessarily or automatically subversive of or outside of historically sedimented ways of seeing.

In *The Postmodern Condition*, Jean-François Lyotard suggests that cultural signification in the twentieth century gains much of its force from a discrediting by the natural and social sciences of the explanatory models, the narratives and myths, what he calls "les grands récits," that gave sense to earlier periods.[9] Against the convenient fictions of premodernist periods, the condition of the postmodern is, for Lyotard, one of language *games*, social meaning dissolved into a vast, spectacular *combinatoire*, a dissociation of cause and effect, a concentration on the seductiveness of means and a concomitant disavowal of ends. One could no doubt challenge Lyotard's contention that this state is universally, inevitably, and now eternally, our condition; but it does seem true that what spectacle particularly aspires to is exactly that postmodern discrediting of significance for the sake of *signifiance*, in Kristeva's sense of the term. Spectacle jettisons a need for narrative myths and opts for an attitude in which the only tenable position seems to be the reveling in the fictiveness of one's own fictive acts. Contradiction itself becomes a new coherence, the modern seduction (see, for example, modern television, which is not afraid to mix genres, so that Mork from the planet Ork first appears in a cameo on a show about everyday life in the fifties, *Happy Days*). Spectacle resolves that Derridean challenge by making non-sense marketable (just as poststructuralism itself has perhaps become a bearable and buyable commodity). Modernist arguments against narrative or against illusionism may well be anachronisms in the face of a new mass culture that adopts many of the strategies of the postmodern and so takes as its very quality forms of antinarrative and antirealism that have been part of the modernist challenge.[10]

Film arrives on the horizon of the nineteenth century out of immediate technological concerns—how to capture motion, how to project that captured motion on a screen—concerns that have a long and well-documented history. But that history depends on a prior, more inclusive one: the history of the desire to project images, to capture images, to see. This history runs with a fascination through the nineteenth and twentieth centuries. For example, both Freud and Marx (among others) use photography and photographic machinery as metaphors for consciousness. Marx, in *The German Ideology*, refers to ideology as inversion of real relations like that inversion in the camera obscura from positive to negative. Freud, as he searches for a way to *represent* the levels of consciousness, tries the metaphor of the camera, seeing the conscious and unconscious as two camera parts.[11] Significantly, what these two metaphoric references most reveal is Marx and Freud's recognition that seeing is not merely a capturing of the world, an imprinting of meaning within an image. There is something more: a production, a transformation, and even an exclusion, a mis-representation that intervenes between the world and the making of images of that world.[12]

What is most important here is the implication that knowing and seeing—even if they are a false seeing, a false knowing—somehow have a privileged connection to each other. As a tired cliché would have it: "A picture is worth a thousand words"—the idea that to see is somehow to know. If Plato in *The Republic* gives central prominence to sight in the constitution of an epistemology, then we can say that the cinema, modern cavern in which images parade before enraptured spectators, realizes a return to Plato's cave, as Jean-Louis Baudry has well analyzed.[13]

In this sense, we can speak of a tendency of the whole signifier of entertainment toward *fiction*, in the way that Hans Vaihinger in his *Philosophy of "As If"* speaks of social constructs as "convenient fictions," symbolizing acts by which subjects alienated from their own realities try fictively to overcome that alienation in *poesis*. The overriding particularity of the fiction film (meaning that term to refer to more than just a film with an imaginary story) is then its *will-to-spectacle*. This *will-to-spectacle* asserts that world only has substance—in some cases, only is meaningful—when it appears as image, when it is shown, when it exists as phenomenal appearance, a look. As a Polaroid ad (cited by Sontag in *On Photography*) would have it, "You see a picture everywhere you look."

The world of spectacle is a world without background, a world in which things only exist or mean in the way they appear. One, but only one, of the ways in which the will-to-spectacle appears is in what we conventionally call *realism*, and as Auerbach suggests in *Mimesis*, a desire to depict actuality does not necessarily have anything to do with the reality of a world depicted. Realism, in Auerbach's reading of the Homeric mode of writing, can become a divorcing of surfaces from an underlying history. In such a world, which is not that far from the phenomenalism of the spectacle film, only that which is pictured exists. In such a world, Auerbach says, "Delight in physical existence is everything. The highest deed is to make the world perceptible to us . . . seeing heroes so that we may take pleasure in their manner of enjoying their present." And here Auerbach makes an especially significant point about our investments in such a world: "So long as we are reading or hearing the poems, it does not matter at all that it is only legend, only make-believe. . . . Homer can be analyzed but he cannot be interpreted."[14] This is also our response to the spectacle film, the triumph of an impression of presence, the realization of a philosophy of realist individuation as the photography of film captures characters in all their immediacy and specificity. The image shows everything, and, because it shows everything, it can *say* nothing; it frames a world and banishes into nonexistence everything beyond that frame. The will-to-spectacle is the assertion that a world of foreground is the only world that matters or is the only world that *is*. Like impressionist literature and painting with whose history it is coincident, the fiction film is an impressionist medium that claims that things described matter more than things understood.[15]

This "vocation of the perceptual" (as Fredric Jameson calls it [*Political Unconscious* 237]) works to divorce ends from means or, rather, to make means vanish in the instantaneity of a perception. Jameson argues that impressionism has a particular function within capitalist production and reproduction; impressionist arts provide a last haven where the senses can enjoy aesthetic play in an age that is all too quickly restricting areas of play:

> [T]he geometrization of science . . . which substitutes ideal qualities for physically perceivable objects of study . . . is accompanied by a release in perceptual energies. The very activity of sense perception has nowhere to go in a world in which science deals with ideal quantities. . . . This unused surplus capacity of sense perception can only reorganize itself into a new and semi-autonomous activity, one which produces its own specific objects, new objects that are themselves the result of a process of abstraction and reification.[16]

Jameson is right to note the reification that can occur in impressionist practice. But I think he goes too far in seeing impressionism as no more than a reaction to economic practice and not as one of its possible forms; in other words, he too readily cuts aesthetic production off from economic practice as its denial. It is certainly true, as Jameson suggests, that impressionism most immediately is readable as a kind of beleaguered entrenchment of perception. At the same time, though, the nomination of certain practices as aesthetic and others as economic is itself reificatory of their potential imbrications and conjunctural exchange. Antieconomic manifesto comes to dominate the publicising organs of modern art and its rhetoric at the very moment when social life itself is taking on the form of an avant-garde, a commitment to an idea and ideal of the modern.[17] The problem of the avant-garde as a reactive force is not only that it has to fight the mechanization, the bourgeoisification of everyday life, but also, in contrast, that it has to fight the aestheticization and avant-gardization of that everyday life. If modern life is undergoing an increasing rationalization (in Weber's and Marcuse's sense), this rationalization goes hand in hand with, and under the guise of, an increasing aestheticization of everyday life, from the pinball-like beeps, glows, and instantaneous readouts of digital gas pumps and cash registers—all of which create a seductive spectacle of/for the commodity—to the introduction of eros into the workplace. In white-collar Silicon Valley, for example, work becomes a big show: everyone smiles benignly at everyone else, bosses are to be addressed by their first names, cubicles are painted in bright colors, and workers are encouraged to use their lunch hours for trysts out in the custom-re-modeled recreational vehicles they have driven to work. (Of course, this conver-sion of work into fun operates along strict class lines; while the companies seduce the bright, young electronic wizards, the low-level workers—usually women—who are actually building the silicon chips are subject to all sorts of occupational hazards, especially chemical and electrical.)

In the "phenomenological" world of spectacle—a world of instant perceptions bracketing out the value of perception—an experience, especially in the ways it becomes little more than a perceptual impulse, is seen to matter in and of itself.[18] The very films that establish cinema explicitly exemplify this virtual condensation of sense into sight. Significantly, Lumière's films—*actualités* as they were called—capture the surface sights of the everyday world of turn of-the-century production, labor, and social reproduction, and, in this sense, one of the Lumière films—*Workers Leaving the Factory* (1895)—is topical in an exceedingly precise way. But instead of probing the connections between production and people, Lumière can only put his camera outside the factory doors and establish his only truth, his only *impression,* about these workers: that they leave.

Jameson refers to aesthetic productions as "strategies of containment" (*Polit-ical Unconscious* 53). The superficiality of spectacle, its inability to mean more than it shows, is an important reason those political films that set out to counteract current political structures simply by *showing* that world fall into the trap of merely confirming ills without offering a path beyond them. Because of the will-to-spectacle, these films end up as the idealist and romantic battle of one sight against another. A movement like neorealism, for example, may show the crush of the modern world, but that is all it can do: beyond revelation or confirmation, spectacle provides no meaningful qualification of a represented situation.

Spectacle is not the same as, or reducible to, specific visual strategies such as illusionism or realism. Rather, the illusion of reality is only one form of spectacle. Auerbach's recognition that Homeric language does not require belief in the reality of a represented world captures this important point.[19] An art of foreground may insist on our attention, but that does not mean that it necessarily insists on our belief (indeed, simultaneous attraction to and disbelief in the actual becomes the source of certain popular art forms such as *camp*). Spectacle demands our attention—a command to "look here" that needs no cognitive assent other than the initial fact of looking. The specific content of a spectacle is only a very small part of its attraction. Rather, the very fact of showing (regardless of what is shown) becomes a spectacle (and specularly seductive) in the ways it blocks, ignores, shuts out, other forms of cognition. While much criticism of the ideological function of art has concentrated on what such art shows (for example, studies of positive and negative images of women), the politics of fiction may reside as much in what such fiction does not say as in what it does show. Spectacle offers an imagistic surface of the world as a strategy of containment against any depth of involvement with that world. This is why, as Constance Penley has convincingly argued, the ostensibly counterhegemonic practice of minimalist cinema (filmmakers like Paul Sharits or Peter Gidal who try to avoid repressive contents by emptying their films of all contents) may still be part of dominant ideology—here the ideology of spectacle which resonates with a faith, virtually Rousseauist, in the purity of acultural sight.[20]

Revealingly, Brecht attacked both naturalism, which he saw as blocked from an engagement with historical situations by its concentration on surfaces, *and* abstract art, which he saw as blocked by its concentration on the sight of its own forms. Both arts ran together for Brecht as examples of the fetish of the spectacular.

Historians of film theory are fond of making a distinction between two traditions of theory (which would correspond to two different film-objects): the realist and formative traditions.[21] As traditional film theory understands it, the realist tradition roots the nature of cinema in its photographic reproduction of prefilmic reality. On the other hand, the formative tradition roots the nature of cinema in an inevitable distortion of reality by filmic techniques. I would suggest that this opposition fades away into a higher order of agreement: both traditions are caught inside a philosophy of the image and its adequation or not to a representation of actuality; whether actuality can or cannot be so represented, both theories have a faith in imagistic powers. Two blockages occur: a naturalist one where photography captures only the look of things and not their meanings, and a formalist one in which any meaning beyond the immediacy of the image is denied.

Form and content come together in a film like *The Pirate* (Vincente Minnelli,

1948), which displays, and literally is, a contagion of spectacle within a world ostensibly geared to rationality.[22] For readers who have not seen *The Pirate*, I have appended a plot summary in the Appendix to this chapter. On the diegetic level, *The Pirate* is about spectacle—the aristocratic Manuela is drawn into a world that she had once disdained: the world of vaudeville, of the stage, and, by extension, of entertainment in general. But more significantly, *The Pirate* represents spectacle at the very level of its mise-en-scène. From its opening shot of Manuela turned away from the camera which can then do no more than peek over her shoulder (an establishing shot of the woman's refusal to be seen, to be narrativised, to become part of spectacle) to the last shot of the film (Manuela in clown costume and in the embrace of a man as she looks straight out at the camera), *The Pirate* enacts the increasing spectaclization (to coin a word) of the world. The stage becomes a central locus for the film as the characters find it necessary literally to *stage* events in order to reveal their truths. For example, at the climax, when Manuela pretends to be hypnotized in order to trap Don Pedro, she has to leave the audience in attendance at Serafin's hanging, and go to the stage that just happens to be there. Only on stage are her actions significant enough to make Don Pedro reveal the truth (that he is Macoco the Pirate) that he has so well hidden under the veneer of bourgeois respectability. And the film can only have Don Pedro reveal that truth by having him step up on the stage too. He must be caught in the world of acting to and for someone else.

This will-to-spectacle reveals itself in such a film as a virtual neurosis, an insistence and overinsistence that things are one way (dominated by spectacle) and not another. The film seems unable to let any chance to reaffirm spectacle and specularity slip by. For example, Don Pedro cannot simply confess; he *must*, for the film's project, do so on a stage. To go further (as the film does), he is not simply captured; rather, he is captured through the use of vaudeville props (juggling pins, hoops, and whatnot) that beat him down and literally surround him. Spectacle becomes an all-pervading, inescapable force.

As a narrative, *The Pirate* seems to be about change, but its development—its diegetic progress—is already determined by its initial commitment to a myth of spectacle that controls the kind of development it can enact. In "The Structural Study of Myth," Claude Lévi-Strauss has described the narrative process of myth as a diachronic presentation of actually synchronic oppositions. Myth here becomes a repetition in different permutations of a basic set, a guiding ideologeme, which, in the case of *The Pirate*, is that of the fundamental rightness of spectacle as a mediation of/for all differences. For example, what appear to be differences in the two versions of "Be a Clown" sung in the film fade in the face of the film's overall project: to insist endlessly on the need for everyone to join the world of spectacle. In the first version, men sing. Their most immediate audience is an acknowledged one *within* the film (the audience that has come to see Serafin hung), and this concentration on a diegetic audience alone is emphasized by the camera angles, which are rarely frontal; Serafin and the Goldsmith Brothers sing in virtually every direction *except to us*. In the second version, the version that closes the film, what was lacking in the earlier version is now present: the complete capturing of woman and real audience (we spectators) in a specular relationship as we get a full frontal view of Manuela and Serafin singing out to us. From one scene to the other, there is no extreme difference but only a filling in (Manuela loses her independence from spectacle and from men) whose inevitability is present from the beginning when Manuela finally becomes visible in the scene and so allows the films to proceed. With the two versions of the song, we move from men singing for other characters to a woman singing for us.

There is one scene in *The Pirate* that is virtually symptomatic in its desire to banish all meanings other than spectacle from its field of attention. This is the moment when Manuela sees the ocean, the ocean that she has long dreamed of. It is also the moment when Serafin first sees her. Here the two sides of the film's central thematic structure—the woman's desire and discourse versus the man's—collide. But the film has already tipped the balance. From the start of the film, Manuela's desire is already a desire for an unreality; the ocean is for her a sign of fantasy, a sign of the male world of adventure that she has read about in books and wants to enter. In the ocean scene, then, what has already been determined is now overdetermined (in Frued's sense of a radical condensation of meanings). Two shots here demonstrate the whole aesthetic project of spectacle. The buildup to these two shots is as follows: Manuela walks toward the sea, the camera tracking before her. Suddenly, her face lights up with rapture. She has evidently seen the ocean . . . but there is as yet no corresponding shot of the ocean to complete her look. Instead, at the precise moment when her rapture bursts out, Serafin pops into the frame from behind some boxes, as if by magic, as if somehow called forth as the object of Manuela's desire (even though she does not yet know that). Manuela proceeds onward out of frame, unaware of Serafin, but she has already lost the game. The film henceforth acts as her unconscious, redirecting her desires to what the film defines as their true goal. Now the true question of the film—the question it has always been asking: how will the two main characters get together?—pushes aside its decoy question: how will Manuela get her pirate dream? We then get two shots in which all the contradictions of film spectacle can be read—two intercut shots of an ocean—each shot about a second long, and separated by a medium-distance shot of Manuela seeing. In the first of the two shots of Manuela seeing, she is alone, she and the ocean forming a virtual dialogue along the lines of a shot/reaction-shot pattern. In the second shot of Manuela, Serafin has entered the frame to stand beside her, and Manuela's gaze reluctantly shifts from the ocean, her ocean, to the man. Manuela's story has become Manuela's *and Serafin's*. The two shots of the ocean are the only two shots of the film not filmed on a set. Only here, for two seconds out of almost two hours, does any world, any other scene, try to insist its way into the action. And, symptomatically, the shots have no force, nothing to make them real. The ocean that opens up to worlds beyond the frame of the story disappears as the diegesis moves inland to the studio-set town in which Manuela lives. On a narrative level, *The Pirate* is then in some way about the loss of a woman's desire under the influence of the world of spectacle for which cinema, the film *The Pirate* itself, is a metonymic representation. The narrative of the film is always a narrative inside spectacle; the film cannot outrun the fact that it is shown.

Could the practice of film present, figure, critical practice without that practice turning into spectacle? The ways filmmakers have tried to answer this question affirmatively might constitute a history of antihegemonic cinema. This brings me to my second visit to the cinema, the visit of Godard's character, Michel-Ange, in *Les Carabiniers* (1963), as he visits the cinema for the first time. Like Gorki, Michel-Ange sees shadows as a kingdom: he flinches as a Lumière-like train arrives on the screen; he fills with delight as a naked woman proceeds to take a bath. Michel-Ange runs to the screen and tries to look over the edge of the tub. Finally, he leans too far and accidentally tears and bursts through the screen, only to confront a grimy wall beyond it. As he faces the wall, the impenetrable barrier before him, Michel-Ange suddenly turns and looks out in panic at the projector and at us, as the film continues to run on his face. Michel-Ange has punctured the signs of spectacle, realized that they are no more than signs. But, at the same time, his lesson about film is *shown* to us in a film. Michel-Ange becomes a spectacle for us, the implications of his discovery of the limits of sight ironically dissipated by our own confidence in sight. *His* grimy wall behind a movie screen is still a movie screen *for us*. Significantly, the scene, which occurs in one unmoving shot, includes spectators, seen from the back, between Michel-Ange and us. They sit impassively, continuing to watch even after Michel-Ange has destroyed the image they are watching; in such a fashion, they mirror our own complacency in the face of filmic deconstruction, our own ability to make deconstructive practices a new form of seductive presence.

Les Carabiniers makes explicit the difficulties of film's attempts to qualify its spectacle through another kind of cognition—a nonspectacular, critical one. Spectacle works to convert the critical into the merely watched and watchable. In his essay, "The Literarization of the Theatre," Brecht described a similar difficulty in political theater: "This [theatrical] apparatus resists all conversion to other purposes, by taking any play that it encounters and immediately changing it so that it no longer represents a foreign body within the apparatus . . . it theatres it all down."[23] Similarly, the problem of cinematic spectacle is the way that, when faced by criticism or critical elements, it "cinemas" them all down.

However, even if *Les Carabiniers* ends up by repeating the apparatus of spectacle, the film does begin to ask explicitly the questions that guide any attempt to create a political and critical art. What Michel-Ange cannot understand, we can begin to understand and analyze. Even in its limitations, the film is an emblematic call for the necessity of critical work on and *in* the cinema—for the transformation of the image through a knowledge that puts fictions inside quotation marks of analytic distance. This transformation would take an art that cannot say everything, that cannot say anything, whose will-to-spectacle is also a will-to-silence, and would try to make this art speak. Criticism, then, is not a contingent activity, but must be built into the work of art as its critical sense, its real guarantee. It expresses the necessity to situate aesthetic practice, its myths, its fiction, its spectacle, within a new and higher coherence: the coherence of history and its knowledge as a totalizing reciprocity of people and their world.

APPENDIX: PLOT SUMMARY OF THE PIRATE

The place: the Caribbean during the age of Spanish colonialism.

In a small inland village, the young Manuela (Judy Garland) dreams of adventures with Macoco the Pirate, whom she has read about in books. But her aunt has arranged for her marriage to Don Pedro Vargas (Walter Slezak), the bland, stay-at-home mayor of the village. Manuela accepts her fate but convinces her aunt to take her to the port where her wedding dress will be arriving. She wants one glimpse of the ocean before the routine of domesticity descends upon her.

Her aunt consents and off they go. The moment Manuela sees the ocean, she is accosted by Serafin (Gene Kelly), a circus performer who claims his undying love for her. Manuela wards off the advances of this lowly and common performer. But she is intrigued, and that night she appears in the circus audience. As part of his act, Serafin hypnotizes her, whereupon Manuela, in her trance, reveals her love for the pirate, Macoco, in a feverish song. Although jealous of her love for Macoco, Serafin is excited by Manuela's performing abilities and he follows her back to the village. There he asks her to join his troupe. At this point, Don Pedro arrives. Sending Manuela out of the room, he is about to whip Serafin when Serafin suddenly recognizes Don Pedro as Macoco the Pirate, now retired and in disguise. Using the still-valid price on Macoco's head as blackmail, Serafin himself claims to be Macoco and has Don Pedro's confirmation to back up this deception. While Serafin seduces Manuela with the guise of the pirate, Don Pedro sneaks off to bring the island's militia to arrest Serafin and frame him as Macoco. Believing Serafin to be Macoco, Manuela is excited that her Macoco fantasy is coming true, but her love turns to anger when one of Serafin's assistants accidentally reveals the truth of the deception. Yet even though she realizes that Serafin is just Serafin, she now also realizes that she loves him anyway.

The militia, led by the governor, arrives. Neither Serafin nor Macoco can convince anyone that Serafin is not Macoco. Serafin is scheduled to be hanged and asks to give one last performance. Over Don Pedro's objection, the Governor agrees. Serafin and several performers sing "Be a Clown." Then Serafin tries to hypnotize Don Pedro to bring out the truth, but, in a scuffle, the hypnotizing lamp is broken. Manuela, however, pretends to be hypnotized and declares her undying love for Macoco. Brought to the point of jealousy, Don Pedro suddenly blurts out that he is Macoco and that he is the one Manuela should love. The circus performers capture Don Pedro with their props.

Manuela and Serafin, in clown outfits, perform in the circus and sing "Be a Clown" to the audience.

NOTES

1. Maxim Gorki, quoted in Jay Leyda, *Kino: a History of the Russian and Soviet Film* (New York: Collier Books, 1973), 407.

2. "Kingdom of shadows" also connotes the underworld, and so Gorki unconsciously antici-pates those critics of cinema, so especially prevalent in the first part of the century, who saw cinema-going as a kind of scandal, a sin against bourgeois propriety, a voyage to a nether world. Edgar Morin analyzes the connections between cinema and the underworld in his *Le Cinéma ou l'homme imaginaire* (Paris: Les Editions de Minuit, 1956) where he suggests that the cinema's anthropological appeal lies in its creation of spectral doubles of our quotidian world.

3. For a useful introduction to the interconnections of film and dream, see Edgar Morin, *Le Cinéma ou l'homme imaginaire*. And for psychoanalytic approaches, see the entire issue of *Communi-cations*, no. 23 (1978) on "Psychanalyse et cinéma" which includes articles by Roland Barthes, Julia Kristeva, Félix Guattari, and others.

4. See Edgar Morin, *Les stars* (Paris: Les Editions de Minuit, 1957). For more recent discussion of the psychology and ideology of star-worship, see Richard Dyer, *Stars* (London: British Film Institute, 1979).

5. See Jacques Derrida, "From Restricted to General Economy: A Hegelianism without Re-serve," in *Writing and Difference* (Chicago: Univ. of Chicago Press, 1978), 251–77.

6. See Jacques Derrida, "Structure, Sign and Play in the Discourse of the Human Sciences," in *Writing and Difference*, 278–93. Derrida's critique of "presence" has been found useful by many film theorists who have seen film's photographic qualities as a potential version of that linking of signifiers with signifieds that Derrida argues is the engendering condition of metaphysics. In the way that Derrida poses the mediations of writing (*écriture*) against the ostensible fullness of speech, Derridean-inspired film theorists have tried to argue that film is not a transparent conduit to a prefilmic reality but a form of writing in which cinematic codes construct, rather than reflect, meanings.

7. See Jacques Derrida, "The Theater of Cruelty and the Closure of Representation," in *Writing and Difference*, 232–50.

8. Claudine Eizykman, *La jouissance-cinéma* (Paris: Union Générale d' Editions, 1976), 15–16.

9. Jean-François Lyotard, *The Postmodern Condition* (Minneapolis: Univ. of Minnesota Press, 1984), trans. Geoff Bennington and Brian Massumi.

10. For the argument that mass and postmodernist cultures are parallel responses to modernity, see Fredric Jameson, "Reification and Utopia in Mass Culture," *Social Text*, no. 1 (1979): 130–48; and Fred Pfeil, "Postmodernism as a 'Structure of Feeling'," in *Marxism and the Interpretation of Culture*, ed. Cary Nelson and Lawrence Grossberg (Urbana: Univ. of Illinois Press, forthcoming). See also Fredric Jameson, "Postmodernism, or the Cultural Logic of Late Capitalism," *New Left Review*, no. 146 (July–August 1984): 53–92.

11. See Sigmund Freud, *Introduction to Psychoanalysis* (New York: Pocket Books, 1975), 305–6. In "Notes on the Mystical Writing Pad," Freud abandons the visual metaphor and tries a textual one to describe consciousness; Derrida argues convincingly that this shift comes from Freud's recognition of the discursive and semiotic, rather than specular and representational, quality of

consciousness. See Jacques Derrida, "Freud and the Scene of Writing," in *Writing and Difference*, 196–231.

12. For an examination of uses and abuses of the camera obscura as a metaphor for consciousness, see Sarah Kofman, *Camera obscura de l'idéologie* (Paris: Editions Galilée, 1973).

13. Jean-Louis Baudry, "The Apparatus," trans. Bertrand Augst, *Camera Obscura* 1 (Fall 1976): 104–26.

14. Erich Auerbach, *Mimesis: The Representation of Reality in Western Literature*, trans. Willard Trask (Princeton, N.J.: Princeton Univ. Press, 1953), 12.

15. On the relations between film and impressionism, see Keith Cohen, *Film and Fiction: Dynamics of Exchange* (New Haven, Conn.: Yale Univ. Press, 1979).

16. Fredric Jameson, *The Political Unconscious: Narrative as a Socially Symbolic Act* (Ithaca, N.Y.: Cornell Univ. Press, 1981), 229.

17. On the spread of specifically artistic impulses into everyday life in the form of "shock" and dissociation of experiences, see Walter Benjamin, *Charles Baudelaire: A Lyric Poet in the Era of High Capitalism*, trans. Harry Zohn (London: New Left Books, 1973).

18. I should make it clear that I do not mean to imply through this idea of containment in/by the visual that sound has no ideological function in spectacle. Sound and image work together in a variety of ways. Although some directors demonstrate a mobile and fluid use of sound, the general historical function of sound has been to confirm and support the image. Mary Ann Doane has well examined the dominant ideology of sound (especially as expressed by Hollywood sound engineers themselves) in her article, "The Voice in the Cinema: The Articulation of Body and Space," *Yale French Studies*, no. 60 (1980): 33–50. Significantly, those filmmakers who must challenge a will-to-spectacle often do so by giving an unheard-of priority to the sound track. With Eisenstein, for example, a silent-film director foreshadows the antispecular powers of speech by trying to make images themselves into linguistic units; for Eisenstein, montage is that process which de-actualizes (or, in his term, de-anecdotalizes) the immediacy of perceptual actuality so that one might go beyond immediacy to understand historical reality. For discussion of this role of linguistics in political film, see my article "Eisenstein as Theorist," *Cinema Journal* 17. 1 (Fall 1977): 14–29; and more broadly, David Rodowick, "The Political Avant-Garde: Modernism and Epistemology in Post-'68 Film Theory," Ph.D. thesis, Univ. of Iowa, 1983.

19. Significantly, Auerbach's discussion of the modernist novel brings *Mimesis* full circle by finding in a writer like Joyce a thwarting of interpretation not finally so different from Homer's. Compare, for example, the following comment on Joyce with his comments on Homer: "even the most painstaking analysis can hardly emerge with anything more than an appreciation of the multiple enmeshments of the motifs but with nothing of the purpose and meaning of the work itself" (*Mimesis*, 551). Surfaces with no depth and "symbols" that resist symbolic reading are, for Auerbach, aspects of the same literary project.

20. See Constance Penley, "The Avant-Garde and Its Imaginary," *Camera Obscura* 2 (Fall 1977): 3–33.

21. See, for example, the most famous study of film theories, Dudley Andrew's *The Major Film Theories* (New York: Oxford Univ. Press, 1976), which is structured according to this distinction.

22. My analysis owes much to those of Ed Lowry in "Art and Artifice in Six Musicals of Vincente Minnelli" (M.A. thesis, Univ. of Texas at Austin, 1977) and Ruby Rich in her program notes from the Art Institute of Chicago, 28 October 1978. As I was first writing this chapter, a study of *The Pirate* appeared that makes many parallel points; see David Rodowick, "Vision, Desire, and the Film-Text," *Camera Obscura* 6 (Fall 1980): 55–89.

23. Bertolt Brecht, "The Literarization of the Theater," in *Brecht on Theatre*, trans. John Willett (New York: Hill & Wang, 1964), 43–46.

Chapter 4
Ezra Pound and the "Economy" of Anti-Semitism
Andrew Parker

To exclude the Jews, no, really, that does not suffice; to exterminate them, that is not enough: they would have to be erased from history, removed from the books in which they have spoken to us. Their presence would have to be obliterated once and for all, before and after all books—their presence which is the inscribed words through which man, as far back as one can remember, where there are no more horizons, already turned towards man. In other words, one would have to suppress "the other" ["*autrui*"].
—Maurice Blanchot (*L'Entretien infini* [Paris: Gallimard, 1969], 190)

There are the Jews and there is something else. But what complicates things is that the "something else" is also Jewish.
—Pierre Vidal-Naquet ("Interpreting Revolutionary Change: Political Divisions and Ideological Diversity in the Jewish World of the First Century A.D.," *Yale French Studies*, no. 59 (1980): 97)

Despite his currently canonical status as a "great American poet,"[1] Ezra Pound remains the name of a persistently embarrassing problem for the institution of literary criticism. *Any* reading of Pound, even one that intends to steer clear from ideological issues by treating his poetry in isolation, ultimately finds itself confronted by the seemingly intractable questions posed by his work—questions concerning the relationship between the language of economy and the economy of language, between political conviction and rhetorical form, between the moment of fascism and the poetics of modernism. Although raised explicitly in both Pound's poetry and his theoretical writings, such questions generally have been "more often noticed than explained" (if not entirely ignored), for most discussions of Pound simply have emphasized one aspect of his oeuvre at the expense of another: "Critics have for the most part preferred either to analyze Pound's work without reference to his ideas, or to analyze his ideas without reference to his work, producing in the first instance largely formalistic analyses and in the second, scathing attacks."[2] Although an immense (and growing) body of commentary has now been devoted to all phases of Pound's career, this arbitrary distinction between "Pound the poet" and "Pound the political economist"—a distinction that surely would have been rejected by Pound himself—nevertheless continues to regulate discussion in scholarly journals as well as in classrooms. [3]

What largely remains unexamined, then, is precisely the nature of the *relationship* between Pound's "work" and "ideas," between his poetry and economics; more than a decade after Pound's death, the difficult question of how his poetics "impel toward his Fascism and anti-Semitism" continues to elude easy answers. [4] The present chapter—in exploring the rhetorical connections between Pound's economics and his anti-Semitism—attempts to outline one possible answer, seeking in the tropology of Pound's economic system certain figures of excess ("usury" and "Judaism") which both motivate and undermine the "economy" of this system and of the poetry in which it is inscribed. In acknowledging as a methodological *a priori* "the formal similarity between linguistic and economic symbolism and production," this study is intended to help "shake the idea that there is a fundamental split in Pound's work" between the province of the poet and that of the economic theorist. [5] Indeed, if any such "split" can be said to inhere in Pound's writing, we shall find it manifest not as some putative barrier separating the literary from the economic but as a structural property of the trope itself. Our discovery of Pound's general association of figurative language with a particular notion of Judaism will enable us finally to reject the widely-held critical position that considers Pound's anti-Semitism as merely a "contingent" phenomenon, ancillary to his poetic achievement. [6] As we shall witness, Pound's animus against Judaism ultimately will be legible as an animus against (his own) writing as such, a "turn" of events that will produce an aberrant economy discernible in the workings of his poetry and prose alike.

I

The basic principles of Pound's economic theories derive almost without exception from Aristotle's classic treatise on government, the *Politics*—one of the few texts with which Pound "would conclude the compulsory studies of every university student" (*SP* 350). [7] In chapters 8 and 9, book I of the *Politics*, Aristotle distinguishes between two systems of exchange that differ in terms of the role played by money in each: "economics" as such (*oikonomikē*), described as "natural," "original," and "proper"; and "wealth-getting" (*chrematistikē*), defined antithetically as "artificial," "secondary," and "improper" (1257a). In the former system, money is employed simply to facilitate the exchange of two heterogeneous commodities; defined strictly as a mediator between commodities rather than as a commodity in its own right, money expends itself "economically" in providing a standardized measure of the values of dissimilar goods. In the latter (chrematistic) system, however, money operates as both the origin and the end of a transaction mediated not by some (ideally transparent) measure of value but by the commodity itself. [8] The "danger" posed by chrematistics thus would be its tendency to fetishize money, to treat money improperly as if it were itself a commodity—a process that, once begun, is without "fixed boundary" since it is not restrained in any referential way to the world of tangible needs and goods: "all getters of wealth increase their hoard of coin without limit" (1257b).

It is precisely this propensity of chrematistics to draw infinite profit from the self-referential capacities of money that Aristotle will "justly censure" (1258a) as a species of "economic incest," a perverted kind of monetary generation whose most virulent form is *usury*:

> Usury is most reasonably hated, because it makes a gain out of money itself, and not from the natural object of it. For money was intended to be used in exchange, but not to increase at interest. And this term "interest" [*tokos*, literally "offspring"], which means the birth of money from money, is applied to the breeding of money because the offspring resembles the parent. Wherefore of all forms of getting wealth this is the most unnatural. (1258b)

The money generated from usurious interest hence "does not stand in the same relation to a monetary deposit as a child (for example, a lamb) stands in relation to a parent (for example, a ram or a ewe),"[9] for the "breeding of money" undermines the natural biological sequence whereby an offspring descends from (and thus does not resemble, is not homogeneous with) its parent. For Aristotle, then, biological generation proceeds according to the (natural) laws of economics, but monetary generation follows the (unnatural) laws of chrematistics—a distinction that subsequently would be reaffirmed by (among many others) Saint Thomas Aquinas in an axiom which helped to form the official policy of the church throughout the later Middle Ages: "to make money by usury is exceedingly unnatural."[10] As we now shall discover, such a designation will underwrite as well the essential terms of Pound's economic theories.

Like Aristotle, Pound would "try to maintain a distinction . . . between the production system, the system of exchange of actual goods [economics], and the wangles or corruptions of accountancy or the money wangles that corrode both the system of production and the processes of exchange [chrematistics]" (*RS* 265). The cardinal point to which Pound returns time after time in his writings is the Aristotelian notion that "true wealth" does not consist in a mere "quantity of money" (*Politics* 1257b) but in "the abundance of nature / with the whole folk behind it.[11] For Pound (as for Aristotle), money "is NOT in itself abundance": it is not itself a commodity but a measure of commodity values, "a ticket for the orderly distribution of WHAT IS AVAILABLE" (*SP* 295) in the same way that "a theatre ticket is not a play, though the circulation of tickets is essential to maintaining Broadway drama."[12] Such a definition implies that money is merely a reflex, a secondary medium whose function is to remain as "irritable and unstable" (Canto 37, 185) as the perishable commodities it represents. For just as "ordinary language" operates most successfully when, in effacing its own materiality, it appears to be transparent, so too should money ideally vanish (as a signifier) when it mediates (as a signified) between the relative worths of commodities. As a "representation of something else" (*SP* 443), money thus does not itself determine but rather is determined by values that derive exclusively "from labour and nature" alone: "It is nature, the actual existence of goods, or of the possibility of producing them, that really determines the [economic] habits of the state. . . . Economic habits arise from the nature of things (animal, mineral, vegetable)" (*SP* 294, 312, 257).

Although rooted ultimately in "the nature of things," money nevertheless will be characterized by Pound as a thoroughly artificial medium the validity of which is guaranteed "not by nature, but by custom, whence the name NOMISA" (*SP* 329). Holding little reverence for the intrinsic (metallic) value of coins, Pound praises such historical figures as Kublai Khan (one of the first to issue paper money) who similarly recognized that there is nothing "natural" in the particular *form* assumed by a given currency (*SP* 204–26). Any plentiful material may be employed as legal tender, for "the guinea stamp, not the metal, is the essential component of the coin." [13] What remains natural for Pound hence is not the material value of money per se but its systematic *correspondence* with the order of commodities. Just as Pound and Fenollosa redrew the Chinese ideogram to "correspond with actions" rather than with "things," so does money, in Pound's conception, designate not the worth of objects in static isolation but the active, systemic relationships that constitute commodity values. [14] This notion of a natural, dynamic correspondence between monetary signs and their commodity referents will underlie all of Pound's writings on economics (and on language as well): "The verbal manifestation on any bank cheque is very much like that on any other. Your cheque, if good, means ultimately delivery of something you want. An abstract statement [like money] is GOOD if it be ultimately found to *correspond* with the facts. [15]

If found, however, not to "correspond with the facts," money no longer serves as a standardized measure of value but becomes instead its ultimate source; transformed into a commodity in its own right, money comes to enjoy "powers that correspond neither to justice nor to the nature of the goods it is issued against or used to purchase" (*SP* 349). In the absence of any natural congruency between sign and referent, money will be created ex nihilo with nothing "real" to back it from the order of commodity values—a process that, if unrestrained, finally results in *usury*, "a charge for the use of purchasing power, levied without regard to production; often without regard to the possibilities of production" (note appended to Canto 45, 230).

As Pound will elaborate, "usury is contra naturam" [16] in the Aristotelian sense whereby economic practices are proscribed by natural laws:

Stonecutter is kept from his stone
weaver is kept from his loom
WITH USURA
wool comes not to market
sheep bringeth no gain with usura
usura is a murrain, usura
blunteth the needle in the maid's hand
and stoppeth the spinner's cunning.
                    (Canto 45, 229)
Usury is against Nature's increase.
                    (Canto 51, 250)

Linked explicitly (as in Aristotle) to "unnatural" sexual practices ("By great wisdom sodomy and usury were seen coupled together" [*SP* 265]), usury is attacked by Pound as a prophylactic that confounds all natural immediacy by inhibiting the biological sequence of generation:

It stayeth the young man's courting
It hath brought palsey to bed, lyeth
between the young bride and her bridegroom
            CONTRA NATURAM
                    (Canto 45, 230)

Usury, moreover, percludes the determination of any "just price"—the economic equivalent of what Pound termed "*le mot juste*"[17]—by blurring all distinctions between objects and values, words and things. "Antithetic to discrimination by the senses" (*GK* 281), usury precipitates a general "failure to keep the different nature of different things clearly distinct in the mind" (*SP* 257):

with usura the line grows thick
with usura is no clear demarcation
and no man can find site for his dwelling.
                    (Canto 45, 229)

By means of this "thickening of lines," usury gradually infests all aspects of civilization, its impact discernible even "in England's versification" as well as in the plastic arts, for economic and cultural decay "move parallel" (*SP* 265): "I suggest that finer and future critics of art will be able to tell from the quality of a painting the degree of tolerance or intolerance of usury extant in the age and milieu that produced it" (*GK* 27). A general debasement of the arts is thus merely one of the effects of "an arbitrary and artificial money system that has no correspondence to reality at all."[18]

In order to remedy this iniquitous situation, to eradicate the usurious "clog" that prevents money from being wholly "honest" (Canto 38, 190), Pound called for the development of a monetary system founded on the same "natural" basis as are the commodities to which it refers. The present system—devised by "the usurocracy" for its own selfish ends (*RS* 265)—is "something against nature, a false representation in the mineral world of laws which apply only to animals and vegetables," for it represents gold as if it could "germinate like grain" (*SP* 346, 249). Believing that a more faithful representation would "make [money] last as long as things last in the material world" (*SP* 349), Pound urged the immediate adoption of Silvio Gesell's "stamp scrip" [*Schwundgeld*, "perishable currency"]. Defined succinctly by Pound as "counter-usury" (*SP* 276), the scrip essentially is a tax on money, in which a stamp (costing, say, a penny) must be attached to a dollar bill at regular (say, monthly) intervals in order to keep the signified worth of the dollar at face value. If, for example, no stamps were attached during the course of a year, the dollar would be worth only eighty-eight cents. Such a system is intended to keep money unhoarded and in rapid circulation, for consumers will want to spend it before having to pay twelve cents per dollar per year. The scrip is thus a nonregressive tax in that "it will never fall due on anyone who does not have in his pocket, *at the very moment* it falls due, one hundred times the sum demanded" (*SP* 315). Gesell's scrip actually was put into effect at Wörgl, a small Tyrolean village, which used the device to help pull itself out of the Depression—until "all the slobs in Europe were terrified" (Canto 74, 441) and the experiment was terminated by the Viennese authorities.[19]

Pound was fascinated by the idea of the scrip, describing the positive effects of its implementation in his projected "country of Utopia": "Because the currency is no more durable than commodities such as potatoes, crops, or fabrics, the people have acquired a much healthier sense of values" (*SP* 336–37). Holding (in Pound's view) the same ontological properties as the goods to which it refers,[20] stamped money is able to participate fully in the flux of commodity values, the former now corresponding to the latter without any apparent trace of arbitrariness. "The simplest possible system for maintaining a monetary *representation* of extant goods" (*SP* 277), the stamp scrip would be fully "economic" rather than merely "chrematistic," for it brings money once more into line with natural processes; its status as a representation thus no longer would be "false," for it enables money to recover its former transparency as an immediate measure of "real" values.

The usurocracy, however, will not so willingly surrender its prerogatives: the government must step in to ensure the "just price" through its implementation of the stamp scrip, as "STATAL MONEY based upon national wealth must replace GOLD manipulated by international usurers" (*SP* 297). Pound reasoned that only a certain kind of government would be able to accomplish such a formidable task, for the Western democracies typically have shown themselves incapable of withstanding the temptations of usury. Indeed, Pound ultimately concluded that "USURY is the cancer of the world which only the surgeon's knife of Fascism can cut out of the life of nations'' (*SP* 300). Pound, however, did not arrive at this position as a consequence of some ''aberration'' in his thought; as we shall begin to acknowledge below, Pound's characteristic identification of the usurer with the Jew proceeds directly from the ''economic'' logic of his monetary policies.

II

As might be anticipated, Pound's anti-Semitism has generated a full spectrum of critical responses ranging in tone from violent denunciations at one extreme to ultimate (albeit usually implicit) endorsements at the other. Most literary critics, however, have preferred to negotiate this issue in one of two ways—either by denying its existence altogether or by ''explaining it away'' as a purely regional phenomenon which must be taken with a grain of salt if one is still to ''read Pound's verse today and find it a source of delight and entertainment.''[21] Representing the former position, William Cookson attempts to exonerate Pound from all charges, insisting that ''although Pound said many critical things about the Jews and particularly the Jewish religion, it is false to label him an anti-Semite'' because ''many of his remarks about other nations and other religions are as derogatory.''[22] Clarence Mullins, in much the same vein, contends that Pound was neither an anti-Semite nor a defender of Italian fascism, citing as evidence the fact that Pound ''met Mussolini only once.'' Mullins further recalls that ''Pound had pointed out some years before [the Bollingen controversy] that his critics would 'use any stick to beat me,' and the issue of anti-Semitism in his work is merely one of the desperate measures to which liberals resort in their ceaseless attempts to discredit him.''[23] In a more temperate fashion, Hugh Kenner nevertheless reaches the similar conclusion that, far from being anti-Semitic, Pound ''correctly or not . . . attempted a diagnosis, and one tending rather to decrease than to encourage anti-Semitism.''[24]

Although each of these critics would deny Pound's animus against Judaism, a second group shows no such reluctance in acknowledging his anti-Semitism— but only on the condition that it not be emphasized too strongly, since it is of a kind that ''never will inspire the faintest urge in anyone to put a torch to a synagogue.''[25] Christine Brooke-Rose is the leading proponent of this notion that Pound's anti-Semitism, though occasionally ''nasty,'' is best regarded as a regrettable error that can and should be dismissed—unless, of course, one were ''not willing to forgive the past'':

Pound did not know about the concentration camps, he was totally out of touch in Italy. This does not excuse him as a public preacher who should be informed. His anti-Semitism is (or was) nasty, an aberration, even if in intention focused on the financial question. But, if I may say so, for I was brought up in the thirties and heard the way grown-ups talked, it was part of the general hysterical, ill-informed atmosphere of propaganda and counter-propaganda of the time. Dear old ladies in Kent villages would talk about Jews in a similar vein, if in more genteel terms.

Brooke-Rose will conclude that, "to the best and most serious part of the younger generation whom I address, and some of whom I teach, these issues are as dead as the religious wars. . . .'Let us forgive the past and get on with the job.'"[26] Such a recommendation has proven to be highly influential, as other critics similarly have concluded that Pound's anti-Semitism is either "highly exaggerated" or without real consequence "for today."[27]

To "forgive the past," however, should not be taken as a license to suppress it deliberately, to free ourselves from the necessity of reading (and writing) it; as Pound himself would warn, one should "suspect anyone who destroys an image, or wants to suppress a page of history" (*SP* 317). Yet it was also Pound himself who seems to have contributed most to the "suppression" of his anti-Semitism—whether through various revisions of his earlier published work (in which anti-Semitic material was deleted silently)[28] or through the famous "retractions" of his senescence, which tended, in their critical impact, to mitigate substantially the polemical thrust of his earlier assertions.[29] On Pound's own behalf, one must record his acknowledgment that "race prejudice is red herring . . . the tool of the man defeated intellectually, and of the cheap politician" (*GK* 242)—a recognition that, perhaps, enabled Pound to treat *individual* Jews with the utmost respect (as Louis Zukofsky reported): "I never felt the least trace of anti-Semitism in his presence. Nothing he ever said to me made me feel the embarassment I always have for the 'Goy' in whom a residue of antagonism for the 'Jew' remains. If we had an occasion to use the word 'Jew' or 'Goy' they were no more or less ethnological in their sense than 'Chinese' or 'Italian'."[30]

What generally is omitted in this context, however, is Pound's persistent belief in the "danger of Jews. Not that they mayn't be O.K. individually. STATE of mind by being surrounded by nothing but."[31] Despite both his and his defenders' many disclaimers to the contrary, it must be recognized that Pound consistently identified the usurer with the Jew—a gesture that assigns to the latter the same "unlimited" powers and influence that he typically associates with the former:

> Just WHICH of you is free from JEW influence? Just which political and business groups are free from JEW influence, or bujayzuz, from JEW control? Who holds the mortgage? Who is a dominating director? Just which Jew has asked what Jew to nominate which assemblyman who is in debt to WHOM? . . . Just which college or university will distinguish itself by adding to its history courses a course in the study of chewish history . . . and the effects of Jewsury and of usury on the history of Europe during the past thousand years? (*RS* 254)

In coining such neologisms as "Jewsury," Pound underscores his belief in the ultimate inseparability of this word's constituent parts. If, for example, he sometimes would have it that the many "poor yitts" should not be held responsible for "a few big jews' vendetta on goyim," Pound immediately effaces this (already dubious) distinction by associating *all* "jews, real jews, chazims [pigs]" with the usurious practice of *neschek* (Canto 52, 257). Similarly, if Pound would maintain that "usurers have no race," he will do so only after appending the following qualifications: "How long *the whole Jewish people* is to be the sacrificial goat for the usurer, I know not. . . . I wish to distinguish between prejudice against the Jew as such and the suggestion that the Jew should face *his own problem*" (*SP* 300n., 299; my emphases). Often cited as "proof" that Pound was, in fact, capable of making "a distinction between the financiers and *the rest of Jewry*,"[32] such statements, rather, clearly demand an antithetical glossing: not only is one of their terms ("financiers") always defined as a synecdoche of the other ("the rest of Jewry"), but these so-called distinctions also leave unchallenged the notion that the Jew does indeed "have his own problem"—one endemic to "the whole Jewish people" even if, in Pound's view, exacerbated by only a few of its representatives through certain "hereditary" economic practices: "It is useless to engage in anti-Semitism, leaving intact the *Hebraic monetary system* which is a most tremendous instrument of usury. . . . Why curse Adolph, why not get down to bedrock? . . . As always jewish outlaw and crook leads the sheriffs posse back to the ghetto."[33]

Far, then, from being able to distinguish between usurers and Jews, Pound employed these words so interchangeably that he ultimately would classify as "Semitic" such non-Jewish figures as "Franklin Finklestein Roosevelt" (according to Pound, one of the worst of the usurocrats).[34] In view of such apparent perversity, we might better appreciate the rationale for Pound's conflation of these terms following a closer analysis of his characterization of the Jew.

Although he acknowledged (as if self-evidently) that "no one will deny that the Jews have racial characteristics, better and worse ones" (*GK* 243), Pound in practice remained predisposed to consider only the "worse ones"—to which he would refer collectively as "the Hebrew disease" (*LE* 154). In Pound's conception, "the Jew is atavistic: [his] psychology, may the stink of your camp drive you onward. [They are] herders, having no care but to let their herds browse and move on, when the pasture is exhausted" (*RS* 302). The very writings of the Hebrews seem to embody "the ethos of a nomadic era" (*SP* 66)—writings that reflect "not a trace of civilization from the first lines of Genesis to the excised account of Holophernes" (*GK* 330). Pound sought continually to register his sense of the inherent "evil" of "all this damn near eastern squish"[35] (the canonical texts of the Jewish religion):

> I think no impartial examiner will deny that the
> ethics of the Old Testament are merely squalid. (*SP* 64)

> The Chronicles record the doings of a thoroughly
> disgusting race of barbarians. (*RS* 117)

> I see almost no spiritual elevation in the Old
> Testament, and the Talmud, if one is to judge by
> current quotations, is not an ethical volume at all
> but a species of gangster's handbook. (*SP* 68)

> The Bolshevik anti-morale comes out of the Talmud,
> which is the dirtiest teaching any race ever codified. (*RS* 117)

Such writings are said, moreover, to project a "brutal and savage mythology" (*SP* 265) most visible by way of contrast to (Pound's version of) Christianity, a religion which "is (or was when real) anti-Semitism"(*L* 340).[36] Doubting that "any single ethical idea now honoured comes from Jewry" (*L* 341), Pound maintained that "all the Jew part of the Bible is black evil. Question is mainly how soon one can get rid of it without killing the patient"(*L* 345)—a question, Pound argued, which T. S. Eliot never seriously raised (to his detriment): "Until [Eliot] succeeds in detaching the Jewish from the European elements of his peculiar variety of Christianity, he will never find the right formula. Not a jot or tittle of the hebraic alphabet can pass into the text without danger of contaminating it" (*SP* 320). Pound similarly charged that Harriet Monroe failed to free herself from the "damn remnants" of "Jew religion, that bitch Moses and the rest of the tribal barbarians" (*L* 182), for he believed that "until a man purges himself of this [Jewish] poison he will never achieve understanding" (*SP* 320).

Perhaps the most significant of the "Jewish elements" that Pound would purge is the *excess* he identified as the primary characteristic of "the Semitic"[37]—an attribution that once more links his conception of the Jew with that of the usurer. Like usury, the Jewish religion would be "antithetic to discrimination by the senses," for "the effect of Protestantism [in Pound's view, a variety of Judaism] has been *semiticly* to obliterate values, to efface grades and graduations" (*GK* 185; my emphasis). Pound, in fact, would demonstrate how Judaism quite literally forces "lines [to] grow thick"—a process represented graphically in Canto 52 (257), where heavily blackened lines substitute for Pound's purportedly libelous remarks concerning the activities of the Rothschilds.[38] In the same way that usury produces a surplus value without direct monetary reference to the world of tangible commodities, so do the texts of Judaism conspire to undermine the efficacy of immediate linguistic reference, to suppress "any interest in verbal precision": "Cabala, for example, anything to make the word mean something it does NOT say" (*RS* 284). This ability of the Jew to efface both verbal and economic boundaries—to contribute to usury whether through financial or hermeneutic practices—is what Pound will condemn pervasively as the "excess" of a people committed to *forging* money out of nothing:

> If or when one hears of the Protocols alleged to be of the Elders of Zion,
> one is frequently met with the reply: Oh, but they are a forgery. Certainly
> they are a forgery, and that is the one proof that we have of their authenticity.

The Jews have worked with forged documents for the past 24 hundred years, namely ever since they have had any documents whatsoever. (*RS* 283)

If Pound thus assumed (however ironically) some inherent connection between the history of the Jews and their alleged possession of "forged documents," we soon shall recognize that such an assumption is not as illogical as it first might appear. In what follows we indeed shall discover (in the words of Hyam Maccoby) that "Pound was right in sensing that the Jew was the chief enemy,"[39] for the rhetorical character of Judaism poses an inescapable threat to the integrity of Pound's policies—a threat that will permit us to reexamine the "economy" of his anti-Semitism in a radically *different* manner.

III

Although, as we have seen, Pound would attack Judaism as a consequence of its tendency toward excess, it is for this very tendency that Judaism has become adopted as the "unofficial religion" of much contemporary writing in France. As thematized by deconstruction, for example, excess would be a property of all written texts, a product of the structural incapacity of any form of discourse to master fully its own rhetorical mode. If this excess by which writing is characterized can be understood (provisionally) as "an experience of the infinitely other"[40]—that is, as an encounter with textual elements that remain irreducibly peripheral with respect to a presiding (authorial) consciousness—we might then infer that Judaism conveys a rhetorically similar experience, for it forms an analogous, unassimilable "excess" on the margins of the dominant Western culture. Just as the linguistic sign both differs from and defers perpetually that which it represents, so may Judaism itself be viewed as a religion of difference and deferral, as an ethos of absence and loss conditioned by the hope for a Messiah who "always already" remains yet to come. The writer and the Jew, by extension, would each become "nomads," exiles displaced from any stable origin or destination—exiles condemned to endless metonymic succession (in which referent and sign can never coincide) without hope for immediate sacramental identity (in which the former incarnates the latter).[41] Given the terms of this analogy, one may consider "the situation of the Jew" to be exemplary of "the situation of the poet, the man of speech and writing," for both figures find themselves inscribed in a common textuality.[42]

As "a race born of the book," the Jews would be related to writing in another sense as well: imprinted with the mark of circumcision "by which they are distinguished from all other nations and peoples,"[43] Jewish men bear upon their own bodies an inscription that transforms them figuratively into the image of *money*—an image of which Marx, for one, was not entirely unaware: "The capitalist knows that all commodities, however scurvy they may look, or however badly they may smell, are in faith and in truth money, inwardly circumcised Jews [*innerlich beschnittene Juden*], and what is more, a wonderful means whereby out of money to make more money." [44] If (as in this instance) both Jews and money can function as alternate figures for "writing," each term will maintain with the other a "relationship of reciprocal metaphoricity in which the Jews represent money and money represents them." [45] We might infer further that such reciprocity can be understood as a metaphor for metaphor, as a figure for figure, for: "the carrying of one term across an equal sign to another"—a process which is doubled in the passage cited above—might be taken as describing the activities of all tropes. [46] Judaism, writing, money, and rhetoric thus would all belong to the same tropological series, each term functioning analogously as a figure of "excess," as an inscription that deflects any immediate connection between the sign and its intended referent. By virtue of this proliferation of interchangeable (rhetorical) parts, one indeed may acknowledge that "the difficulty of being Jewish . . . is the same as the difficulty of writing, for Judaism and writing are but the same waiting, the same hope, the same wearing out [*une même usure*]." [47]

Une même usure: it is surely not fortuitous that the word *usure* figures in this tropological network, rhetoric and usury having been defined perennially as synonymous terms for the production of interdicted (linguistic or economic) values. As noted by Derrida, for example, *usure* seems to be "systematically connected with the theme of metaphor" and of tropes in general, for usury and rhetoric both derive a heterogeneous and discontinuous surplus from their respective "capital" investments. [48] In deviating improperly from all correspondence with the natural world, both usury and rhetoric can be said to indicate "the *spacing*, both graphic and temporal, which marks the transgression of the origin, the text's ill-gotten gains." [49] If, then, it were admitted that usury and rhetoric share an identical structure of "excess," it would not be unreasonable to expect that Pound will fulminate against rhetoric and writing in the same ways that he attacks usury and Judaism.

Such an expectation is, in fact, confirmed, as Pound condemns incessantly the "habit of defining things always 'in terms of something else.'" [50] Just as he would determine the degree of usury extant in any particular age from the quality of its cultural achievements, so will Pound link the decline of a civilization to its willingness to indulge itself in rhetoric:

> Rome rose through the idiom of Caesar, Ovid, and Tacitus, she declined in a welter of rhetoric, the diplomat's "language to conceal thought," and so forth. (*ABC* 33)

> And in the midst of these awakenings Italy went to rot, destroyed by rhetoric, destroyed by the periodic sentence and the flowing paragraph, as the Roman Empire had been destroyed before her. For when words cease

to cling close to things, kingdoms fall, empires wane and diminish. Rome went because it was no longer the fashion to hit the nail on the head. (*G-B* 113–14)

The Renaissance sought a realism and attained it. It rose in a search for precision and declined through rhetoric and rhetorical thinking. (*G-H* 117)

Pound's preference for "precision" (presumably, when words cling close to things) is evidenced, moreover, in his definition of the "Image" as "the furthest possible remove from rhetoric" (*G-B* 83) and in his admonition to "use no ornament or good ornament" (*LE* 5). Such statements also reflect Pound's disdain for poets who "have used symbol and metaphor / and no man learned anything from them / for their speaking in figures" (Addendum for [Canto] 100, 799).[51]

Pound, in short, would attempt to eradicate the "nomadic" play of rhetoric in the same way that he sought to purge himself of "the Jewish poison"; he similarly would "go in fear of abstractions" (*LE* 5), for abstract terms (like rhetoric and "Judaism") render problematic the supposedly natural connection between sign and referent. Such "fear" was perhaps sufficient motivation for Pound to be drawn to Fenollosa's manuscript, *The Chinese Written Character*, for both men deplored the abstraction inherent in Western forms of phonetic writing. Pound argued that "writing in Europe, etc." exists merely as the sign of a sign, as graphic marks which by "more or less approximate agreement" represent "various noises" (*ABC* 28). Speech, in this conception, would be anterior to writing, less removed from the presence of those living entities that remain forever banished from the enervating realm of script. Expressing his dissatisfaction with "the feeble cohesive force of our phonetic symbols"—with the arbitrariness of characters that can never represent things in their plenitude but only as if "stunned"—Pound would complain "What's the use of writing"[52] in remaining conscious of the fact that "we have no communication system worthy of the name" (*CWC* 25, 26; *GK* 55). Refusing to accept such arbitrariness as the structural condition of writing in general, Pound directed his efforts instead to the development of "a more natural way of writing" in order to:

> Free us, for we perish
> In this ever-flowing monotony
> Of ugly print marks, black
> Upon white parchment.[53]

Pound would discover this "more natural way of writing" in the Chinese written chracter, a pictographic script that (he believed) manifests visibly the "natural" phenomena to which it refers. As opposed to Western phonetic writing, the Chinese ideogram "is *not* abstract," for it "brings language close to things," "closer to the concreteness of natural processes" (*CWC* 13, 18, 24): "Chinese notation is something much more than arbitrary symbols. It is based upon a vivid shorthand picture of the operations of nature. In the algebraic figure and in the spoken word there is no natural connection between things and signs: all depends upon sheer convention. But the Chinese method follows natural suggestion" (*CWC* 8). Following, for example, the "natural suggestions" of the character ⊟ ["dawn"], Pound will read this image iconically as "the sun above the horizon" (*CWC* 39). More natural, then, even than speech, the ideogram enables one to read without "juggling mental counters," to witness "*things* [working] out their own fate" (*CWC* 9). Chinese thus seemed to Pound "the ideal language of the world" (*CWC* 31): by virtue of its ability not merely to "stand for" but actually to imitate the natural phenomena that it represents, the Chinese character would remotivate the connection between sign and referent that Western phonetic writing continually threatens to obscure.

As "a vivid shorthand *picture* of the operations of nature," however, the Chinese character may remind us of another figure previously encountered in Pound's writings—the stamp scrip, "a 'money *picture*' of extant goods" (*SP* 277; my emphases). Indeed, the stamp scrip and the Chinese character not only have an identical synecdochic structure (in which each term forms part of the totality that it represents) but also perform identical rhetorical functions within their respective signifying economies, each device being geared to repel any intrusion of abstraction, figuration, usury, writing, "Judaism"—in a word, *différance*—by safeguarding the natural correspondence between (monetary and linguistic) sign and (commodity and phenomenal) referent. The intention with which Pound employed the ideogram thus applies as well to his proposals for the scrip, since both devices were directed to "[do] away with abstractions, classifications, codes"—anything, in short, that might inhibit *immediacy*—in order to ensure that "meaning would not endlessly ooze and spread." [54]

And yet, paradoxically, both the stamp scrip and the Chinese character may themselves comprise instances of the very problems they were intended to eliminate; irreducibly figural, these synecdoches inevitably join ranks with the tropes against which they were issued to contend. The stamp scrip, for example, cannot possibly succeed in its project of bringing money "once more into line with natural processes," for (quite simply) there is nothing "real" or "natural" to back that additional twelve cents exacted on every dollar per year—nothing, that is, except for the arbitrary power of the state which must underwrite the production of this irreducible "difference." The scrip's purported ability to remedy the vagaries of monetary reference thus is undermined by its antithetical tendency to propel money more forcefully than ever into an *abyme* of self-referentiality. Containing within its own structure the very chrematism it would eradicate, the scrip from the outset would already be a scrip*t*, would "turn" itself figurally toward the camp of its enemy.

A similar rhetorical situation prevails in the case of the Chinese character, for it too cannot permit us to witness the singularity of "things working out their own fate." Even in a so-called iconic sign like the ideogram "the thing itself always escapes," its "pictographic [reference] has never been simply 'realistic' '":

> Is it not evident that no signifier, whatever its substance and form, has a "unique and singular reality"? A signifier is from the very beginning the possibility of its own repetition, of its own image or resemblance. It is the condition of its ideality, what identifies it as a signifier, and makes it function as such, relating it to a signified which, for the very same reasons, could never be a "unique and singular reality." From the moment that the sign appears, that is to say from the very beginning, there is no chance of encountering anywhere the purity of "reality," "unicity," "singularity."[55]

The ideogram, in other words, has always belonged to the order of *writing*: although Pound believed Chinese to be "the ideal language of the world" in terms of its supposed ability to circumvent the arbitrariness of phoneticism, the fact remains that *no* writing (whether phonetic or pictographic) has ever remained unaffected by such arbitrariness. If, for example, the ideogram of a woman holding a child "represents not only the thing it pictures, but love, and by extension, the adjective good,"[56] then the Chinese character seems to admit the very ambiguity and abstraction that Pound hoped to abolish. Why, moreover, must the character 旦 necessarily mean "dawn," when this sign just as easily can be read as "dusk"? Pound's very distinction between "abstract phonetic writing" and "motivated nonphonetic writing" must therefore be revised—on the one hand, because "largely nonphonetic scripts like Chinese and Japanese included phonetic elements" at the origin of their development; on the other hand, because "there is no purely phonetic writing (by reason of the necessary spacing of signs, punctuation, intervals, the differences indispensable for the functioning of graphemes, etc.)."[57] In other words, if no single script can be purely (non)phonetic, the relationship between Western and Chinese writings is less a product of some hard and fast distinction between "arbitrariness" and "motivation" than of the interimplication of each of these qualities as the other's condition of possibility. Phonetic writing thus does not comprise the sole preserve of arbitrariness (as Pound contended); it rather forms the *différance* of its equally rhetorical other, "the other as 'differed' within the systematic ordering [*l'économie*] of the same"—a development that undermines Pound's project from the start, identifying it as the "offspring" of a persistent "sort of European hallucination" determined at any cost to efface the workings of such differences.[58]

The stamp scrip and the Chinese character would both obey what Derrida has termed the uncanny logic of the *supplement*, for each attempts to "compensate for a primordial nonself-presence" in the orders of monetary and linguistic reference—only to discover belatedly that the referentiality in question "had already from the start fallen short of itself," had already come into play not at the behest of some natural plenitude but as an inescapable effect of rhetorical differentiation.[59] Since, in Derrida's words, "writing will appear to us more and more as another name for this structure of supplementarity"—and since we previously discovered that "usury," "rhetoric," and "Judaism" may figure as alternate names for this structure as well—we then may infer that this supplementary logic would equally subvert all the dichotomies on which Pound's writings are founded (specifically: economics/chrematistics, "precision"/rhetoric, Christianity/Judaism). For just as the stamp scrip and the ideogram are both inhabited by the very properties that each was intended to eliminate, so may we conclude that each of Pound's privileged terms inevitably contains its "opposite" within itself, thereby establishing "a relationship to the absolutely other [*différance*] that apparently breaks up any economy."[60]

The "economy" of Pound's economics thus is "broken up" by its hostility toward *writing*—toward a Judaism which, condemned by Pound for lacking any "trace of civilization," may now be acknowledged as the "civilization of the trace." If Pound's intuition of the "danger of contamination" posed by the Hebraic alphabet can be said to reflect a generalized fear of writing, we thus can reject the conventional hypothesis that Pound's anti-Semitism was simply a contingent phenomenon, ancillary to his achievements as a writer—for Judaism constitutes an unavoidable threat to those "natural" orders whose integrity, Pound insisted, it is the duty of the writer to defend. Yet Judaism ultimately will secure its own revenge, undermining the system of reference in which both his poetry and prose are inscribed; Pound could no more purge his texts of the "Jewish poison" than he could isolate them from all contact with the "excess" by which (his own) writing is conditioned. If Pound's attempts to write against writing seem to indicate an aporia that he remained unable to resolve, we might consider his animus against Judaism as a sign of a similar contradiction, as an oblique confirmation of Pound's irreducible Jewishness—evidence for which can be deduced even from his proper name, for "in writing a man's 'name' is his reference" (*ABC* 25).

"Ezra," of course, was a "scribe skilled in the law of Moses" (Ezra 7:6), the leader of that group of Hebrews who, throughout their period of exile in Babylon, never relinquished the dream of returning to Palestine and restoring the Temple. During the reign of the Persian emperor Cyrus, this return was accomplished and work was begun on the Temple's reconstruction. Yet certain fundamental "differences" were to impede these efforts at restoration, for "the Temple was not constructed exactly in accordance with the First Temple plan, and it lacked numerous items (the most striking omission being the Ark of the Covenant)"—an "omission" which indicated that "the invisible presence of God was no longer attached to a man-made object as it had been to the ark."[61]

Failing, by reason of this interior absence, to repossess that which they desired most fervently, the Hebrews discovered that such a void could be negotiated only through an act of reading—an act that, far from restoring a lost presence, demonstrates instead the inability of any text (like the Temple) to coincide completely with itself. This "turn to reading" inaugurated the era of Rabbinic Judaism, a period marked by the compilation of the *Midrash* ["interpretation"], the origins of which are ascribed traditionally to the moment when Ezra read aloud from the Torah (Nehemiah 8:8). From this moment on, the Jew becomes "he who knows how to read—which means that he withdraws from his literal utterance so as to find an interval which allows for the play of interpretation."[62] The return of the Jews from Babylon to their "origin" in Palestine thus marks the beginning of their exile from the fullness of the Word, of their inscription within a diaspora of textuality.

Like his biblical namesake, Pound would be caught in this rift between an irrecuperable presence and the necessity of its remembrance; he too would be condemned to "uneconomical" expenditures that transform all intended truths into the most questionable of interpretations. Denied access to an originary unity in which sign would be connected naturally to referent—forced to wander nomadically without any stable "site for his dwelling"—Pound would find *himself* to be the author of those forgeries he attempted in vain to repudiate. The ultimate irony, however, is not simply that such should be the fate of this most virulent of anti-Semites; it is, moreover, that Pound's ultimate destiny would link him once more to the very people he most despised: "Vous êtes tous Juifs, même les antisémites, car vous avez été designés pour le martyre."[63]

NOTES

1. Donald Davie, *Ezra Pound* (New York: Penguin, 1976), 23.

2. Frank Kermode, *The Sense of an Ending* (New York: Oxford Univ. Press, 1967), 108, and William M. Chace, *The Political Identities of Ezra Pound and T. S. Eliot* (Stanford, Calif.: Stanford Univ. Press, 1973), 4. This critical dichotomy is evidenced as well in the celebrated controversies surrounding Pound's nominations for literary awards: "The Bollingen Prize Committee, in 1949, resolved the Pound dilemma by separating the man from his work and giving the work the prize; the Council of the American Academy of Arts and Sciences, deciding twenty-three years later not to give the Academy's Emerson-Thoreau Medal to Pound, did just the opposite" (C. David Heymann, *Ezra Pound: The Last Rower* [New York: Viking, 1976], 311).

3. Pound, in fact, wrote the following to Louis Zukofsky: "My poetry and my econ are NOT separate or opposed. Essential unity" (cited in Charles Norman, *Ezra Pound* [New York: Macmillan, 1960], 333). The attitude of most literary critics remains, however, that of Christine Brooke-Rose, who argues that Pound's "extra-literary" concerns are of secondary importance to the poetry "itself": "It is time we stopped accusing Pound of being a lousy historian, economist, anthropologist, scientist, etc., whatever impression he may himself have given at various times—in his prose and in the more strident or dully dogmatic parts of [*The Cantos*]—that he took himself seriously in these roles. Let us not fall into the intentional fallacy" (*A ZBC of Ezra Pound* [Berkeley: Univ. of California Press, 1971], 179). By so "defending" Pound from any pedagogic intention, by attempting to separate the "serious" poetic work from its "nonserious" counterparts, Brooke-Rose sustains the prevailing image of Pound as solely "a prime-mover of modernist aesthetics"—an image with which Pound himself broke as early as "Hugh Selwyn Mauberly" (1920).

4. Michael Sprinker, review of *Charles Olson and Ezra Pound: An Encounter at St. Elizabeth's*, ed. Catherine Seelye, in *Western American Literature* 11 (1976): 68. In recent years, however, a

number of pathbreaking studies have appeared that begin to address this thorny issue. See, for example, Ian F. A. Bell, ed., *Ezra Pound: Tactics for Reading* (Totowa, N.J.: Barnes & Noble, 1982); Robert Casillo, "Anti-Semitism, Castration, and Usury in Ezra Pound," *Criticism* 25. 3 (Summer 1983): 239–65; Alan Durant, *Ezra Pound: Identity in Crisis* (Totowa, N.J.: Barnes & Noble, 1981); Maud Ellmann, "Floating the Pound: The Circulation of the Subject of *The Cantos*," *Oxford Literary Review* 3. 3 (Spring 1979): 16–27; Marcelin Pleynet, "La Compromission poétique," *Tel Quel* 70 (1977): 11–26; and Paul Smith, *Pound Revised* (London: Croom Helm, 1983). Ellmann's and Smith's writings are especially provocative in this regard.

5. Marc Shell, *The Economy of Literature* (Baltimore: Johns Hopkins Univ. Press, 1978), 7, and William Cookson, "Introduction" to his edition of Pound's *Selected Prose: 1909–65* (New York: New Directions, 1973), 7 (cited hereafter as *SP*).

6. Clement Greenberg, for instance, maintains that Pound's poetry "degenerates as art" when it gives voice to anti-Semitic sentiments: "Anti-Semitism is not intrinsic to [*The Cantos*] because hardly anything is—not even Pound's apparent obsession with usury—except their art, at its best and at its worst" ("Reply to Hyam Maccoby," *Midstream* 22 [June/July 1976]: 64). This chapter will be arguing, on the contrary, that "Pound's anti-Semitism and the literary uses to which he repeatedly puts it may be evaluated most productively as an altogether logical corollary to his philosophical and aesthetic principles, not as an inexplicable divergence from them" (Chace, *Political Identities*, 81).

7. Pound's frequent allusions to the *Politics* serve as one measure of the importance he accorded this text. See, for example, *SP* 172, 181, 182; *The Cantos of Ezra Pound* (New York: New Directions, 1972), nos. 53, 74, 76–78; and *"Ezra Pound Speaking": Radio Speeches of World War II*, ed. Leonard W. Doob (Westport, Conn.: Greenwood Press, 1978), 82, 178, 263, 391 (cited hereafter as *RS*). All references to the *Politics* are to the 2nd ed. of Richard McKeon's *Introduction to Aristotle* (Chicago: Univ. of Chicago Press, 1973); tacit alterations in this translation will be made where appropriate. My discussion of the *Politics* is indebted heavily to Shell, *Economy of Literature*, 89–96.

8. "Instead of simply representing the relations of commodities, [money] enters now, so to say, into private relations with itself" (Karl Marx, *Capital*, ed. Frederick Engels [New York: International Publishers, 1967], vol. I, 154).

9. Shell, *Economy of Literature*, 94.

10. "Usuraria acquisitio pecuniarum est maxime praeter naturam" (*Summa theologica* II–II, q. 78, a. I, ad 3). Cf. Aquinas's comments in the *Politicorum expositio* (I, lect. 8, n. 134): "Thus, a kind of birth takes place when money grows from money. For this reason the acquisition of money is especially contrary to Nature, because it is in accordance with Nature that money should increase from natural goods and not from money itself." See also Benjamin Nelson, *The Idea of Usury: From Tribal Brotherhood to Universal Otherhood*, 2nd ed. (Chicago: Univ. of Chicago Press, 1969), 3–28, and John T. Noonan, Jr., *The Scholastic Analysis of Usury* (Cambridge, Mass.: Harvard Univ. Press, 1957), 11–57, for detailed accounts of the vicissitudes of the concept of usury within the medieval church.

11. Canto 52, 257; all subsequent references to *The Cantos* will be cited in this manner.

12. Hugh Kenner, "Ezra Pound and Money," *Agenda* 4 (October–November 1965): 52.

13. Pound as cited in Hugh Kenner, *The Pound Era* (Berkeley: Univ. of California Press, 1971), 412.

14. Kenner, *Pound Era*, 225. See Ernest Fenollosa, *The Chinese Written Character as a Medium for Poetry*, ed. Ezra Pound (San Francisco: City Lights, 1964; originally completed in 1918); cited hereafter as *CWC*.

15. Ezra Pound, *ABC of Reading* (New York: New Directions, 1960; originally completed in 1934), 25 (cited hereafter as *ABC*).

16. Ezra Pound, *Guide to Kulchur* (New York: New Directions, 1970; originally published in 1938), 281 (cited hereafter as *GK*).

17. On the notion of *le mot juste*, see Ezra Pound, *Literary Essays*, ed. T. S. Eliot (New York: New Directions, 1968; originally published in 1954), 7, 373, 409 (cited hereafter as *LE*).

18. Hugh MacDiarmid (a poet greatly influenced by Pound's economic thought) as cited in Cookson's "Introduction" to *SP*, 12.

19. See Brooke-Rose, *ZBC*, 277, and Lewis Hyde, "Ezra Pound and the Fate of Vegetable Money," in *The Gift: Imagination and the Erotic Life of Property* (New York: Vintage, 1983), 216–72.

20. It should, perhaps, come as no surprise that such a formulation recalls Coleridge's definition of "the symbolical" as "always itself a part of that, of the whole of which it is representative" (*Coleridge's Miscellaneous Criticism*, ed. T. M. Raysor [London: Everyman's Library, 1936], 29). Both Pound's (economic) and Coleridge's (linguistic) conceptions thus depend on what Paul de Man has termed "the organic coherence of the synecdoche"—a coherence that will prove difficult in practice to sustain (see "The Rhetoric of Temporality," in *Interpretation: Theory and Practice*, ed. Charles S. Singleton [Baltimore: Johns Hopkins Univ. Press, 1969], 176–78).

21. Michael Reck, *Ezra Pound: A Close-Up* (New York: McGraw-Hill, 1967), 131.

22. Cookson, "Introduction" to *SP*, 14.

23. Clarence Eustace Mullins, *This Difficult Individual, Ezra Pound* (New York: Fleet, 1961), 227, 275, 279.

24. Kenner, *Pound Era*, 465.

25. James Kilpatrick as cited in Harry M. Meacham, *The Caged Panther: Ezra Pound at St. Elizabeths* (New York: Twayne, 1967), 137–38.

26. Brooke-Rose, *ZBC*, 250, 252.

27. See, for further examples, Clark Emery, *Ideas Into Action* (Coral Gables, Fla.: Univ. of Miami Press, 1958), 68, and Michael Alexander, *The Poetic Achievement of Ezra Pound* (Berkeley: Univ. of California Press, 1979), 17, 226.

28. Chace, for example, notes that the book version of Pound's *Patria Mia* omits the following sentence that appeared in the original serial edition: "The Jew alone can retain his detestable qualities, despite climatic conditions" (Chace, *Political Identities*, 7n.). Chace adds that the poem "Salutation the Third" was also reprinted "with the more offensive [anti-Semitic] language expunged" (13n.).

29. Late in his life, Pound was quoted as stating that "the worst mistake I made was that stupid, suburban prejudice of anti-Semitism" (Michael Reck, "A Conversation between Ezra Pound and Allen Ginsberg," *Evergreen Review* 55 [June 1968]: 29).

30. Louis Zukofsky as cited by William Van O'Connor and Edward Stone in their *Casebook on Ezra Pound* (New York: Thomas Y. Crowell, 1959), 10.

31. Pound as cited in Heymann, *Ezra Pound*, 75.

32. Kenner, *Pound Era*, 465 (my emphasis).

33. *SP* 351 (my emphasis), and Pound as cited in Heymann, *Ezra Pound*, 75. On the topic of Hitler, see *GK* 134: "Form-sense 1910–1914. 15 or so years later [Wyndham] Lewis discovered Hitler. I hand it to him as a superior perception. Superior in relation to my own 'discovery' of Mussolini." See also Canto 104, 741, where "Adolph" is described as "furious from perception."

34. Chace, *Political Identities*, 84. Cf. *RS* 62, where Roosevelt's name is linked with those of Baruch, Morgenthau, Cohen, Lehman, and others.

35. Ezra Pound, *Selected Letters: 1907–1941*, ed. D. D. Paige (New York: New Directions, 1971), 183, 342 (cited hereafter as *L*).

36. Although in his early writings Pound condemned all forms of monotheism, he ultimately would dissociate Protestantism from Catholicism, attacking the former as a species of "Jehovism" while praising the latter's "Dantescan light" as "the best canned goods that can be put on the market immediately in sufficient quantity for general pubk." (*L* 345). See Richard Sieburth, *Instigations: Ezra Pound and Remy de Gourmont* (Cambridge, Mass.: Harvard Univ. Press, 1978), 86.

37. Ezra Pound, *Impact: Essays on Ignorance and the Decline of American Civilization*, ed. Noel Stock (Chicago: Henry Regnery, 1960), 125; cited in Ellmann, "Floating the Pound," 26.

38. Kenner, *Pound Era*, 465.

39. Hyam Maccoby, "The Jew as Anti-Artist: The Anti-Semitism of Ezra Pound," *Midstream* 22 (March 1976): 70n.

40. Jacques Derrida, *Writing and Difference*, trans. Alan Bass (Chicago: Univ. of Chicago Press, 1978), 152.

41. In the context of recent French thought, the term "nomadism" is often employed as a figure for the unrestricted economy of writing. See, for example, Gilles Deleuze, "Pensée nomade," in *Nietzsche aujourd'hui?* (Paris: 10/18, 1973), vol. I ("Intensités"), 159–74, and the special issue of *Change* (Février 1975) entitled "L'imprononçable: l'écriture nomade." On the contrasting rhetorical codes of Christianity and Judaism, see Susan Handelman, "Freud's Midrash: The Exile of Interpretation," *New York Literary Forum* 2 (1978): 99–112, and her "Interpretation as Devotion: Freud's Relation to Rabbinic Hermeneutics," *Psychoanalytic Review* 68 (Summer 1981): 201–18.

42. Derrida, *Writing and Difference*, 65.

43. Isidore of Seville as cited in Ruth Mellinkoff, *The Mark of Cain* (Berkeley: Univ. of California Press, 1981), 94. Mellinkoff traces the exegetical history of Genesis 4:15 ("And the Lord set a mark upon Cain, that whosoever found him should not kill him"), finding that this "mark" was often defined as circumcision and hence as a sign of Jewishness (*Mark of Cain*, 92–98). See also Jacques Derrida's *Spurs: Nietzsche's Styles*, trans. Barbara Harlow (Chicago: Univ. of Chicago Press, 1979), 69, concerning Nietzsche's identification of Jews and women: "The fact that Nietzsche often considers them in parallel roles might in fact be related to the motif of castration and simulacrum for which circumcision is the mark, indeed the name of the mark."

44. Marx, *Capital* I, 154. See Elisabeth de Fontenay, *Les figures juives de Marx* (Paris: Galilée, 1973), 96, which reads the phrase "inwardly circumcised Jews" as a function of Marx's Lutheran glossing of Romans 2:28–29: "For he is not a real Jew who is one outwardly, nor is a true circumcision something external and physical. He is a Jew who is one inwardly, and real circumcision is a matter of the heart, spiritual and not literal." In passing here from the letter to the spirit, from the outside to the inside, circumcision reaffirms its irreducibly figural nature.

45. De Fontenay, *Les figures juives*, 29.

46. Richard Klein, "Straight Lines and Arabesques: Metaphors of Metaphor," *Yale French Studies*, no. 45 (1970): 64.

47. Edmond Jabès, *The Book of Questions*, trans. Rosemarie Waldrop (Middletown, Conn.: Wesleyan Univ. Press, 1976), 122.

48. Jacques Derrida, "White Mythology: Metaphor in the Text of Philosophy," trans. F. C. T. Moore, *New Literary History* 6 (Autumn 1974): 13. See also Marc Shell, "The Wether and the Ewe: Verbal Usury in *The Merchant of Venice*," *Kenyon Review* ns. 1 (Fall 1979): 65–92.

49. Ellmann, "Floating the Pound," 25.

50. Ezra Pound, *Gaudier-Brzeska: A Memoir* (New York: New Directions, 1970), 117 (cited hereafter as *G-B*).

51. Imagism's emphasis on "the referential function of the verbal sign in order to convey the 'thing' as directly and transparently as possible" (Sieburth, *Instigations*, 65) thus forms an analogue to Pound's insistence on the referential function of the monetary sign. As in Pound's theory of money, "the plain style of Imagism requires a theory of language in which the relationship of word to thing is ultimate and correspondent" (John T. Gage, "Paradoxes of Objectivity and Argument in Imagist Theory," *Philosophy and Rhetoric* 12 [Summer 1979]: 172).

52. Pound as cited in Max Nänny, "Oral Dimensions in Ezra Pound," *Paideuma* 6 (1974): 14, n. 4.

53. Pound as cited in Herbert N. Schneidau, *Ezra Pound: The Image and the Real* (Baton Rouge: Louisiana State Univ. Press, 1969), 14, and "The Cry of the Eyes," *Collected Early Poems of Ezra Pound*, ed. Michael John King (New York: New Directions, 1976), 24.

54. Michel Beaujour, "Is Less More?" *New York Literary Forum* 2 (1978): 240.

55. Derrida, *Speech and Phenomena*, trans. David B. Allison (Evanston, Ill.: Northwestern

Univ. Press, 1973), 104, and *Of Grammatology*, trans. Gayatri Chakravorty Spivak (Baltimore: Johns Hopkins Univ. Press, 1976), 90, 91.

56. Robert Pattison, *On Literacy* (New York: Oxford Univ. Press, 1982), 34.

57. Derrida, *Of Grammatology*, 90, and *Positions*, trans. Alan Bass (Chicago: Univ. of Chicago Press, 1981), 25–26.

58. Derrida, *Speech and Phenomena*, 148, and *Of Grammatology*, 80.

59. Derrida, *Speech and Phenomena*, 87. For an extended analysis of supplementarity, see *Of Grammatology*, 141–64.

60. Derrida, *Of Grammatology*, 245, and *Speech and Phenomena*, 150.

61. Adin Steinsaltz, *The Essential Talmud*, trans. Chaya Galai (New York: Bantam, 1977), 15, and *The New Oxford Annotated Bible*, eds. Herbert G. May and Bruce M. Metzger (New York: Oxford Univ. Press, 1973), 1543.

62. Jacques Lacan as cited in Jeffrey Mehlman, "The 'Floating Signifier': Lévi-Strauss to Lacan," *Yale French Studies*, no. 48 (1972): 32.

63. Jabès, *Le Livre des Questions* (Paris: Gallimard, 1963), 180: "You are all Jews, even the anti-Semites, for you are all marked for martyrdom."

Chapter 5
The Scene of the Other: Theodor W. Adorno's Negative Dialectic in the Context of Poststructuralism
Rainer Nägele

I

When in the summer of 1979 a group of people, mainly connected with *New German Critique* and the newly founded *Social Text*, met in Madison, Wisconsin, for a three-day discussion centered on problems of cultural theories, somebody jokingly called it an assembly of Frankfurters and French fries. To the gourmet of culinary and intellectual subtleties, such a menu must raise all the horror clichés about products from the American kitchen and culture industry. Thus the constellation indicated by the title of this chapter might suggest an eclectic concoction of ill-suited ingredients or, to use an Adornian phrase, a forced reconciliation (*erpresste Versöhnung*) and harmonization of vastly different modes of thinking.[1] It seems particularly ironic to inscribe in an identical field Adorno's uncompromising insistence on nonidentity and Derrida's play of difference and *différance*. However, it is not an identity we are searching for, but the probing of a constellation.

In writing the word "constellation," I have already entered into a constellation. It is a central term of Adorno's *Negative Dialectics* as well as of his *Aesthetic Theory*,[2] and it shapes the very form of his philosophical discourse. It was, however, Walter Benjamin who introduced and unfolded the term as a philosophical idea in his epistemological introduction to the *Ursprung des deutschen Trauerspiels*.[3] In a first (Platonic) move, Benjamin insists on the radical difference between truth and knowledge (*Erkenntnis*), between idea and concept (*Begriff*). In a second move he differentiates his notion of "idea" from the Platonic idea through the image of the constellation. (He first uses the term "configuration," but, after an explicit comparison to the stellar constellation, he shifts to "constellation."[4]) In this image Benjamin traces the relationship between phenomena and ideas: "Phenomena are not embodied in ideas. They are not contained in them. Rather ideas are the objective, virtual arrangement of phenomena, they are their objective interpretation. . . . Ideas relate to things as stellar constellations relate to the stars."[5] Benjamin's project is a messianic reinterpretation of both Plato and the Hegelian sublation (*Aufhebung*): the phenomena are annihilated and saved at the same time: "Ideas are eternal constellations, the elements are seized as points in such constellations, and thus the phenomena are dissolved and saved at the same time. . . . The collecting of phenomena is the task of concepts, and their dissolution which takes place in them through the differentiating reason (*Verstand*) is all the more significant, because in this same event a double task is performed: the deliverance of the phenomena and the representation (*Darstellung*) of the ideas."[6] When Adorno takes up the image of the constellation, he introduces at the same time an important difference. For Benjamin "ideas are eternal constellations"; Adorno speaks of "historically changing constellations" (*AT* 11). "Aesthetics," he says, "must not go on a fruitless hunting for the primal essence (*Urwesen*) of art, but must think such phenomena in historical constellations" (*AT* 523). Adorno thus secularizes Benjamin's messianic project, without, however, giving up the pathos of salvation that is the moving force of the radical negativity of his aesthetics as well as his *Negative Dialectic*.[7] At stake is the theological, eschatological, historical, and philosophical question of the status of the empirical world which includes also the central Marxist problem of theory and praxis.

To formulate the epistemological and ontological problem of phenomena and idea also as a sociopolitical problem of theory and praxis is one of the unifying elements of the Frankfurt school. It might also be the pièce de résistance for any attempt to mediate between the critical theory of the Frankfurt school and French poststructuralism. At least in the United States and in West Germany this creates the most immediately perceptible dividing point.

In the United States, the reception of French structuralism and poststructuralism was mainly mediated through literature departments, which incorporated the new theories in an institutional context that traditionally was little concerned with problems of sociopolitical implications, whether of literature or of the academic discourse on literature. Only recently have such questions begun to emerge from within poststructuralist discussions.[8] In West Germany, on the other hand, the student movement of the sixties had created a strong politicization and an eager openness for neo-Marxist theories, particularly the critical theory of the Frankfurt school. This meant at the same time a radical distrust of "text-immanent," "formalistic," self-indulgent academic practices. The sporadic appearance of structuralist and poststructuralist texts in Germany seemed to many as the intensified reemergence of an academic, ahistorical, apolitical formalism. Sartre's early attack on structuralism as the last theoretical bastion of the late bourgeoisie against Marxism and socialism confirmed such fears. To probe our constellation we have to trace at least their major lines.

II

At stake are historical scars, particularly strong in Germany and for the German left. This might, at least in part, account for the paradoxical situation that a mode of thinking which is strongly informed by the reading of German texts (Hegel, Marx, Nietzsche, Freud, and Heidegger) has had much less impact in Germany than in other countries. Two of the names mentioned, Nietzsche and Heidegger, both eminently important for poststructuralist theory, touch on a particularly sensitive spot of German political and intellectual history. Both philosophers and philosophies are overshadowed by a historical association with fascism and national socialism. At stake, however, is not simply the historical association—the use and abuse of Nietzsche by the Nazis and Heidegger's public support of the Third Reich—but the question to what degree the partial integration of both philosophies is not merely due to a historical accident, but to an immanent element of both philosophical discourses. It is the same question directed at philosophy that, in the so-called expressionism debate of the thirties,[9] was directed at expressionism and modernism in general, after some of the expressionists, Gottfried Benn in particular, had turned to fascism. At the basis of such debates are not so much specific contents and concepts, but rather certain modes of discourse, frequently opposed in a rigorous scheme of rationality versus irrationality.

In the philosophical as well as in the literary debates George Lukács played a major role. Already in the expressionism debate he attempted to construct a systematic relationship between the antihumanistic barbarism of fascism and what he considered the irrationalism and dehumanizing art forms of expressionism. Two decades later, his book *Die Zerstörung der Vernunft (The Destruction of Reason,* 1954)[10] traces the philosophical history of irrationalism from Schelling through Nietzsche to Heidegger, Jaspers, and Rosenberg. The history of irrationalism becomes the prehistory of fascism.

The dichotomy thus established has developed its own dynamic far beyond the Marxist field as well as beyond the German context. As a dynamic, the dichotomy works like a repetition compulsion, shaping every debate and distributing the roles according to the scenario of an anxiety of exclusion and inclusion. If, within the German context, the anxiety speaks in the name of the fear of fascism against what seem to be uncontrolled, wild discourses, the same anxiety in America and other countries speaks in the name of humanistic scholarship and scientific objectivity. "How not to dig our own graves,"[11] the warning voices preach, and they conjure up the "always dangerous and nearly always disastrous" "disregard for traditional disciplinary boundaries."[12] To say that anxiety speaks is not an attempt at simply discrediting a discourse. The discourse of anxiety is part of *our* institutional praxis and acknowledging it is necessary if we are to probe the differences and possible common basis of theoretical positions that are also elements of institutional praxis.

III

The structuralist and poststructuralist questioning and problematization of such categories as "the subject" and "history" and their insistent occupation with "text," "discourse," and "writing" seem indeed to go against the grain of any Marxist theory for which history and the subject are central, and text, discourse, writing secondary elements of the superstructure. Our first move thus seems to have led us to an unpromising nonconstellation. But what appears in the discourse of anxiety as the mutually exclusive opposition of Marxist theory versus structuralism and deconstruction is already part of an explosive tension *within* both discursive modes. And it might well be possible that there is a mutual inter-est: an immanent element, unarticulable within each discourse, but articulable through the other. If poststructuralism is able to articulate and reinvestigate the problematic of history, language, and the subject in a way that lays bare some of the unacknowledged, repressed, and therefore very effective bourgeois heritage in Marxist theory, Marxism on the other hand is able to acticulate some of the unacknowledged, repressed political and institutional implications in poststructuralist thought. That there is such a common inter-est, is due to the common family romance of a struggle with the history of the bourgeois European Enlightenment.

The explicit critique of Enlightenment in Horkheimer and Adorno's *Dialectic of Enlightenment* and the implicit critique of Enlightenment in poststructuralist discourses mark the constellation of a family romance in which the parents are both denied and reinvented, negated and reaffirmed. The very notion of critique, particularly for Adorno, involves that double move of negation and affirmation: "Philosophy demands today, as it did in Kant's times, critique of reason through reason, not the banishment or annihilation of reason" (*ND* 85). And: "Self-reflection of Enlightenment is not its revocation: this would be its corruption under the present status quo" (*ND* 158). It is a move that at least in its most general outlines resembles that of deconstruction. In order to trace the more subtle moves, however, we have to enter into Adorno's critique as it unfolds in his *Negative Dialectics*. The shape of our reading will be outlined by those elements of the Enlightenment in and through which the critique constitutes itself.

Three large themes emerge dominantly in the eighteenth century: teleology of a universal history, teleology of the autonomous subject, and teleology of a universal discourse as the language of a universal spirit: the exorcism of the spirits in favor of the one spirit, as Friedrich Kittler neatly summarized the Enlightenment.[13] This involves specific procedures that could be summarized schematically as: centralization (clear hierarchies of center and margin, of inclusion and exclusion, definite boundaries); spiritualization and sublimation; unifi-cation of language games. Unification out of a need for universal control and domination is the underlying principle.

Point by point, these elements, shaped by the economic and social needs of emerging capitalism and the bourgeoisie, reappear in the Marxist political and ideological structure as well as in Habermas's model of free communication. I mention this model because it had a remarkable impact on the theoretical articu-lation of the New Left during the sixties and because Habermas in a certain sense represents the last generation of the Frankfurt school. Thus his model reinscribes into critical theory those elements that Adorno and Horkheimer tried to exorcise: the ghosts come back in the name of the universal spirit and its grammar.

The broadest and most general attack against structuralism, poststructuralism, and deconstruction has been carried out in the name of "history" both by conservative "humanists" and by Marxists. Thus one of the more recent and widely read polemics on this ground, Gerald Graff's *Literature against Itself*, has obviously appealed to a wide ideological spectrum from the left to the right.[14] Graff's argumentation is marked by the same strong moralistic gesture that characterizes most of the major discussions concerning history: the decision for or against history is not simply a methodological question but a moral and political decision. This moral quality is indeed inseparable from the concept of history as developed in the European Enlightenment. History and moral-aesthetic education have formed an "organic" cultural-ideological unity since the eighteenth century. Thus any argumentation within this ideological constellation must consider any critique of this constellation as an attack on history itself. In the moralistic gesture speaks the anxiety of closure against the threat of an opening that no longer ensures full control.

Paradigmatic for this anxiety, and all the more telling because performed by a highly intelligent critic, is Hans Robert Jauss's critique of Kristeva:

The turning around (*Umschlag*) of aesthetic negativity into a metaphysics of *rupture* is unavoidable, if an unlimited textual productivity in the literary process is considered as the only process producing meaning and if each text is supposed to be nothing more than the ever renewed rejection of tradition and dissolution of the subject, so that negation becomes abstract and at the end leaves nothing of the negated. That such a permanent aesthetic revolution unavoidably cancels all historical dialectic, becomes evident in *La révolution du langage poétique*, where Julia Kristeva thinks she can add to the triad of Hegelian logic a fourth element (hardly approved by Hegel): *le rejet,* a negation emerging from the depth of the genotext which thwarts the closure (*Abschliessung*) of the subject in the phenotext, and which supposedly is nothing else but Freud's death drive turned into a source of aesthetic pleasure.[15]

The anxiety of closure produces a vocabulary of compulsion and of negative/positive totality: the "turning around" into metaphysics is as "unavoidable" as the cancellation of *all* historical dialectic.[16] The addition of *one* negative element, one break and rupture, is enough to threaten everything: the phantasm of total death and annihilation crashes down to silence the soft luring traces of death in the aesthetic pleasure.

Jauss's critique is part of a critique of Adorno's aesthetic negativity and at the same time an attempt to separate Adorno's "historical dialectic" from his own negativity and from poststructuralist "loss of history." Critical theory's and Adorno's insistence on "history" seems indeed to be the line that separates them from "New French Theory." However, Jauss is perceptive enough to see that he has to trace the line already within the Adornian text. Adorno's insistence on history also inscribes into its definition the anxiety of identity and closure and thus breaks it open:

History is the unity of continuity and discontinuity. Society keeps alive not despite its antagonism but because of it; profit interests and class relations are objectively the motor of the production process on which the life of all depends and whose primacy has its focal point in the death of all. This implies a reconciling element in non-reconciliation because it alone permits people to live; without it there wouldn't even be the possibility to change life. That which historically created this possibility can also destroy it. The world spirit, a worthy object of definition, would have to be defined as the permanent catastrophe. Under the totalizing, subjugating principle of identity, everything that is not subsumed by identity and escapes the planning rationality in the realm of means turns into anxiety (*wird . . . zum Beängstigenden*), revenge for the calamity (*Unheil*) which the non-identical suffers from identity. Philosophically, history could hardly be interpreted in a different way, without bewitching it (*verzaubern*) into an idea. (*ND* 320)

The witch's name, one might add, is metaphysics which robs the material life and death in history of its materiality and of the reality of its suffering. Adorno thus reverses Jauss before Jauss: If Jauss conjures the shadow of metaphysics where the ruptures and discontinuities open up, Adorno uses the rupture as a magic wand against the totalizing bewitching power of metaphysics.

Adorno attacks a concept of history as "grand récit," as Jean-François Lyotard has called those totalizing narratives that tell history as the unified story of one universal subject with one origin and one telos.[17] Universal history does not become problematic for Adorno because it contradicts empirical history, but, to the contrary, because it uncannily becomes more and more reified reality: "The concept of universal history, which inspired Hegel's philosophy as Kant's philosophy was inspired by the mathematical sciences, has become the more problematic the more the unified world approximates a totalizing process" (*ND*

319). In such a world, which increasingly, despite the antagonism between capitalist and socialist industrialized countries and the Third World, develops under the unifying signature of instrumental reason, Lyotard's "petits récits" and Adorno's heterogeneous stories of nonidentity become the last subversive arsenal. Positivism, despite its apparent renunciation of the grand narratives of metaphysical history, is all the more blindly carrying out the totalizing design of instrumental reason. But Adorno, in contrast to Lyotard and to most poststructuralist thinking, does not simply cross out the notion of universal history: "Discontinuity and universal history have to be thought together. To cross out universal history as a remnant of metaphysical superstition would confirm mere facticity as the only thing to be recognized and accepted, just in the same way as before that sovereignty, which subsumed the facts in the totalizing march of the One Spirit and thus affirmed them. Universal history has to be construed and negated" (*ND* 319f.). The "world spirit," despite its fetishism, has also its truth, a negative truth, but nevertheless a truth. To negate it abstractly in theory would only lead to its blind affirmation in praxis: "The prevalence of totality over appearance has to be grasped in the appearances over which that which tradition calls world spirit, in fact rules. . . . The world spirit is, but is nobody, is not spirit, but that negativity which Hegel took away from Him in order to load it on the shoulders of those who have to serve to Him. . . . The irrational element in the notion of the world spirit comes from the irrationality of the course of the world. Nevertheless it remains a fetishistic concept. History up till now has no construable total subject" (*ND* 303f.). In this figure of affirmation in the negation, an element of acknowledgment and recognition (*Anerkennung* not only in the Hegelian but also in the Freudian sense) emerges that perhaps marks the most important difference between Adorno and poststructuralist discourses. It creates that difference in the gesture of the discourse which Jochen Hörisch in one of the few knowledgeable comparisons has noted: "If Critical Theory and Poststructuralism both describe 'that other scene of the production of meaning preceding meaning,' the gesture of description is notably different. The 'happy positivism' of the French contrasts all the more with the depressive gesture of Critical Theory, as their themes and motives have close affinity."[18] The contrast of the gestures is only fully understood if one recognizes in the "happy positivism" (a formula used by Foucault, but applicable also to the underlying gesture of Derrida's style, despite significant differences in their philosophies) the element of rejection (the crossing out, essential to all positivism) and the element of irreducible affirmation in the depressive gesture of irreducible negativity.

Thus Adorno's critique of history and historicism is carried out in the name of historicity, which for Adorno, according to its own immanent logic, has to free itself from all invariability; it has to un-define itself. Anything else is ideology: "The popular question concerning 'Man,' prevalent still in Marxism of the Lukácsian version, is ideological, because it dictates already in its form the invariancy of a possible answer, even if it were historicity itself. What 'Man' in himself is supposed to be is always only what he was: he is nailed to the rock of the past'' (*ND* 51). To liberate history from the ideological invariability of a grand story, Adorno unhinges that point on which all stories depend: the beginning whose arbitrariness is covered up in the fiction of a necessary and natural origin. Adorno's critique of the metaphysics of origin speaks in the name of history: "The world, objectively knotted to totality, does not give freedom to consciousness. Unremittingly it fixates consciousness to that from which it wants to escape; a thinking, however, which happily and carelessly wants to start from the beginning again, unconcerned with the historical form of the problem becomes all the more its prey. Only through its thinking breath (*vermöge ihres denkenden Atems*) does philosophy participate in the idea of depth'' (*ND* 17). No name is mentioned at this point, but there is no doubt that Adorno speaks to and against Heidegger, from whom he sets himself all the more insistently apart as his philosophy shows close affinity to Heidegger. The small differences are all the more important. Condensed, differences and affinity appear in the strange metaphor of philosophy as "thinking breath." Heidegger liked to emphasize the concreteness of his ontology through metaphors and similes from the peasant world, thus claiming that his philosophy was rooted in the depth of the language and in the depth of the folk and its soil: a philosophy that walks in wooden shoes through the forest of being and knows the dead-endedness of the wood-tracks (*Holzwege*) in the woods. Against the heavy pace of the wooden shoes, Adorno, with some ironic malice, invokes the evanescent grace of the breath that moves with the wind. In doing so, he also invokes the Greek and Latin etymology of the spirit: *pneuma* or *spiritus* is breath, wind, air.

Adorno's philosophy as thinking breath locates it in a zone of a particular mediation, a mediation through negation; breath is the *topos* of transience and translation, the evanescent point of materiality and immateriality, of exteriority and interiority, of negation and affirmation. Adorno thus inscribes in his philosophy of negative dialectic the same originary movement that Freud in his late essay on negation claims as the origin not only of negation, but implicitly of all propositions and thus of all thinking: the opposition, differentiation, and rhythm of acceptance and rejection: "This I want to introduce into me, this I want to exclude from me."[19] I inhale, I exhale, I breathe, I think. For Adorno, the philosophy of the wooden shoe and the wood-tracks is both an abstract reification of the ontological and an abstract negation of the ontic. While agreeing with Heidegger that the ontic is a façade, Adorno nevertheless does not simply give it over to contempt. The deconstruction of the façade implies also a crushing violence: "The power of the existing erects façades, against which consciousness bounces. It must attempt to crash through them. Only thus the postulate of depth can escape ideology'' (*ND* 17). When Adorno later enters into an explicit setting-apart of his own (*Auseinandersetzung*) of his own philosophy from Heidegger's, he criticizes Heidegger's notion of historicity as simply the reversal of the orthodox Marxist notion: if the latter fetishizes historicity to an invariant category of humankind, Heidegger brings history to a stop in the invariancy of an ontological ahistoricity:

> The ambivalence of the philosophy of being: to talk about the existing and to ontologize it. This determines its relationship to history. On the one hand, historicity is deprived of the salt of history by transposing it into an existential category; the demand of all *prima philosophia* for invariants is extended over that which varies: historicity brings history to a stop in the realm of ahistoricity. On the other hand, [Heidegger's philosophy of being] permits the ontologizing of history, thus investing historical power with the authoritative power of being and thus justifying the subordination under historical situations as if it were demanded by being itself. (*ND* 129f.)

These are only fragments of a continuous struggle in which Adorno tries to delineate the difference between his philosophy and Heidegger's, despite his affinity with Heidegger. Given the eminent presence of Heidegger, particularly in Derrida's and Lacan's thinking, a careful reading of this setting-apart (*Auseinandersetzung*) might be the best beginning from which to trace the constellation of critical theory and deconstruction. In that case, this essay is only the beginning of a beginning, the pointing toward a beginning.

Adorno's proximity to Derrida and his conflictual affinity to Heidegger show most clearly in his critique of "origin": "Thought fascinated by the phantasm of an absolute first will tend to reclaim the irreducible itself as an ultimate. In Heidegger's concept of being the reduction to irreducibility is still implied" (*ND* 103). Adorno is aware how careful Heidegger is to avoid any reification of being in a crude sense. Heidegger thus "escapes the critique, without, however, giving up the advantages of origin, which he places so far back, that it is outside time, but because of that appears omnipresent" (*ND* 106). Adorno's critique of Heidegger's ontology is carried out not in the name of something else, but in the name of pure difference: "Critique of ontology does not aspire to another ontology, not even a nonontology. If it would do that it would simply posit an Other as the absolute first; in this case not absolute identity, being, or a concept, but nonidentity, existence, facticity. It would hypostasize thus the concept of nonconceptuality and act against its own intention" (*ND* 136). If nevertheless the *Negative Dialectic* is permeated, if not dominated, by the word "nonidentity" and the critique of identity, nonidentity has to be thought of not in terms of a concept, but of a differential marker which in fact is the motor of the text's movement and which in turn points beyond the textual praxis, setting it both apart from and in conflictual relations to political praxis.

If Hegel's dialectic is the attempt to master the heterogeneous in philosophical concepts, negative dialectic is the attempt to reinscribe the heterogeneous as heterogeneous also in thought. "To think is to identify" (*ND* 5), but it does not remain in abstract opposition to the heterogeneous, nor does it simply abdicate in the face of it. Thought constitutes itself through its own insufficiency which for Adorno is also a guilt and a debt (*Schuld*): thought is driven to dialectic by "its unavoidable insufficiency and guilt/debt (*Schuld*) in relation to that which it thinks" (*ND* 5). Thus the praxis of negation in negative dialectic is not an originary moment, but already derivative, an originary sin and part of an economy. At the same time, to think is also "in itself, before any particular content, negation, resistance against that which is forced upon it. This is the heritage which thought takes over from the relationship of labor to its material" (*ND* 19). The concrete praxis of labor is thus the constitutive model for the thinking of negative dialectic. But any attempt to short-circuit the conflictual relationship between theory and praxis would collapse both. Thought "inherits" something from its model; the relationship to heritage doubles the originary negative relationship between labor and material. Thought uses praxis as its material, just as labor does to its raw material, and in doing so negates it in its given form. Theory is negation of praxis. That is its unavoidable guilt and debt, which it must acknowledge. Adorno's refusal to "forget" the debt and guilt of thought marks an incisive difference from Heidegger, a difference that is not by chance more evident in the style and gesture of their writing than in their themes and motives.

If the negating labor of thought finds its model in the relationship of material labor to its material, the identifying and affirming element of thought finds its model in the economic principle of exchange and its relationship to labor:

> The principle of exchange, the reduction of human labor to the abstract
> concept of the average working time is intimately related to the principle
> of identification. Exchange is its social model, and without it there would
> be no identification; through it nonidentical singular beings and
> achievements become commensurable, identical. The expansion of this
> principle pushes the whole world toward identity and totality. (*ND* 146).

But the reproduction of the social model of exchange in thought not only affirms it as the totalizing form, it also sets itself apart from it and affirms a *particular* element of exchange and identity that is covered up under the existing socioeconomic conditions. Adorno, always careful not to fall back into the trap of totalizing identity in the shape of simple oppositions, dissolves the mere duality of (negative) identity and (positive) nonidentity. Just as he refuses to simply negate universal history, he warns of the abstract negation of exchange and identity:

> If one would preach, as a positive ideal, that there should be no longer an
> exchange of equal to equal in honor of an irreducible quality, this would

only create the pretext for a relapse into the old injustice. The exchange of equivalences always implied that one exchanged in its name unequal things, that one appropriated the surplus value of labor. If one simply annuals the measuring category of comparability, this would only be a replacement of rationality, which inhabits the principle of exchange as ideology but also as a promise, by unmediated appropriation and violence, today: the naked privilege of monopolies and clans. Critique of the principle of exchange as identifying thought claims that the ideal of free and just exchange up till today has been realized only as a pretext. This alone transcends exchange.[20]

In an implicit play on the German words *verwerfen* (to throw away, to reject) and *vorwerfen* (to reproach; literally: to throw in front of, to throw ahead), Adorno condenses paradigmatically the dialectic of rejection and negation: "Hubris is, that identity is; that the thing is equivalent to its concept. But its ideal must not simply be rejected (*wäre nicht einfach wegzuwerfen*): in the reproach (*Vorwurf*), that the thing is not identical with its concept, also lives its desire, that it should come true" (*ND* 149). In the phonematic difference of e/o (*verwerfen/vorwerfen*)[21] utopian thinking, as an essential element of Adorno's thinking, inscribes itself as pure difference, as "the difference from that which exists" (*ND* 313). "Not the extirpation of difference, but the reflection upon it might be a help toward the reconciliation of the general and the particular" (*ND* 347). This utopian dimension of difference, which differentiates Adorno's dialectic from the "happy positivism" of Foucault's version of poststructuralism, might also be a point to displace immanently the deconstructive position of difference.

Adorno's critique and analysis of identity implies and is accompanied by a critique and analysis of subjectivity. This is the point where his writing overlaps most obviously with the poststructuralist field, and also the point which the anxiety of closure reacts most vehemently against. Thus even within critical theory, there is a strong attempt either to reject Adorno's critique of the self-identical subject or to neutralize it. Bernhard Lypp sees in the "lack of a subject" (*Subjektlosigkeit*) the "misery of Critical Theory" which has to be overcome.[22] Hans Robert Jauss would like to differentiate Adorno's "dialectical" procedure from French theories, which, according to him, act upon the undialectical "expulsion of the subject," a phrase several times repeated in his essay, and once explicitly given as a translation of the French "*décentrement du sujet.*"[23] "*Dé-centrement*" = expulsion (*Austreibung*): one could hardly find a more telling paradigm for the anxiety of exclusion/inclusion. Decentering, a topological and hierarchical transformation, can only be read as a dichotomy of inclusion or exclusion, just as the admittance of one opening, of one irreducible negativity, into the triadic closure of Hegelian dialectic, explodes the whole dialectic and *all* of history.

Part of the problem might be in the difficulty of differentiating between structuralism and poststructuralism, which is due not only to bad and superficial reading but also to an immanent problem of theoretical movements that are not identical or clearly opposed or even differentiated, but rather complex transformations of one within the other. However, some of these transformations, particularly concerning such key notions as "history" and "subject," are graspable as indicators of a differential mark. Thus, particularly in its earlier phases, structuralism tended toward an abstract opposition of diachronic versus synchronic perspective and, indeed, took a rather crude ahistorical position. In a similar way, there was (and still is) a tendency in structuralism simply to replace the human agents and heroes of humanistic models of (hi-)story with the dynamic of structural constellations. And to the degree that this was a mere substitution, structuralism was vulnerable to a relapse into the old dichotomy between the pretended autonomy of the subject and the real power of social structures and their forces. In its crudest form, structuralism could even become an ontological justification for the existing structural forces of the concrete power constellations. Much of the present mistrust on the left against French theories is based on this possibility of an ideological justification of the status quo through structuralism. At the same time, however, the structuralist displacement of the subject, even in its cruder form, is also a threat to the ideological discourse of the autonomous subject, which is needed by the ruling class to cover up the real destruction of subjectivity and autonomy in the social praxis. Thus, structuralism has provoked even more angry reactions on the right than on the left of the political spectrum.

Poststructuralism and Adorno's negative dialectic no longer speak in terms of a simple dichotomy, but more toward and through a reflective displacement and transformation of that which constitutes subjectivity. It is a reflective moment that differs from Hegel's insofar as it never closes upon itself. Adorno does not cancel the subject; he reclaims it through a postulate of transgressions: "The subject has to make good for what it has done to the nonidentical. In doing that it becomes free of the appearance of its absolute being-for-itself" (*ND* 145f.). Making "good for what it has done to the nonidentical": Adorno's thinking, from its beginnings, has been concerned with the analysis and critique of power, domination, and violence. To end domination is the utopian motive that permeates all of critical theory. It is the magnetic force that arranges the constellations of negation and affirmation and also assigns the double role of the subject. Subjectivity, for Adorno, is both the resistance against and the principle of domination. Any philosophy that does not acknowledge this double role and instead claims an absolute subject, from Hegel to existentialism, remains locked in contradictions: "The absolute subject cannot escape its ensnarement: the fetters it wants to tear apart, the fetters of domination, are identical with the principle of absolute subjectivity" (*ND* 50). Adorno articulates in philosophical terms what Lacan pointed out in the phantasmatic productions of the autonomous subject: that it phantasizes itself by preference in fetters and prison walls.[24] Whereas Lacan dissolves the self-identical subject in the constellation of the child, the mirror, and the mother, Adorno's analysis puts it into a Darwinian phylogenetic constellation: "The primacy of subjectivity continues in spiritualized form the Darwinian struggle for survival. The oppression of nature for human purposes is a mere natural relationship; therefore the superiority of reason as domination over nature and its principle: appearance" (*ND* 179). In other words: the very principle of domination over nature is in fact the ensnarement in it; the seeming transcendence of reason above nature, its blind tribute to it. Thus the qualities that the development of subjectivity brings forth are already its subversion: "That which objectivated itself from and against pure reflexes in human beings: character or will, the potential organ of freedom, subverts freedom because it embodies the principle of domination, to which human beings progressively subject themselves. Identity of the self and self-alienation accompany each other from the beginning; therefore the concept of self-alienation is bad romanticism" (*ND* 217). In such a constellation the promise of freedom, attached by the Enlightenment to the autonomous self and I, moves away from the I to its other: "The dawning consciousness of freedom nourishes itself on the memory of an archaic impulse not yet governed by a definite I. . . . Without the anamnesis of an unconstrained, pre-ego impulse which later is banished to the zone of unfree bondage of nature, the idea of freedom could not be created" (*ND* 221). But the sentence does not stop here; a relative clause abruptly turns the movement around: "the idea of freedom could not be created which on its part however finds its goal (*terminiert*) in the strengthening of the I" (*ND* 222). The movement of this passage can be read as a parallel to the Lacanian reinterpretation of the Freudian sentence: "Where It was, I should become."[25] Both Adorno and Lacan undermine the traditional and dominant interpretation, according to which the I is supposed to appropriate "It" and replace "It." Adorno and Lacan instead read the "where It was" as the constitutive ground in which the I is rooted and founded. If Adorno affirms the necessity of the I in a phrase that seems to come straight from ego-psychology: "*Stärkung des Ichs*" (strengthening of the I), one has to read this alongside an earlier passage about the fortified I:

> The philosophical emphasis on the constitutive power of the subjective element always also closes off the truth. Thus certain animal species, such as the dinosaur Triceratops and the rhinoceros, carry along their armor, which protects them, as a prison, which—to speak anthropomorphically— they in vain try to get rid of. The imprisonment in the apparatus of survival might explain the particular ferociousness of rhinoceroses as well as the unadmitted and therefore all the more terrifying ferociousness of homo sapiens. (*ND* 180)

In light of this passage, the strengthening of the I can no longer be read as the phantasmatic fortification of ego-psychology but rather, paradoxically, as a liquification, a playfulness which, in one of his better moments, Schiller dreamed of in his aesthetics as the true essence of human beings, who are truly human only when they play. Against such an ideal, our historical status is still that of the rhinoceros.

One of the fundamental differences between contemporary French thinking and German critical theory seems to be indicated by the different positions that language takes in each. This is only partly due to the process of politicization in the sixties. Although it is true that the political movement and the traditional Marxist emphasis on art as representation tended to distrust the concern with language as "formalistic," the situation is more complicated. On the one hand, the so-called text-immanent criticism, which dominated West German criticism during the fifties and early sixties, was only marginally interested in language and signification processes as such; close reading in that context meant mainly empathy and a certain "sensitivity" for the text rather than the tracing of its literality. On the other hand, the student movement created a new and keen interest in language and its performance, particularly as an instrument of power and ideology. But this instrumental emphasis on language among Germans has tended to block out the very different French linguistic and semiological interests. Thus the dominant trends in linguistics and semiotics in Germany are either language as communication or linguistics as a method to eliminate "subjective" literary criticism and replace it by an objective functional "science."[26]

The conflict, which erupted within the Enlightenment, between the demand for rational control over language and the real, disruptive effects of semiosis, has led to a repression, which is continued up to the present by a concept of scientific and scholarly discourse that pretends the full control of the speaking subject over its speaking. This conflict Adorno, always on the track of the dialectic of enlightenment, took up again in *Negative Dialectic*, but under the renewed force of the dialectic of enlightenment this conflict runs the danger of being buried again by Habermas's project of reducing language to transparent communication.[27] Adorno locates this desire for transparency and the resulting negation of language even in Hegel, who lets language play its games more than any philosopher of his time, because he wants to negate that which is not sayable: "In an emphatic sense, [Hegel] didn't need language, because everything, even that which has no language (*das Sprachlose*) and the opaque, for him, was supposed to become spirit, and spirit coherence (*Zusammenhang*)" (*ND* 163).

The dialectic of the sayable and the unsayable is at the center of Adorno's thinking in and about language. In this context, it is interesting to note that one of the best and most knowledgeable recent German investigations on poststructuralist theories appeared under the title *Das Sagbare und das Unsagbare* (The Sayable and the Unsayable).[28] The dominant trend in the Marxist tradition has been to exclude the unsayable as false mystification and at the same time to delimit language to an instrument of representation and communication. Language thus is strictly confined, definable, and distinguishable as a system of signs against an equally definable and distinguishable system of referents. Because of this defined relation, the confined language enables total articulation of the confined system of "reality." From this perspective, poststructuralist discourses both over- and under-estimate language. On the one hand, everything seems to turn into language, "text," "écriture"; but it is, on the other hand, precisely this "blurring" of the bar between signifiers and signified and the ensuing "textualization" of the "world" which also sets up the horizon of language and thus a "beyond" language, which, however, is not a beyond outside language but in its core: its crypt.[29]

Meditation on that crypt of silence encounters the taboo of rational discourse against "irrationalism." As he did in the *Dialectic of Enlightenment*, Adorno breaks the taboo, not by privileging silence against articulation, but by tracing their mutual constitution, although it is and remains conflictual. It is the immanent contradiction of philosophy: "contrary to Wittgenstein: to say what cannot be said. The simple contradiction of this desire is that of philosophy itself" (*ND* 9). The path to the nonconceptual, to the crypt, leads not through rejection of concepts; rather, it is constituted by them. What concepts articulate points beyond them to a scene of the Other: "The truth which is met through concepts beyond their abstract content, can have no other scene (*Schauplatz*) than the scene of that which has been repressed, neglected, and rejected by concepts. The utopia of cognition (*Erkenntnis*) would be to open that which has no concept through concepts, without assimilating it to them" (*ND* 9f.). The scene here invoked by Adorno is that which the discourse of enlightenment wants to exclude. It also marks a certain political praxis: the more exclusion is denied in the name of reason, liberality, and pluralism, the more exclusions become necessary; the greater the anxiety of the ego, which likes to phantasize itself as an engineer of dams, the greater the paranoia of a public consciousness that cannot erect enough walls and dams for the protection of our rights and our freedom. Dialectic of enlightenment: the prison house as the ultimate safeguard of the autonomous subject and its "freedom."

Friedrich Kittler, in a book mentioned earlier,[30] calls the poststructuralist knowledge a knowledge of refuse (*Abfall*). Indeed, that which has been refused and rejected by the public discourse permeates poststructuralist theories and those texts from which poststructuralism has emanated. Dreams, parapraxes, jokes constitute the discourse of psychoanalysis. Saussure's systematization of linguistics is driven by his obsession with anagrams and glossolalia. Roman Jakobson developed the systematic character of linguistic phenomena through children's language and aphasia: the logic of linguistic degeneration articulates the logic of linguistic generation, just as the esoteric literality of the mad Hölderlin spells the order of poetic logic.[31] Historiography is turning increasingly toward local histories and histories of marginalized phenomena: histories of small provincial towns, histories of death, of sexuality, of women, of children—all those (hi-)stories that a totalizing History has displaced to silence and darkness.

Emphatically, Adorno re-calls the rejected, the "refuse" into philosophy as its true inter-est: "Philosophy has, in its present historical status, its true interest there, where Hegel, in consonance with tradition, shows no interest: in the nonconceptual, in the singular and particular" (ND 8). This interest is motivated by the insistent urgency of the rejected which presses because it has been repressed and oppressed: "Urgent (Dringlich) has become, for the concept, that which it does not reach, that which its mechanism of abstraction eliminates/secretes (ausscheidet). That which is not already an example of the concept" (ND 8). It is, however, not an abstract glorification of the singular against the universal (which would fall back behind Hegel's analysis of the "here" and "now" of the so-called concrete), but a movement which has as its model Walter Benjamin's interweaving of speculative thought with micrological proximity to details. For Adorno this implies the necessity of thought to "dwell on smallest details," more even, to immerse itself in the concrete in order to transcend it: "One must not philosophize about the concrete, but from out of it (aus ihm heraus)" (ND 33). This movement of thought through the detail leaves a rupture which does not close in a transcendent synthesis. That is, again, Adorno's difference from Hegel: "The philosophical demand, to immerse oneself into the detail, which cannot be directed by any philosophy from above . . . was already one side of Hegel. But the actual execution got entangled tautologically: his mode of immersion in the detail produced, as if prearranged, the same spirit which, as totality and the absolute, was posited from the beginning" (ND 303).

To philosophize out of the concrete implies that the speaking subject immerses itself in its refuse, that the spirit descends from the sublime heights of its discourse into the corporeality of the speaking subject as well as into the literality and materiality of the signifiers. If the discourse of enlightenment declares war with Paulinian zeal against the "dead letter" in the name of the living spirit, Lacan asks how this self-confident spirit would live without the letter. And he goes even further by claiming that the letter performs its effects of truth without the spirit's intervention. Foucault's analyses of power are centered on discourse, sexuality and the body. Sociologists and anthropologists interested in institutional structures and social organizations are becoming aware of the physical, architectural dimension of such organizations of power and experience.

This seems, at first glance, a direct countertendency to Brecht's famous phrase (directed against the naturalists) that a photograph of the Krupp factories says nothing about capitalist production mechanisms. On the other hand, it was Marx himself who saw the concrete physical appearance of industry as the open book of human consciousness and read it as the visible script of human psychology. Paradox after paradox: Brecht, who liked to say that truth is the concrete, seems to deny the sensual and visible; Marx, whose analysis of the fetishism of commodities radicalizes Hegel's critique of sensual immediacy and inscribes it in a systematic nexus of ideological deception, wants to read the truth in the empirical appearance. At stake in these seeming paradoxes is the dialectic of that which philosophical tradition has put into the opposition of being and appearance. If such different texts as "Marx," "Nietzsche," "Freud" have had a strong impact on poststructuralist thought, one of the reasons is their rethinking of the dialectic of appearance and being, of surface and depth.

All three have in common a structure of thinking in which the "positive facts" of positivism are not "given" but are produced by a systematic nexus of deception, displacement, reversal. Truth is not on the surface, but neither is it behind or beneath. All three radically criticize the meta-physical search for a world behind the world (the *Hinterweltler* and *Hinterwäldler* as Nietzsche called them). Freud's procedure shows this move particularly clearly: whatever appears in speech acts and utterances is product of a displacement, of a cover-up, a secondary process; however, the truth is not simply behind this deceptive surface and process, it will not be found by a simple act of uncovering and particularly not by negating the surface. The truth is nowhere else but *in* the deceptive secondary process itself. The process of hiding *is* the structure of truth. The great detectives in the detective novels—a genre emerging from the age of enlightenment—knew it all along, or perhaps did not know it in their ideology of pure deduction, but they always performed it.

Because of this particular structure of truth and appearance, there is also no simple reversal possible, no naive return to the sensual, material, to the body. Benjamin's thought of the constellation already said it: the phenomena are saved, but in an act of negation. Thus the body speaks in Adorno's *Negative Dialectic* insistently in the language of suffering. *Schmerz* is the voice of the phenomenal world. Dialectic hurts, because it negates: "The impoverishment of experience through dialectic is the adequation of the abstract monotony of the administered world. The dialectic suffering is the suffering about that world, elevated to concept (*zum Begriff erhoben*)" (*ND* 6). The need to let suffering speak is the condition of all truth (*ND* 17f.). The constitutive wound of all thought is the inadequacy of concept and truth, the bar between the signifier and the signified, their asymmetry, but thought is also the attempt to heal the wound, through concepts, not in them, but in their *constellation*: "Only concepts can fulfill what concepts prevent. Cognition (*Erkenntnis*) is a *trōsas iasetai*. The fault of all concepts necessitates the call for other concepts; thus those constellations arise which alone carry something of that hope which is in the name" (*ND* 53). The strange Greek words are not a demonstration of scholarly erudition, but a gesture of shame to speak the utopian. If we would translate the two words, they would read as a "healing of wounds," but such a translation would already falsify the utopia, because it would inscribe it in the language of our administered world, in which "healing the wounds" is inseparably linked to the functionalization of body and soul for further exploitation: the dilemma of any conscientious physician or psychoanalyst. All positively articulated utopias are already marred by that against which they are articulated. Only the words of a "dead" language, removed from the functionalized, administered process of "communication," can point toward it. It is the language of an other scene, not because it is Greek, but because it is ancient Greek, i.e., the language of the dead. Only the dead can speak the language of that no-place, utopia, as long as the living do not live yet. This other scene, as the Other of consciousness, is not outside consciousness but is inserted in it: "The seeming constitutive facts of consciousness are something other than consciousness. In the dimension of pleasure and displeasure something corporeal is inserted. All pain and all negativity, motor of dialectical thought, are the multiply mediated and sometimes unrecognizable shape of the physical, just as all happiness aims at sensual fulfillment in which it has its objectivity" (*ND* 202). It is this other scene, where the utopian speaks to consciousness: "The corporeal moment announced to cognition that suffering should not be, that it should become different." Here is where "materialism merges with critique, with the praxis of social change" (*ND* 203).

The reflection on this penetration of thought by the other entangles it in such a way that it can no longer pretend to be sovereign master of that about which it thinks and of which it speaks. This makes perhaps the greatest difference between poststructuralism and structuralism and the closest affinity between poststructuralism and the meditative discourses of Benjamin and Adorno. They are involved in a semiosis that does not pretend to be a metalanguage above the semiotic effects; rather it stages them, it plays the signs[32] and thus displaces them. It is this semiotic praxis, more than any content, that irritates and provokes the anxiety of closure, the anxiety of institutionally acceptable discourse.

Adorno's first major work, his dissertation on Kierkegaard,[33] begins with a reflection on philosophic and poetic discourse. While insisting on the difference between philosophic and poetic truth, Adorno nevertheless emphatically avoids the relegation of philosophy into the realm of systematic closure and fixed, self-identical signifiers free of the risks of the language game. The *Negative Dialectic* returns again and again to the problem of discursive praxis.

At a very early point of the text, Adorno introduces the play of language as the necessary risk of philosophical discourse: "Against the total domination of method philosophy contains, as a corrective, the moment of play, which the tradition of scientification (*Verwissenschaftlichung*) would like to expel. . . . The unnaive thought knows how little it approaches its object and must nevertheless speak as if it had it completely. This approximates thought to the clownesque" (*ND* 14). Admitting play, clownery, as a necessary moment of thought does not free it from its obligation to truth; it also does not remove the difference between philosophy and art: play and liability to truth are the poles that shape the movement of philosophical process and discursive praxis. What Hegel called the *Anstrengung des Begriffs* (effort of the concept) is not in the rigidity of concepts, but in the sustained effort to remain in the tension of these two poles. This differentiates the discursive praxis of Derrida, Lacan, Adorno from epigonal imitations which simply give in to the play of language without taking any responsibility. Choosing one pole means the cancellation of all truth values in favor of the phantasmatic, be it the phantasmatic delirium of the scientific sovereign subject, be it its mere mirror reversal: the shady spectacle of rhetoric.

The form of philosophical discourse for Adorno is therefore not deductive logic, the hierarchy of universal, particular, and singular, but a concentric *constellation*, parataxis, the metonymic chain of language itself: "Model for it (the constellation) is the behavior of language, which does not offer simply a system of signs for cognitive functions. Where it appears essentially as language, where it becomes presentation (*Darstellung*) it does not define its concepts. The objectivity of the concepts is the effect of their relation, in which they are arranged through a constellation centered on an object (*eine Sache*)" (*ND* 162). The constellation, as mere form, is, to speak in the traditional metaphors, pure exteriority, but this exteriority invokes an otherwise negated interiority: "Constellations alone represent, from the outside, that which the concept has erased inside, that "more," which it wants to be as much as it cannot be it" (*ND* 162). The condition for such an effect lies in the structure of the signified "itself," whose interiority is not constituted in itself, but, as Hegel already pointed out, the "thing itself" is already its nexus (*Zusammenhang*), it is "this" thing only through its differential relations to others, therefore not reducible to pure identity. The constellation, as we mentioned earlier, is for Adorno always historical; and it marks a double historicity of the "thing": history is sedimented in its interior as well as being that which surrounds it and gives it its place: "To perceive the (historical) constellation of an object, that in which it has its place, means at the same time to decipher the history which it carries within as something that has become" (*ND* 163). The constellation makes the world readable as a kind of *écriture:* "The similarity to writing (*das Schriftähnliche*) of such constellations is the turning point of subjective thought and constructs into objectivity through language" (*ND* 165).

We have thus arrived at a key notion of some of poststructuralist thought. However, it is not the identity of a concept or word, which neither for Derrida nor for Adorno can have an identity, that would justify an attempt to think them together; the attempt is justified only by the constellations that I have tried to trace and that indicate the nexus of such notions as part of an immanent problematic in both discourses, constituted by their specific historical position.

NOTES

1. It is a constellation that so far has been given little attention. One exception is Jochen Hörisch, "Herrscherwort, Geld und geltende Sätze: Adornos Aktualisierung der Frühromantik und

ihre Affinität zur poststrukturalistischen Kritik des Subjekts," in *Materialien zur äesthetischen Theorie, Th. W. Adornos Konstruktion der Moderne*, ed. B. Lindner and W. M. Lüdke (Frankfurt am Main: Suhrkamp, 1979), 397–414. Han Robert Jauss also makes a few suggestions of similarity in the same volume on Adorno's aesthetics, but immediately inscribes the constellation into a hierarchical and historical linearity of "first" and "second," of more and less progressive.

2. References to both works appear in the text as *ND* (*Negative Dialektik*) and *AT* (*Ästhetische Theorie*). Quotes of *AT* are based on the German edition with my own translation: Theodor W. Adorno, *Ästhetische Theorie* (Frankfurt am Main: Suhrkamp, 1973). (There is now an English translation, *Aesthetic Theory* [London: Routledge & Kegan Paul, 1984] trans. C. Lenhardt.) Page references for *ND* are to the English-language edition (although I use generally my own translation): Theodor W. Adorno, *Negative Dialectics* (New York: Seabury Press, 1973), trans. E. B. Ashton.

3. Walter Benjamin, *Ursprung des deutschen Trauerspiels*, in *Gesammelte Schriften* (Frankfurt am Main: Suhrkamp, 1980), I.1: 203–430.

4. Benjamin, *Ursprung*, 214–15. All translations from this work are my own.

5. Benjamin, *Ursprung*, 214.

6. Benjamin, *Ursprung*, 215.

7. This is one of the elements that has created some uneasiness in the reception of Adorno by the German left. See, for example: Karl Markus Michel, "Versuch, die 'ästhetische Theorie' zu verstehen," in *Materialien zur äesthetischen Theorie* (note 1), 41–107; especially 75. In the same volume: Irving Wohlfahrt, "Dialektischer Spleen. Zur Ortsbestimmung der Adornoschen Ästhetik," 310–47.

8. Gayatri Spivak has in recent publications increasingly strongly attempted to reflect on the political implications of deconstruction. See also Michael Ryan, "New French Theory in *New German Critique*," in *New German Critique*, no. 22 (1981): 145–161; and *Marxism and Deconstruction* (Baltimore: Johns Hopkins Univ. Press, 1982).

9. See *Die Expressionismusdebatte. Materialien zu einer marxistischen Realismuskonzeption*, ed. Hans-Jürgen Schmidt (Franklin am Main: Suhrkamp, 1973); in English, see Ernst Bloch et al., *Aesthetics and Politics* (London: NLB, 1977).

10. English translation: Georg Lukács, *The Destruction of Reason*, trans. Peter Palmer (London: Merlin Press, 1980).

11. Wayne C. Booth, "Preserving the Exemplar: Or How Not to Dig Our Own Graves," in *Critical Inquiry* 3 (1977): 407–23.

12. Thus the words of an anonymous reviewer of the *Oxford Literary Review* in *Times Literary Supplement*, 6 June 1980, 646.

13. Friedrich Kittler, in *Die Austreibung des Geistes aus den Geisteswissenschaften* (Paderborn: Schöningh, 1980), 8.

14. Gerald Graff, *Literature against Itself* (Chicago: Univ. of Chicago Press, 1979). For a critical discussion of the book, see Michael Sprinker, "Criticism as Reaction," *Diacritics* 10 (Fall 1980): 2–14; Donald G. Marshall, "Truth or Consequence," *Diacritics* 10 (Winter 1980): 75–85.

15. H. R. Jauss, "Negativität und ästhetische Erfahrung. Adornos ästhetische Theorie in der Retrospektive," in *Materialien zur ästhetischen Theorie* (note 1), 153. My translation.

16. A careful reading of Kristeva can show that she is far from canceling historical dialectic, but that she rather reformulates it.

17. Jean-François Lyotard, *The Postmodern Condition* (1979) (Minneapolis: Univ. of Minnesota Press, 1984), trans. Geoff Bennington and Brian Massumi, especially chapters 6 and 7.

18. Hörisch (note 1), 409. My translation.

19. Sigmund Freud, "Negation," in *The Standard Edition of the Complete Psychological Works* 19, ed. and trans. James Strachey (London: Hogarth Press, 1961), 237 (my translation, from "*Die Verneinung*," in *Gesammelte Werke* 14 [London: Hogarth Press, 1940–52], 11–15.

20. Here perhaps Derrida's analysis of the gift (*don, cadeau*), which already in its freest form

opens the chain that binds, might be the point of an immanent critique and further development of Adorno's dialectic. See Jacques Derrida, *Glas* (Paris: Editions Galilée, 1974), 170–72, left column.

21. The phonematic difference is repeated as a temporal difference in the semantics of *Vorwurf*: it is an ob-jection to the present status and a projection into the future, a present negation in the name of a future affirmation.

22. B. Lypp, "Selbsterhaltung und ästhetische Erfahrung. Zur Geschichtsphilosophie und ästhetischen Theorie Adornos," in *Materialien zur Ästhetik* (note 1), 198.

23. H. R. Jauss (note 15, 160); see also 152.

24. Jacques Lacan, "Le stade du miroir comme formateur de la fonction du Je," in *Ecrits* (Paris: Editions du Seuil, 1966), 99.

25. I prefer to use, as Freud does in German, the common pronouns instead of the artificial Latinized and also substantialized "ego" and "id" used in the standard English-language translation, which only support the false reification of a topology that in Freud's text is still recognizable as a linguistic function of shifters.

26. If one wants to use Julia Kristeva's differentiation between semiotics as a technical discourse about signs and semiology as a self-reflective discourse reflecting upon the ideological preconditions of "scientific" and technical discourses, semiotics would definitely be the dominant trend in Germany. Cf. Julia Kristeva, "La sémiologie comme science des idéólogies," in *Semiotica* 1 (1969): 196–204.

27. The emphasis on communication also explains the strong impact of reception theory in Germany. It is not by chance that one of its main representatives, Hans Robert Jauss, criticizes Adorno's aesthetics mainly for its failure to understand art as "a communicative activity" (note 15), 139.

28. Manfred Frank, *Das Sagbare und das Unsagbare: Studien zur neuesten französischen Hermeneutik und Texttheorie* (Frankfurt am Main: Suhrkamp, 1980).

29. For the notion of "crypt" see Jacques Derrida's introduction ("Fors") to Nicolas Abraham and Maria Torok, *Cryptonymie. Le verbier de l'homme aux loups* (Paris: Editions Aubier Flammarion, 1976).

30. See note 12.

31. Roman Jakobson, *Kindersprache, Aphasie und allgemeine Lautgesetze* (Frankfurt am Main: Suhrkamp, 1978) (first published in 1944); Roman Jakobson and Grete Lubbe-Grothues, "Ein Blick auf *Die Aussicht* von Hölderlin," in Roman Jakobson, *Hölderlin. Klee. Brecht. Zur Wortkunst dreier Gedichte* (Frankfurt am Main: Suhrkamp, 1976).

32. See Roland Barthes, *Leçon* (Paris: Editions du Seuil, 1978), 39.

33. Theodor W. Adorno, *Kierkegaard. Konstruktion des Ästhetischen* (Frankfurt am Main: Suhrkamp, 1962) (first published in 1933).

Chapter 6
Raymond Williams and the
Problem of Ideology
John Higgins

The last time I saw Raymond Williams speak was in a social-history seminar given at King's College, Cambridge. His topic seemed at first ironic in that context: the Bloomsbury group, in the college most associated with them; but the transformation of that irony into something more serious is what I want to record here as a way of introducing the seriousness of Williams's work. His voice was remarkable; the voice of an authority. It was conversational, almost to the point of dullness, but sustained throughout by that curiously academic power, the intellectually cautious assertion of the radical. His final judgment on the Bloomsbury group was damning: "The social conscience, in the end, is to protect the private consciousness." A questioner asked how he could bear to study such an awful group of people, and Williams replied, with a vivid ferocity, that it was a necessary task because that same kind of cultural fraction was still so powerful an enemy. The tone of that reply did not belong to the conventional smoothness of an academic discourse: it held instead the necessary anger of the political. It was, in the Cambridge context of a politely intellectual wit, a welcome shock of the real. It is precisely that tone which you have to imagine if you are to understand the seriousness of Williams's assertion in *Politics and Letters*: "If you look at the implied relationships of nearly all the books I have written, I have been arguing with what I take to be official English culture." I want to examine the argument as it is in two books: *Problems in Materialism and Culture* (London NLB, 1980) a collection of Williams's most important essays; and *Politics and Letters,* a series of interviews with Williams conducted by several members of the editorial board of the *New Left Review.* I shall particularly be concerned with Williams's responses to the central problem of English Marxism since the seventies, the problem of ideology.[1]

There are two main periods to Williams's work. In the first, his argument against official English culture takes place in isolation from any active Marxist tradition. In *Politics and Letters*, Williams records his extreme frustration with English studies by the end of part one of the Tripos. Williams found that the cultural line of the Communist party could not be used to argue successfully against an established critic like E. M.W. Tillyard. "People often ask me why I didn't carry on from the Marxist arguments of the thirties. The reason is that I felt they had led me into an impasse. I had become convinced that their answers did not meet the questions, and that I had got to be prepared to meet the professional objections. I was damned well going to do it properly this time" (52). Coming back to Cambridge in 1945, Williams, along with Wolf Mankowitz and Clifford Collins, founded a journal, *Politics and Letters*, which failed in 1948. This failure only made Williams more determined to succeed, as he records: "I pulled back to do my own work. For the next ten years, I wrote in nearly complete isolation" (77). *Culture and Society* was published in 1958, the first fruit of the attempt to meet the "professional objections" of the establishment. Here the attempt was to confront the Leavisite critics of *Scrutiny* with an alternative view of the notion of culture. Looking back at *Culture and Society*, Williams describes it as "a book which is negatively marked by elements of a disgusted withdrawal . . . from all immediate forms of collaboration, combined with an intense disappointment that they were not available" (106). At the same time, he is ready to defend its originality, as a book that made an important intervention in the definition of cultural studies. This first period, then, is the period of isolation and withdrawal and continues up to the publication in 1971 of *Orwell*, where Williams dissects the dangerous appeal of the figure of Orwell, what he calls Eric Blair's "successful impersonation of the plain man who bumps into experience in an unmediated way and is simply telling us the truth about it" (385). *Orwell* can also be seen as Williams's farewell to a mode of academic writing removed from any active relation to Marxism (Williams's own impersonation of the plain man untouched by Marxism), the last of the books of that first period and the beginning of the second period, during which there is a more direct relationship with Marxist theory.[2]

This second-period work is more complicated, as Williams continues his arguments against the establishment view of literature, but at the same time begins to place his own work more creatively in the context of a developing Marxist theory, one that he sees at times as dangerously idealistic. In *Politics and Letters*, he attributes the occasional opacity of his *Marxism and Literature* (1977) to its double opposition. It is directed both against the older conventional view of literature in the universities, and "against the limits of the newly dominant mode of critical structuralism, because this was taken as Marxist literary theory all

over Western Europe and North America." Williams stood against the "danger
. . . of the eruption of a mode of idealist study claiming the authority of Marxism
and the prestige of association with powerful intellectual movements in many
other fields" (339–40). The struggle in the first period of work was against the
isolation of the text in the vacuum of Practical Criticism; in the second period,
the struggle is to remove the text from the void of deconstructive jouissance,
and once again assert the necessity for a historical and materialist study of cultural
production. Williams calls his current theoretical position "cultural materialism,"
which he defines as "the analysis of all forms of signification, including quite
centrally writing, within the actual means and condition of their production."
His recent *Culture* (London: Fontana, 1981) provides a practical program of
such a cultural materialism as a potential new direction in the sociology of
culture. This practical program can be seen as Williams's final response in his
opposition throughout the seventies to Louis Althusser's idealist theories of
cultural and ideological reproduction.[3]

The beginnings of the second period of Williams's work can be seen with his
acknowledgment, in a memorial lecture of 1971, of the importance of the work
of Lucien Goldmann ("Literature and Sociology," *Problems* 11–30). Williams
argues that a major weakness of the English literary tradition is its lack of any
coherent theoretical center, its active ignorance of philosophy and sociology. He
also notes the absence in Marxism of any nonreductionist account of cultural
reproduction and points out the weaknesses of the base and superstructure model.
These he attempts to remedy in the 1973 essay, "Base and Superstructure in
Marxist Cultural Theory" (*Problems* 31–49). This essay can be regarded as the
single most important essay in *Problems*, marking both Williams's renewal of
interest in Marxist theory, and his active engagement in contributing directly to
its development.

The most important point Williams has to make in this essay is to see the base
and superstructure model not as a model of a static structure, but as the model
of an active process. The static model reduces the cultural to the status of an
effect: the ideological, illusory reflection of activities in the real economic base.
What Williams is keen to emphasize (as also in the following essay, "Means
of Communication as Means of Production") is the constitutive status of the
cultural in the reproduction of the social totality. In this active process, the
concept of hegemony has a crucial role: that of explaining the dominance of
particular class interests. Williams's point is that this dominant system of meanings and values is experienced as practice: hegemony is "the central, effective
and dominant system of meanings and values, which are not merely abstract but
are organized and lived" (*Problems* 38). Hegemony, then, is not the name of
an abstraction, but the name of an active social process, the practice of human
sociality. The ideological, for Williams, is always the result of human practice.
It is the notion of ideology as practice that most differentiates Williams from

the position taken by a most influential figure in the seventies in England, Louis Althusser. For Althusser, ideology is not the human practice of sociality; it is instead the condition for human sociality. Let us now examine the work that best represents what Williams sees as dangerous idealist developments in Marxist theory, Althusser's structuralist theory of ideology.

Althusser's theory of ideology is based on a certain reading of Lacanian theory. In "Freud and Lacan," Althusser writes: "Lacan has shown that [the] transition from (ultimately purely) biological existence to human existence (the human child) is achieved within the Law of Order, the law I shall call the Law of Culture, and that this Law of Culture is confounded in its *formal* essence with the order of language." He emphasizes that "the Law of Culture . . . is not exhausted by language; its content is the real kinship structures and the determinate ideological formations in which the persons inscribed in these structures live their function." Althusser does not clarify, however, the nature of the relation between these "real kinship structures" and the "determinate ideological formations," nor the relation of these to language.[4]

This failure to specify any differences between the "real kinship structures" and "determinate ideological formations" is compounded in the later essay, "Ideology and Ideological State Apparatuses," where the implicit reductionism of Althusser's position ("live their function") becomes explicit. We shall see that Althusser's interpellation theory suffers the vicious circularity of all functionalisms.[5]

The central thesis of Althusser's theory of ideology is "Ideology interpellates individuals as subjects."[6] By ideology, Althusser means "the imaginary relationship of individuals to their real conditions of existence." Interpellation is the name of the process that places the individual in an imaginary relationship to society, as a social subject. Interpellation is the name of the transition from "abstract" presocial individual to this ideological and social subject and it is also the name of the constant process of ideology: "The existence of ideology and the hailing or interpellation of individuals as subjects are one and the same thing" (163). They are one and the same thing owing to Althusser's conception of the subject, which he admits is the center of his theory: "there is no ideology except by the subject and for subjects. Meaning, there is no ideology except for concrete subjects, and this destination for ideology is only made possible by the subject: meaning, *by the category of the subject* and its functioning" (160).

The category of the subject is what makes possible the transition from "abstract individual" to "concrete subject": Althusser supposes a causal correspondence between individuals and subjects such that "ideology has always-already interpellated individuals as subjects" (164). As Paul Hirst explains, "The concrete individual is 'abstract,' it is not yet the subject it will be. It is, however, *already* a subject in the sense of the subject which supports the process of recognition. Thus something which is not a subject must already have the faculties necessary to support the recognition which will constitute it as a subject."[7] Althusser's argument is circular. The category of the subject is essential to the functioning of ideology as misrecognition. What is even more curious about Althusser's notion of the subject is that the transition from presocial to social is also seen as a complete transformation: once a subject, always a subject. Althusser emphasizes that, once individuals enter the structure of interpellation as subjects, they "'work by themselves'" (169). Interpellation is an uninterrupted process: "I must now suppress the temporal form in which I have presented the functioning of ideology, and say: ideology has always-already interpellated individuals as subjects" (164). This is quite at odds with the psychoanalytic account of the subject, which emphasizes above all the lacunary nature of consciousness, the "flickering in eclipses" of the subject.

Althusser's subject is a subject without an unconscious. He sees the moment of repression, that castrating moment of transition from pre-social to social existence, as one of successful and complete repression, inaugurating a homogenous and unbroken process of interpellation which then requires the dropping of any temporal description. Ideology is eternal; it has no history, says Althusser. The consequence of this, for the subject, is that it has no history either, and, in an important sense, is free from contradiction. Althusser's account lacks the most crucial element of psychoanalysis for a Marxist theory of ideology, the idea of the history of the production of the subject, and the related notions of ideological struggle (its very possibility) as constituted in the sphere of representation, where precisely what is at stake is the bind of the subject in representation, the conditions for particular acts of interpellation. By seeing interpellation as an eternal process, as timeless as the unconscious itself, Althusser removes the potentially radical account of the subject in process in language, constituted precisely in the refusal or acceptance of particular acts of interpellation. Seeing language only as a subjection to the Law of Culture, Althusser lacks any notion of language as agency.

There is no correspondence in Althusser's theory to Lacan's insistence on the rejection of the idea of a unified subject, epitomized for Lacan by the Cartesian *cogito*. In fact, Althusser's "concrete subject," the subject of ideology and interpellation, is a very strong form of the unified subject, the only difference from the position of Cartesian certitude being that the terms of the subject's unity in Althusser's theory are terms of misrecognition. The experience of the subject is a unity, but the experience of the subject is false, illusory. The whole position is epitomized in a passage of Althusser's *Letter on Art*:

> When we speak of ideology we should know that ideology slides into all human activity, that it is identical with the "lived" experience of human existence itself: that is why the form in which we are "made to see" ideology in great novels has as its content the "lived" experience of individuals. But this "lived" experience is not a *given*, given by a pure

"reality," but the spontaneous "lived experience" of ideology in its peculiar relations to the real.[8]

The critical weight of Althusser's account of ideology falls, then, on the notion of experience, which is, for Althusser, a structure of inevitable misrecognition. In "Notes on Marxism in Britain since 1945," Williams states his opposition to that "fashionable form of Marxism which makes the whole people, including the whole working class, mere carriers of the structures of a corrupt ideology" (*Problems* 241). The opposition can be understood politically: Althusser's theory is untenable as the basis for any idea of ideological struggle. And this is sharpened by the centrality of experience in Williams's own theory. Terry Eagleton has claimed: "It is precisely this insistence on experience, this passionate premium placed upon the 'lived' which supplies one of the centrally unifying themes of Williams's oeuvre—which supplies at once the formidable power and drastic limitation of his work."[9]

Eagleton is writing here from within the Althusserian problematic. The limitations he sees are the limitations of those who lack Theory. Eagleton accuses Williams of a "consistent over-subjectivising of the social formation." He notes that Williams relies on an experiential definition of hegemony and that Williams attempts to substitute the theoretically vacuous notion of "structure of feeling" for a full-fledged account of ideology. These are the limitations of a vulgar empiricism, which can only be overcome by a Marxist science of the text, on the lines of Pierre Macherey's *Pour une théorie de la production littéraire* (Paris: François Maspero, 1974.) Eagleton has since acknowledged a certain unease with this position, but he says he "would still for the most part defend its essential critique of the work of Williams." The questions that remain concern the category of experience in a materialist theory of ideology.[10]

In *Politics and Letters*, Williams is questioned about his work on the lines set out by Eagleton. Experience, notes the interviewer, "must be the only word you use recurrently that is not given an entry in *Keywords*" (166–67; there is now an entry in the 1983 revised edition) and seems at times to "presuppose a kind of pristine contact between the subject and the reality in which the subject is immersed" (167). Williams denies this, noting that experience has become a "forbidden word, whereas what we ought to say about it is that it is a limited word, for there are many kinds of knowledge it will never give us, in any of its ordinary senses" (172). Williams accepts the interviewer's point that certain kinds of historical process are not immediately experienced and can be described only from a conceptual or scientific discourse, but he goes on to add that "just as I am moving in that direction, I see a kind of appalling parody . . . beyond me—the claim that all experience is ideology, that the subject is wholly an ideological illusion, which is the last stage of formalism—and I even start to pull back a bit" (172). What is at stake is the relationship between experience and explanation. Eagleton attributed the "formidable power" of Williams's work to its appeal to personal experience, and noted the importance of certain concepts of personal identity in Williams's work. Eagleton saw this as a part of the work's ideological appeal, for the very notion of personal identity seems to be outlawed by the Althusserian theory of the subject. Yet we have already seen some of the deficiencies in Althusser's account of subjectivity, and it is at precisely this point, the account of the subject, that theoretical links between experience and explanation can be made, though they still need to be explored. For, if, with Williams, we reject as "formalism" the Althusserian critique of the subject, the claim that the subject is "wholly an ideological illusion," we still need to establish a satisfactory account of the subject's role in explanation. Such an account would be based on a thorough examination of the relations between the semantic properties of natural languages and the social relations of subjectivity involved in the production of meaning." [11] One element of Williams's work that can be seen as a contribution to such an account is his interest in historical semantics.

A significant part of Williams's work has been devoted to historical linguistics, the investigation of the conflictual meanings of words, the changes and differences in the meanings of words both synchronically and diachronically. *Keywords* (London: Fontana, 1976) is the most obvious example. It can be seen above all as an investigation of the social determination of the meaning of words, and the process of that determination through conflict and assertion. Several of the essays in *Problems in Materialism and Culture* are extended accounts of the differences in usage and meaning of concepts such as "materialism," "nature," and "Social Darwinism." Such accounts of conflictual meanings are quite at odds with Althusser's notion of language as an all-dominating ideological instance. It is a curious paradox of Althusser's account that at the same time as identifying the ideological as a discrete instance for political struggle, he also defined the ideological in such a way as to make the idea of effective struggle in the ideological domain impossible. For Althusser, language is always subjection, and never a matter of agency. Williams's semantic investigations are also directed against what he sees (with Timpanaro) as an idealist trend in linguistics: Saussure's creation of a scientific concept of language that excludes any determination of the language by individual speakers. An opposing account might begin with an investigation of the importance of what J. L. Austin has called performatives. Austin begins with a distinction between performatives, acts of speech where the issuing of the utterance is the performing of an action ("I promise," "I protest"), and constatives, acts of speech that describe or report something. But he later suggests that closer attention to the situation in which even simple statements are made tends to dissolve that distinction and to raise instead the *problem* of truth. Such an emphasis on the conditions of production of statements would be of great significance for a materialist theory of language. [12]

Williams seems to be moving toward such an account in *Marxism and Liter-*

ature. Williams acknowledges in *Politics and Letters* the development of his interest in language while writing *Marxism and Literature*: "The book was originally based on lectures which started in Cambridge about 1970. But it's very significant that in those lectures there was nothing on the theory of language, whereas now it is the longest section of the book, and I would say the most pivotal. . . . There particularly I felt the limitations of length, because by then I could have written a whole book on that subject alone" (324).

Such a study would have to go beyond the impasse of currently available positions that share, paradoxically, the view of language as an essentially static system which I have described here in its Althusserian form. From one position, the system of language is seen as coextensive with an anonymous system of power which necessarily incorporates any act or utterance against itself because it provides the very conditions of existence for all such acts and utterances. The second position may be seen in part as a reaction to, and in part simply as a variant of, the first. Here, the task is to avoid or deflect the consequences of entry into the system of language by exposing the terms of its operation. Apparently, the subject can be liberated from the consequences of its entry into the system by reversing the status of the crucial category of difference. In psychoanalytic theory, difference has a constitutive status. It is difference that structures the chaos of the ineffable real into the social order of discourse and representation. In its reversed form, difference is held to dissolve that social order of discourse and representation into the formal play of signifiers and the endless unravelings of textuality. Both of these positions share—what I have tried to describe here in relation to Althusser's work—the refusal of the psychoanalytical account of the subject as a process, and not as a product, as dynamic rather than static. It is hardly surprising that both versions cannot discuss the crucial question (for any theory of ideology) of agency, for agency is precluded by their reduction of language to its textual and systematic aspects and their ignorance of the social and discursive components of language practice. Williams's opposition to Althusser is perhaps best understood in relation to the difference between discussions of language as discourse and treatments of language as textuality.[13]

Although Althusser's theory of ideology fails in part because of its assigning a merely static and repressive place for the subject, it does succeed in its emphasis on the materiality of ideological practice. Such a notion is not very far removed from Williams's insistence on the necessity for a cultural materialism that would confront the historical and theoretical problems of the "precise constituted materiality" (*Problems* 108) of human agency. What is lacking in Williams's account of ideological production is any clear notion of human subjectivity: Williams's reading of psychoanalysis remains too much within the confines of Timpanaro's limiting problematic of a biological, rather than a linguistic or semantic, Freudianism. What is now needed is a productive coupling of historical semantics and a coherent theory of the production of subjectivity in discourse, a point of contact which Williams has seen between his own work and current work in radical semiotics: "I remember saying that a fully historical semiotics would be very much the same thing as cultural materialism."[14]

The emphasis in Williams's work on experience seems to place him, as we have seen, as a substantial target for Althusserian-style accusations of empiricism. It is certainly true that Williams can be situated in the historical tradition of English empiricism. But one can distinguish between two kinds of empiricism. There is that vulgar empiricism which is Althusser's target in *Reading Capital*. Vulgar empiricism takes for granted the existence of a knowing subject with an unmediated access to experience; its idea of language is language as a transparent means of communication. Radical empiricism questions the terms of the construction of that knowing subject and interrogates in particular the semantics of natural languages in relation to questions of human sociality; its object is always (borrowing Edward Said's useful terms) "worldly" discourse rather than "systematic" textuality. This is the radical empiricism of John Locke and David Hume, whose political philosophies are precisely concerned with the problems of ideological reproduction across questions of subjectivity and knowledge. Such also is the radical empiricism of Raymond Williams. *Politics and Letters* and *Problems in Materialism and Culture* are excellent introductions to the conflicts in the seventies around the theory of ideology which can be seen as focusing once again the conflict between two important components of Marxist theory: the idealism of the young Marx and the empiricism of the mature Marx and of Friedrich Engels.[15]

NOTES

1. *Politics and Letters* (London: NLB, 1979), 316. The interviewers were Perry Anderson, Anthony Barnett, and Francis Mulhern. See Perry Anderson, *Arguments within English Marxism* (London: NLB, 1980); Anthony Barnett, "Raymond Williams and Marxism" in *New Left Review* no. 99 (1976); and Francis Mulhern, *The Moment of "Scrutiny"* (London: NLB, 1979). For the English version of ideology that Williams rejects, see Rosalind Coward and John Ellis, *Language and Materialism: Developments in Semiology and the Theory of the Subject* (London: Routledge and Kegan Paul, 1977).

2. See *Politics and Letters*, 50–52, 73–77, 97–98; and *Orwell* (London: Fontana, 1971). Williams was unaware of Edward Thompson's work toward *The Making of the English Working Class* (London: Victor Gollancz, 1963) at the time of writing *Culture and Society, 1780–1950* (London: Chatto and Windus, 1958) and acknowledges its subsequent influence. See *Politics and Letters*, 108–9: "Today, for example, I would like to write about the extraordinary transposition of varieties of radicalism that occurred between 1790 and 1840—which I never mentioned in the book" (108).

3. *Politics and Letters*, 112. For Williams's definition of cultural materialsm, see "Crisis in English Studies," in *Writing in Society* (London: Verso, 1984), 210; and also my review of Williams, *Minnesota Review* (forthcoming).

4. Louis Althusser, "Freud and Lacan" in *Lenin and Philosophy and Other Essays*, trans. Ben Brewster (London: New Left Books, 1971), 193–94. A useful introduction to Lacan's blending of

concepts from structuralist linguistics and anthropology is Anika Lemaire's *Jacques Lacan*, trans. David Macey (London: Routledge and Kegan Paul, 1977).

5. On the circularity of functionalist arguments, see David Goddard, "Anthropology: The Limits of Functionalism" in *Ideology and Social Science: Readings in Critical Social Theory*, ed. Robin Blackburn (London: Fontana, 1972).

6. Louis Althusser, "Ideology and Ideological State Apparatuses (Notes towards an Investigation)" in *Lenin and Philosophy*, 160.

7. Paul Hirst, *On Law and Ideology* (London: Macmillan, 1979), 65. Hirst provides the best critical introduction to Althusser's theory of ideology.

8. See Jacques Alain Miller, "La Suture: Eléments de la logique du signifiant" in *Cahiers pour l'analyse*, no 1 (1966): 39–51 (English translation in *Screen* 18.4 [1977/78]: 24–34). See also Stephen Heath, *Questions of Cinema* (London: Macmillan, 1981), "On Suture," 76–112. For Lacan on Descartes see, for example, *Les quatre concepts fondamentaux de la psychanalyse* (Paris: Seuil, 1973), 36–37 (English translation by Alan Sheridan [Harmondsworth: Allen Lane, 1977], 35–37). Althusser, "A Letter on Art" in *Lenin and Philosophy*, 204–5. And more generally, see Stephen Heath, *Three Essays on Subjectivity* (London: Macmillan, forthcoming).

9. Terry Eagleton, *Criticism and Ideology* (London: New Left Books, 1976), 22. I shall deal more fully with this problem in a forthcoming book on Williams (to be published by Croom Helm). See also chapter 8 of this volume, by Bruce Robbins.

10. Eagleton, *Criticism and Ideology*, 32. For his relation to Macherey see chapter 3, "Towards a Science of the Text." Eagleton, *Walter Benjamin, or Towards a Revolutionary Criticism* (London: New Left Books, 1981), 97.

11. Compare, for example, Hilary Putnam, "Is Semantics Possible?" in his *Mind, Language and Reality: Philosophical Papers* 2 (Cambridge: Cambridge Univ. Press, 1975), 152: "A general and precise theory which answers the questions (1) why do words have the different sorts of functions they do? and (2) exactly how does conveying the core facts enable one to learn the use of a word? is not to be expected until one has a general and precise model of a language-user; and that is still a long way off." A starting point for such a theory could be Luce Irigaray, "Communications linguistique et speculaire" in *Cahiers pour l'analyse*, no. 3 (May–June 1966): 39–55. See also M. A. K. Halliday, *Language as Social Semiotic* (London: Edward Arnold, 1978).

12. See J. L. Austin, *How to Do Things with Words* (Oxford: Oxford Univ. Press, 1962), especially 52: "We must consider the total situation in which the utterance is issued—the total speech act—if we are to see the parallel between statements and performative utterances, and how each can go wrong. Perhaps indeed there is no great distinction between statements and performative utterances." See also 138: "Once we realize that what we have to study is *not* the sentence but the issuing of an utterance in a speech situation, there can hardly any longer be a possibility of not seeing that stating is performing an act." See also Michel Pêcheux, *Les Vérités de la Palice* (Paris: François Maspero, 1975); *Stating the Obvious: From Semantics to Discourse* (London: Macmillan, 1982), trans. Harbans Nagpal. The crucial philosophical category for such semantic investigation is belief, and, in particular, what Bernard Williams refers to as "full-blown belief" and its relations to assertoricity. See "Deciding to Believe," in *Problems of the Self*. (Cambridge: Cambridge Univ. Press, 1973), especially 147: "We need the possibility of deliberate reticence, not saying what I believe, and of insincerity, saying something other than what I believe. So in a sense we need the will; for it is only with the ability to decide to assert either what I believe or what I do not believe, the ability to decide to speak rather than to remain silent about something, that we can get the dimension which is essential to belief." And, of course, to ideology.

13. On this distinction see especially Edward W. Said, "Criticism between Culture and System," in *The World, the Text, and the Critic* (Cambridge, Mass.: Harvard Univ. Press, 1983), 178–225. On the context of critical theory in recent years, see Perry Anderson, *In the Tracks of Historical Materialism* (London: Verso, 1983).

14. Williams, *Writing in Society*, 210. Williams gives a sympathetic assessment of Timpanaro's *On Materialism* (London: New Left Books, 1975) and *The Freudian Slip* (London: New Left Books, 1976) in "Problems of Materialism" in *Problems in Materialism and Culture*. Timpanaro's aggressive attack on Freud's theories through a linguistic analysis of the parapraxes in Freud's *Jokes and their Relation to the Unconscious* is accepted by Williams; but Timpanaro's attack on Freud's popularization of his theories never really comes to grips with Freud's notion of the unconscious. Compare Williams's attitude toward Vološinov's *Freudianism: A Marxist Critique* (New York: Academic Press, 1976) with the account given by Heath in *Questions of Cinema*, 208-12. In the same way that Williams's work has benefited from a closer relation to Marxist theory, it might also benefit from a more sustained engagement with the radical elements of psychoanalytic theory. For the elements of such a position, see Colin MacCabe, "On Discourse," in *Tracking the Signifier: Theoretical Essays: Film, Linguistics, Literature* (Minneapolis: Univ. of Minnesota Press, 1985), 82–112.

15. For Althusser on empiricism, see *Reading Capital* (1968; London: New Left Books, 1970), 34–46. On Locke, see John Dunn, *The Political Thought of John Locke* (Cambridge: Cambridge Univ. Press, 1969) and James Tully, *A Discourse on Property* (Cambridge: Cambridge Univ. Press, 1980). On Hume, Gilles Deleuze, *Empirisme et Subjectivité* (Paris: Presses Universitaires de France, 1953) and David Miller, *Philosophy and Ideology in Hume's Political Thought* (Oxford: Clarendon Press, 1982). For the effect of Engels's empiricism on Marx, see Gareth Stedman Jones, "The Originality of Engels," *New Left Review*, no. 106 (1977): 79–104.

Chapter 7
Ethics and Action in Fredric Jameson's Marxist Hermeneutics
Cornel West

Fredric Jameson is the most challenging American Marxist hermeneutic thinker on the present scene. His ingenious interpretations (prior to accessible translations) of major figures of the Frankfurt school, Russian formalism, French structuralism, and poststructuralism as well as of Georg Lukács, Jean-Paul Sartre, Louis Althusser, Max Weber, and Louis Marin are significant contributions to the intellectual history of twentieth-century Marxist and European thought. Jameson's treatments of the development of the novel, the surrealist movement, of Continental writers such as Honoré de Balzac, Marcel Proust, Alessandro Manzoni, and Alain Robbe-Grillet, and of American writers, including Ernest Hemingway, Kenneth Burke, and Ursula Le Guin, constitute powerful political readings. Furthermore, his adamantly antiphilosophical form of Marxist hermeneutics puts forward an American *Aufhebung* of poststructuralism that merits close scrutiny.

In this chapter I shall highlight Jameson's impressive intellectual achievements, specific theoretical flaws, and particular political shortcomings by focusing on the philosophical concerns and ideological aims in his trilogy.[1] Jameson is first and foremost a loyal, though critical, disciple of the Lukács of *History and Class Consciousness* in the sense that he nearly dogmatically believes that commodification—the selling of human labor power to profit-maximizing capitalists—is the primary source of domination in capitalist societies and that reification—the appearance of this relation between persons and classes as relations between things and prices—is the major historical process against which to understand norms, values, sensibilities, texts, and movements in the modern world.[2]

The central question that haunts Jameson is "How to be a sophisticated Lukácsian Marxist without Lukács's nostalgic historicism and highbrow humanism?" A more general formulation of this question is "How to take history, class struggle, and capitalist dehumanization seriously after the profound poststructuralist deconstructions of solipsistic Cartesianism, transcendental Kantianism, teleological Hegelianism, genetic Marxism, and recuperative humanism?" In Anglo-American common-sense lingo, this query becomes "How to live and act in the face of the impotence of irony and the paralysis of skepticism?" The pressing problem that plagues Jameson is whether the Marxist quest for totalization—with its concomitant notions of totality, mediation, narrative (or even universal) history, part/whole relations, essence/appearance distinctions, and subject/object oppositions—presupposes a form of philosophical idealism that inevitably results in a mystification which ignores difference, flux, dissemination, and heterogeneity. Jameson's work can be read as a gallant attempt at such a quest which hopes to avoid idealist presuppositions and preclude mystifying results.

Jameson initiates this quest by examining the major European Marxist thinker for whom this problematic looms large: Jean-Paul Sartre.[3] Yet Jameson's project takes shape in the encounter with the rich German tradition of Marxist dialectical thought best exemplified in the works of Adorno, Benjamin, Marcuse, Bloch, and, of course, Lukács. His dialectical perspective first tries to reveal the philosophical and political bankruptcy of modern Anglo-American thought. In the preface to *Marxism and Form* he writes:

> Less obvious, perhaps, is the degree to which anyone presenting German
> and French dialectical literature is forced—either implicitly or explicitly—
> to take yet a third national tradition into account, I mean our own: that
> mixture of political liberalism, empiricism, and logical positivism which
> we know as Anglo-American philosophy and which is hostile at all points
> to the type of thinking outlined here. One cannot write for a reader formed
> in this tradition—one cannot even come to terms with one's own historical
> formation—without taking this influential conceptual opponent into
> account; and it is this, if you like, which makes up the tendentious part
> of my book, which gives it its political and philosophical cutting edge, so
> to speak. (*MF* x)

Jameson's battle against modern Anglo-American thought is aided by poststructuralism in that deconstructions disclose the *philosophical* bankruptcy of this bourgeois humanist tradition. Yet, such deconstructions say little about the *political* bankruptcy of this tradition; further, and more seriously, deconstructions conceal the political impotency of its own projects. In short, Jameson rightly considers poststructuralism an ally against bourgeois humanism yet ultimately an intellectual foe and political enemy. His tempered appreciation and subsequent rejection of structuralism and poststructuralism are enacted in his superb critical treatment of their roots and development in *The Prison-House of Language*. For example, he writes in the preface of this text:

> My own plan—to offer an introductory survey of these movements which might stand at the same time as a critique of their basic methodology—is no doubt open to attack from both partisans and adversaries alike. . . .
> The present critique does not, however, aim at judgments of detail, nor at the expression of some opinion, either positive or negative, on the works in question here. It proposes rather to lay bare what Collingwood would have called the "absolute presuppositions" of Formalism and Structuralism taken as intellectual totalities. These absolute presuppositions may then speak, for themselves, and, like all such ultimate premises or models, are too fundamental to be either accepted or rejected. (*PHL* x)

Jameson's first lengthy treatment of the Marxist dialectical tradition focuses on the most intelligent thinker and adroit stylist of that tradition: Theodor Adorno.[4] Adorno presents Jameson with his most formidable challenge, for Adorno's delicate dialectical acrobatics embark on the quest for totalization while simultaneously calling such a quest into question; they reconstruct the part in light of the whole while deconstructing the notion of a whole; they devise a complex conception of mediation while disclosing the idea of totality as illusion; and they ultimately promote dialectical development while surrendering to bleak pessimism about ever attaining a desirable telos. In short, Adorno is a negative hermeneutical thinker, a dialectical deconstructionist par excellence: the skeleton that forever hangs in Jameson's closet.

In this way, Adorno is the most ingenious and dangerous figure for Jameson. Adorno ingeniously makes and maintains contact with the concrete in a dialectical demystifying movement that begins with the art object and engages the psychological, that moves from the psychological and implicates the social, and then finds the economic in the social. Yet he refuses to ossify the object of inquiry or freeze the concepts he employs to interrogate the object. This intellectual energy and ability is characterized by Jameson in the following way:

> It is to this ultimate squaring of the circle that Adorno came in his two last and most systematic, most technically philosophical works, *Negative Dialectics* and *Aesthetic Theory*. Indeed, as the title of the former suggests, these works are designed to offer a theory of the untheorizable, to show why dialectical thinking is at one and the same time both indispensable and impossible, to keep the idea of system itself alive while intransigently dispelling the pretensions of any of the contingent and already realized systems to validity and even to existence. . . . Thus a negative dialectic has no choice but to affirm the notion and value of an ultimate synthesis, while negating its possibility and reality in every concrete case that comes before it . . . negative dialectics does not result in an empty formalism,

but rather in a thoroughgoing critique of forms, in a painstaking and well-nigh permanent destruction of every possible hypostasis of the various moments of thinking itself. (*MF* 54–55, 56)

Adorno is dangerous for Jameson because his deconstructionist strategies and political impotence resemble the very poststructuralism with which Jameson wrestles. Jameson never adequately settles this deep tension with Adorno. In his later work, he circumvents this tension by reducing Adorno's negative dialectics to an aesthetic ideal, and this reduction minimizes Adorno's philosophical challenge to Jameson's own antiphilosophical hermeneutics. Jameson tries to disarm Adorno's position by construing it as a perspective that reconfirms the status of the concept of totality by reacting to and deconstructing "totality."[5] In Jameson's view, the antitotalizing deconstructionist strategies of Jacques Derrida and Paul de Man also "confirm" the status of the concept of totality since such strategies "must be accompanied by some initial appearance of continuity, some ideology of unification already in place, which it is their mission to rebuke and to shatter" (*PU* 53). Jameson seems to be employing a rather slippery notion of how the idea of totality is confirmed, since powerful projects which "rebuke" and "shatter" this idea appear to "confirm" it. On this crucial point, Jameson presents neither a persuasive argument against deconstructionists nor a convincing case for his own position, but rather a defensive recuperative strategy that co-opts the deconstructionists in a quest for totality unbeknownst and unrecognizable to them. This ad hoc strategy reflects Jameson's unsettled tension with Adorno and his reluctance to come to terms with Paul de Man's rigorous version of deconstruction.[6]

Yet what is missing in Adorno, Jameson finds in Benjamin, Marcuse, and Bloch: a theoretical mechanism that sustains hope and generates praxis in the present moment of the historical process. Such hope and praxis are promoted by a *politicized notion of desire* that is sustained by a "nostalgia conscious of itself, a lucid and remorseless dissatisfaction with the present on the grounds of some remembered plenitude" (*MF* 82). For example, Jameson is attracted to Benjamin primarily because Benjamin's conception of nostalgic utopianism as a revolutionary stimulus in the present delivers Jameson from the wretched pessimism of Adorno.

For Jameson, Benjamin's notion of nostalgic utopianism—best elucidated in his masterful essay on Nikolai Leskov, "The Storyteller"—unfolds as storytelling that does justice to our experience of the past, as nonnovelistic (hence, nonindividualistic) narrative that makes contact with the concrete, with an authentic form of social and historical existence quickly vanishing owing to the reification process in late monopoly capitalism. Following Benjamin, Jameson holds that reification destroys the conditions for storytelling, for meaningful destinies and common plots that encompass the past, present, and future of the human community. Therefore one-dimensional societies do not simply domesticate their opposition; they also deprive such opposition of the very means to stay in touch with any revolutionary past or visionary future. Such societies present no stories but rather "only a series of experiences of equal weight whose order is indiscriminately reversible" (*MF* 79).

Jameson conceives the politicized notion of desire—found first in Friedrich Schiller and then more fully in Herbert Marcuse—as the transformative élan repressed and submerged by the reification process in late monopoly capitalism. This conception of desire constitutes the central component of Jameson's notion of freedom, a notion that he argues can never be conceptually grasped but rather symptomatically displayed in the dissatisfaction of the present, in a Faustian Refusal of the Instant, or in a Blochian ontological astonishment that renders us aware of the "not-yet" latent in the present. To put it crudely, Jameson's politicized notion of desire promises access to a revolutionary energy lurking beneath the social veil of appearances, an energy capable of negating the reified present order.

This notion of freedom—or negational activity motivated by the desire for freedom—serves as the "center" that Jameson's Marxist hermeneutics dialectically discloses and decenters. This is what makes his viewpoint *political* and *hermeneutical* as opposed to *idealistic* and *philosophical*. For example, he states,

> For hermeneutics, traditionally a technique whereby religions recuperated the texts and spiritual activities of cultures resistant to them, is also a political discipline, and provides the means for maintaining contact with the very sources of revolutionary energy during a stagnant time, or preserving the concept of freedom itself, underground, during geological ages of repression. Indeed, it is the concept of freedom which . . . proves to be the privileged instrument of a political hermeneutic, and which, in turn, is perhaps itself best understood as an interpretive device rather than a philosophical essence or idea.[7] (*MF* 84)

Jameson's totalizing impulse is seen quite clearly in his claim that this political hermeneutic approach is the "absolute horizon of all reading and all interpretation" (*PU* 17). This approach preserves, negates, and transcends all prevailing modes of reading and interpreting texts, whether psychoanalytic, myth-critical, stylistic, ethical, structural, or poststructural. Jameson unequivocally states,

> One of the essential themes of this book will be the contention that Marxism subsumes other interpretive modes or systems; or, to put it in methodological terms, that the limits of the latter can always be overcome, and their more positive findings retained, by a radical historicizing of their mental operations, such that not only the content of the analysis, but the very method itself, along with the analyst, then comes to be reckoned into the "text" or phenomenon to be explained. (*PU* 47)

This totalizing impulse can be best understood in the crucial links Jameson makes among the notions of desire, freedom, and narrative. In a fascinating and important discussion of André Breton's *Manifesto*, Jameson writes,

> It is not too much to say that for Surrealism a genuine plot, a genuine narrative, is that which can stand as the very *figure* of Desire itself: and this not only because in the Freudian sense pure physiological desire is inaccessible as such to consciousness, but also because in the socioeconomic context, genuine desire risks being dissolved and lost in the vast network of pseudosatisfactions which makes up the market system. In that sense desire is the form taken by freedom in the new commercial environment, by a freedom we do not even realize we have lost unless we think of it in terms, not only of the stilling, but also of the awakening, of Desire in general. (*MF* 100–101)

In Jameson's sophisticated version of Lukácsian Marxism, narrative is the means by which the totality is glimpsed, thereby preserving the possibility of dialectical thinking. This glimpse of totality—disclosed in a complex and coherent story about conflicting classes and clashing modes of production—constitutes the "very figure of Desire" in the present, a desire that both enables and enacts the negation of the present. Unlike the function of the notion of desire in poststructuralism, Jameson understands this notion to result in a will to freedom, not in a will to presence. In fact, Jameson's conception of the function of desire is much closer to the Christian view of a will to salvation than the deconstructionist "will to presence"; that is, Jameson's perspective more closely resembles a transcendental system which regulates human action than a rhetorical system which circumscribes epistemological moves.

Jameson's American Marxist *Aufhebung* of poststructuralism posits the major terrain—the primal scene—of contemporary criticism as not epistemology, but ethics. Instead of focusing on the numerous Sisyphean attempts to construct a metaphysics of presence, he highlights the various efforts to negate the present and shows how such negations point toward a society of freedom. For example, Jacques Derrida, the preeminent deconstructionist, brilliantly unmasks the binary oppositions in traditional and contemporary Western thought, such as speech and writing, presence and absence, and so forth. Yet Derrida remains oblivious to similar binary oppositions in ethics such as good and evil.

> To move from Derrida to Nietzsche is to glimpse the possibility of a rather different interpretation of the binary opposition, according to which its positive and negative terms are ultimately assimilated by the mind as a distinction between good and evil. Not metaphysics but ethics is the informing ideology of the binary opposition; and we have forgotten the thrust of Nietzsche's thought and lost everything scandalous and virulent about it if we cannot understand how it is ethics itself which is the ideological vehicle and the legitimation of concrete structures of power and domination. (*PU* 114)

Jameson's attempt to shift the fierce epistemological and metaphysical battles in contemporary Continental philosophy and criticism to ethics is invigorating and impressive. This shift is prompted by his de-Platonizing of the poststructuralist notion of desire—which freely floats above history like a Platonic form only to be embodied in various versions of metaphysics of presence—and his placing it in the underground of history which emerges in the form of a negation of the present, as an "ontological patience in which the constraining situation itself is for the first time perceived in the very moment in which it is refused" (*MF* 84–85). Of course, Jameson recognizes that this shift replaces one metaphysical and mythical version of desire with his own. Yet, in his view, his politicized notion of desire has crucial historical consequences and therefore it is more acceptable than the poststructuralist conception of desire.

> Yet, it will be observed, even if the theory of desire is a metaphysic and a myth, it is one whose great narrative events—repression and revolt—ought to be congenial to a Marxist perspective, one whose ultimate Utopian vision of the liberation of desire and of libidinal transfiguration was an essential feature of the great mass revolts of the 1960s in Eastern and Western Europe as well as in China and the United States. (*PU* 67)

Jameson's project of politicizing the notion of desire is rooted in Schiller's *Letters on the Aesthetic Education of Mankind*, which sidesteps the Kantian epistemological question of the necessary conditions for the possibility of experience and instead raises the more political question of the speculative and hypothetical (or utopian) conditions for the possibility of a free and harmonious personality. In attempting to answer this question, Schiller presents analogies between the psyche and society, between the mental divisions of impulses (*Stofftrieb*, *Formtrieb*, and *Spieltrieb*) and the social divisions of labor (Work, Reason and Art). In the same vein, Jameson's reading of Marcuse's *Eros and Civilization* sees Marcuse as replacing Freud's inquiry into the structure of actual mental phenomena with an inquiry into the speculative and hypothetical conditions for the possibility of an aggression-free society in which work is libidinally satisfying. As in Benjamin's nostalgic utopianism, the primary function of memory is to serve the pleasure principle; the origin of utopian thought resides in the remembered plenitude of psychic gratification. Jameson quotes Marcuse's famous formulation of the origins of thought, "The memory of gratification is at the origin of all thinking, and the impulse to recapture past gratification is the hidden driving power behind the process of thought." [8] Jameson then adds,

> The primary energy of revolutionary activity derives from this memory of a prehistoric happiness which the individual can regain only through its externalization, through its reestablishment for society as a whole. The loss or repression of the very sense of such concepts as freedom and desire takes, therefore, the form of a kind of amnesia or forgetful numbness,

which the hermeneutic activity, the stimulation of memory as the negation of the here and now, as the projection of Utopia, has as its function to dispel, restoring to us the original clarity and force of our own most vital drives and wishes. (*MF* 113–14)

It should be apparent that Jameson is, in many ways, a traditional hermeneutical thinker; that is, his basic theoretical strategy is that of recuperation, restoration, and recovery.[9] Furthermore, his fundamental aim is to preserve the old Christian notion—and Marxist affirmation—that history is meaningful,

> Only Marxism can give us an adequate account of the essential *mystery* of the cultural past, which, like Tiresias drinking blood, is momentarily returned to life and warmth and allowed once more to speak, and to deliver its long-forgotten message in surroundings utterly alien to it. This mystery can be reenacted only if the human adventure is one. . . . These matters can recover their original urgency for us only if they are retold within the unity of a single great collective story; only if, in however disguised and symbolic form, they are seen as sharing a single fundamental theme—for Marxism, the collective struggle to wrest a realm of Freedom from a realm of Necessity; only if they are grasped as vital episodes in a single vast unfinished plot.[10] (*PU* 19–20)

Jameson recognizes the deep affinity of his Marxist project with religious *Weltanschauungen*. And since he is not afflicted with the petty antireligious phobia of scientistic Marxists, Jameson develops his affinity by juxtaposing the medieval Christian allegorical method and Northrop Frye's interpretive system with his own project.[11] In fact, the system of four levels—the literal, allegorical, moral, and anagogical levels—of medieval Christian allegorical interpretation constitutes a crucial component of his theoretical framework. This model provides him a means by which to come to terms with the persistent problem for Marxism: the problem of mediation, the task of specifying the relationship between various levels and of adapting analyses from one level to another in light of a meaningful story of the past, present, and future of the human community.

The first (or literal) level permits Jameson to retain the historical referents of events and happenings (such as human suffering, domination, and struggle) and the textual referents of books and works—such as conflict-ridden historical situations, class-ridden social conditions, and antinomy-ridden ideological configurations. In this way, Jameson accepts the antirealist arguments of poststructuralists, yet rejects their textual idealism.[12] He acknowledges that history is always already mediated by language, texts, and interpretations, yet he insists that history is still, in some fundamental sense, "there." He conceives of history as an "absent cause" known by its "formal effects." In the crucial paragraph that directly replies to textual idealists and completes his theoretical chapter in *The Political Unconscious* he writes,

History is therefore the experience of Necessity, and it is this alone which can forestall its thematization or reification as a mere object of representation or as one master code among many others. Necessity is not in that sense a type of content, but rather the inexorable *form* of events; it is therefore a narrative category in the enlarged sense of some properly narrative political unconscious which has been argued here, a retextualization of History which does not propose the latter as some new representation or "vision," some new content, but as the formal effects of what Althusser, following Spinoza, calls an "absent cause." Conceived in this sense, History is what hurts, it is what refuses desire and sets inexorable limits to individual as well as collective praxis, which its "ruses" turn into grisly and ironic reversals of their overt intention. But this History can be apprehended only through its effects, and never directly as some reified force. This is indeed the ultimate sense in which History as ground and untranscendable horizon needs no particular theoretical justification: we may be sure that its alienating necessities will not forget us, however much we might prefer to ignore them. (*PU* 102)

The second (or allegorical) level sets forth the interpretive code, which is for Jameson the mediatory code of the reification process in capitalist societies.[13] This mediatory code takes the form of a genealogical construction characterized by neither genetic continuity nor teleological linearity, but rather by what Bloch called *Ungleichzeitigkeit* or "nonsynchronous development." This conception of history and texts as a "synchronic unity of structurally contradictory or heterogeneous elements, genetic patterns, and discourses" allows Jameson to identify and isolate particular aspects of the past as preconditions for the elaboration of reifying elements in the present.[14]

The third (or moral) level constitutes an ethical or psychological reading in which, following Althusser's conception of ideology, representational structures permit individual subjects to conceive their lived relationships to transindividual realities such as the destiny of humankind or the social structure. The fourth (or anagogical) level—which is inseparable from the third level—provides a political reading for the collective meaning of history, a characterization of the transindividual realities that link the individual to a fate, plot, and story of a community, class, group, or society.

Jameson's appropriation of the medieval system leads him to redefine the activity of interpretation in allegorical terms; that is, his own political allegorical machinery, with its aims of ideological unmasking and utopian projection, dictates the way in which interpretation and criticism ought to proceed.

We will assume that a criticism which asks the question "What does it mean?" constitutes something like an allegorical operation in which a text is systematically *rewritten* in terms of some fundamental master code or "ultimately determining instance." On this view, then, all "interpretation" in the narrower sense demands the forcible or imperceptible transformation of a given text into an allegory of its particular master code or "transcendental signified": the discredit into which interpretation has fallen is thus at one with the disrepute visited on allegory itself.

Yet to see interpretation this way is to acquire the instruments by which we can force a given interpretive practice to stand and yield up its name, to blurt out its master code and thereby reveal its metaphysical and ideological underpinnings. (*PU* 58)

Jameson's redefinition of the allegorical model also draws him closer to Northrop Frye. In *Marxism and Form*, Jameson invokes, in a respectful yet somewhat pejorative manner, Frye's interpretive system as "the only philosophically coherent alternative" to Marxist hermeneutics.[15] In a later essay, "Criticism in History," Jameson harshly criticizes Frye's system as ahistorical and guilty of presupposing an unacceptable notion of unbroken continuity between the narrative forms of "primitive" societies and those of modern times.[16] Yet in *The Political Unconscious*, there is some change of heart.

In the present context, however, Frye's work comes before us as a virtual contemporary reinvention of the four-fold hermeneutic associated with the theological tradition. . . .

The greatness of Frye, and the radical difference between his work and that of the great bulk of garden-variety myth criticism, lies in his willingness to raise the issue of community and to draw basic, essentially social, interpretive consequences from the nature of religion as collective representation. (*PU* 69)

In fact, Jameson's central concept of the political unconscious—though often defined in Lévi-Straussian language as a historical *pensée sauvage* and influenced by the Feuerbachian and Durkheimian conceptions of religion—derives from Frye's notion of literature (be it a weaker form of myth or a later stage of ritual) as a "symbolic meditation on the destiny of community."[17] What upsets Jameson about Frye is no longer simply Frye's ahistorical approach, but, more important, Frye's Blakean anagogy—the image of the cosmic body—which Jameson claims privatizes a political anagogy and hence poses the destiny of the human community in an individualistic manner, in terms of the isolated body and personal gratification.[18]

Frye's conflation of ethics and politics gives Jameson the opportunity both to congratulate and to criticize him. Jameson congratulates Frye—the North American liberal version of structuralism—because Frye conceives the central problematic of criticism to be not epistemological but rather ethical, namely the relation of texts to the destiny of human communities. In this sense, Frye is preferable to the French structuralists and poststructuralists since he understands that there is a crucial relationship among desire, freedom, and narrative.

Jameson criticizes Frye because Frye understands this relationship too idealistically and individualistically. In this sense, Frye stands halfway between the *Platonized* notion of desire employed by those who deconstruct the metaphysics of presence and the *politicized* notion of desire promoted by Jameson's Marxist hermeneutics. Frye's *moralized* notion of desire dictated by his "anatomy of romance" (to use Geoffrey Hartman's phrase) constitutes a halfway house.[19] As Jameson notes, "Frye's entire discussion of romance turns on a presupposition—the ethical axis of good and evil—which needs to be historically problematized in its turn, and which will prove to be an ideologeme that articulates a social and historical contradiction" (*PU* 110).

By contrast, the principal attraction of Jameson to the project of Gilles Deleuze and Félix Guattari in *Anti-Oedipus* is precisely their *politicized* notion of desire, which does not simply relegate it to the subjective and psychological spheres. Jameson acknowledges that the "thrust of the argument of the *Anti-Oedipus* is, to be sure, very much in the spirit of the present work, for the concern of its authors is to reassert the specificity of the political content of everyday life and of individual fantasy-experience" (*PU* 22). But Jameson objects to their Nietzschean perspectivist attack on hermeneutic or interpretive activity, and hence their antitotalizing orientation and micropolitical conclusions.

The major problem with Jameson's innovative Marxist hermeneutics is that, like Frye's monumental liberal reconstruction of criticism or M. H. Abrams's magisterial bourgeois reading of romanticism, his viewpoint rests on an unexamined metaphor of translation, an uncritical acceptance of transcoding. In this sense, Geoffrey Hartman's incisive criticisms of Frye and J. Hillis Miller's notorious attack on Abrams render Jameson's project suspect.[20] In an interesting manner, the gallant attempts of Frye to resurrect the romance tradition and the Blakean sense of history, of Abrams to recuperate the humanist tradition and the bourgeois conception of history, and of Jameson to recover the Marxist tradition and the political meaning of history all ultimately revert to and rely on problematic methodological uses of various notions of analogy and homology.[21]

For example, Jameson presupposes homologous relations between ethics and epistemology. This presupposition permits him to distinguish himself from Frye by articulating the differences between moralizing and politicizing the notion of desire. As I noted earlier, Jameson ingeniously shifts the primal scene of criticism from epistemology to ethics. Yet, his attempt to historicize the moralistic elements of Frye encourages him to follow the Nietzschean strategies of the poststructuralists in the realm of ethics. Therefore he arrives at the notion that he must go beyond the binary opposition of good and evil in order to overcome ethics and approach the sphere of politics. This notion leads him to the idea that such overcoming of ethics is requisite for a "positive" hermeneutics and a nonfunctional or anticipatory view of culture.

Three principal mistakes support Jameson's presupposition that analogous and homologous relations obtain between ethics and epistemology. First, he believes that the epistemological decentering of the bourgeois subject can be smoothly translated into the moral sphere as an attack on individualistic ethics of bourgeois subjects. This plausible case of analogy seems to warrant, in his view, more general considerations about the homologous relation between ethics and epistemology. Second, he assumes that the poststructuralist attacks on epistemological and metaphysical binary oppositions can be simply transcoded en bloc to ethical binary oppositions. This assumption rests on the notion that these attacks are merely "misplaced"[22] rather than misguided. Third, Jameson misreads three important moments in modern philosophy, namely, Nietzsche's ill-fated attempt to go beyond good and evil, Hegel's critique of Kantian morality, and Marx's rejection of bourgeois ethics.

There is a fundamental link between the epistemological decentering of the subject and an attack on the individualistic ethics of bourgeois subjects, for the arguments by Spinoza and Hegel against individualistic ethics were accompanied by epistemological hostility to the isolated subject. And as Jameson rightly argues, the distinctive Marxist contribution to the current discourse, which takes "decentering" as its center, is to show that both the subject decentered and the decentering itself are modes of ideological activity that are always already bound to particular groups, communities, and classes at specific stages of capitalist development.

In my view, Jameson goes wrong in trying to relate epistemological moves to ethical ones in ideological terms without giving an account of the collective dynamics that accompany these moves. From the Marxist perspective, all metaphysical, epistemological, and ethical discourses are complex ideological affairs of specific groups, communities, and classes in or across particular societies. These discourses must not be understood in their own terms (which Jameson rightly rejects), nor may one discourse become primary and consequently subordinate other discursive nets (which Jameson often insinuates). Rather, the Marxist aim is to disclose the ideological function and class interest of these evolving discourses in terms of the collective dynamics of the pertinent moment in the historical process. Jameson moves two steps forward by eschewing the metaphysical and epistemological terrains of the poststructuralists; his strategy discredits rather than defeats them, which is appropriate since poststructuralist defeatism is impossible to defeat on its own grounds. Yet Jameson moves a step backward by shifting the battleground to ethics. This shift, as I shall show later, prevents him from employing the Marxist logic of collective dynamics and leads him to call for a "new logic of collective dynamics" (*PU* 294).

Jameson's second mistake is to believe that the poststructuralist attacks on binary oppositions are enacted in the wrong terrains, rather than being wrong attacks. Instead of calling into question the very theoretical attitude or unmasking the ideological activity of "going beyond" binary oppositions, Jameson appropriates the same machinery and directs it to ethical binary oppositions. In this way, his project is akin to poststructuralist ones in the bad sense—or akin to idealist projects, in the Marxist sense. Jameson mistakenly does not object to deconstructionist strategies but rather to where they have been applied. In short, his critique does not go deep enough; that is, he does not disclose *the very form of the strategies themselves as modes of ideological activity* that both conceal power relations and extend mechanisms of control by reproducing the ideological conditions for the reproduction of capitalist social arrangements.

Jameson's third mistake is a threefold misreading: of Nietzsche's attempt to go beyond good and evil, of Hegel's critique of Kantian morality, and of Marx's rejection of bourgeois ethics. For Jameson, Nietzsche's attempt to go beyond good and evil is the ethical analogue to the poststructuralist attempt to go beyond the binary oppositions in metaphysics and epistemology. But surely this is not so. Nietzsche's attempt to go beyond good and evil is, as the subtitle of his text states, "Vorspiel einer Philosophie der Zukunft" (Prelude to a Philosophy of the Future). Nietzsche hardly rests with the aporias of deconstructionists, but rather aligns himself with the genealogical concerns of the "historically minded" in order to get his own positive project off the ground. His profound transvaluation of values is not enacted in order to transcend the moral categories of good and evil, but rather to unmask them, disclose what they conceal, and build on that which underlies such categories. And for Nietzsche, the "reality" that lies beneath these categories is the will to power. *Ressentiment* is one particular expression of the will to power of the weak and oppressed toward the strong and oppressor within traditional Judeo-Christian culture and to a certain extent modern bourgeois European culture.[23] Unlike the deconstructionists, Nietzsche's aim is to debunk and demystify in order to build anew—and the springboard for his "countermovement," his "new gospel of the future," is the will to power.

> Suppose, finally, we succeeded in explaining our entire instinctive life as the development and ramification of *one* basic form of the will—namely, of the will to power, as *my* proposition has it; suppose all organic functions could be traced back to this will to power and one could also find in it the solution of the problem of procreation and nourishment—it is *one* problem—then one would have gained the right to determine *all* efficient force univocally as—*will to power*. The world viewed from inside, the world defined and determined according to its "intelligible character"—it would be "will to power" and nothing else.[24]

Jameson's emulation of poststructuralist strategies in the realm of ethics leads him to root Nietzsche's project in the isolated subject of bourgeois epistemology and offer the doctrine of eternal recurrence as the Nietzschean solution to the problem of good and evil. He writes,

Briefly, we can suggest that, as Nietzsche taught us, the judgmental habit of ethical thinking, of ranging everything in the antagonistic categories of good and evil (or their binary equivalents), is not merely an error but is objectively rooted in the inevitable and inescapable centeredness of every individual consciousness or individual subject: what is good is what belongs to me, what is bad is what belongs to the Other . . . The Nietzschean solution to this constitutional ethical habit of the individual subject—the Eternal Return—is for most of us both intolerable in its rigor and unconvincingly ingenious in the prestidigitation with which it desperately squares its circle. (*PU* 234)

It is necessary to note four points, against Jameson, however. First, like Marx, Nietzsche realizes that all ethical discourse is a communal affair; ethics is a group response to particular historical circumstances. Therefore, bourgeois ethics (tied to the individual subject) is but one communal response among others and certainly not identical or even similar to expressions of traditional Christian morality.[25] Second, Nietzsche's doctrine of eternal recurrence grounds his affirmative attitude toward life (an alternative to that of Christianity, in his view); it is itself an expression of his will to power, but not a "solution" to the binary opposition of good and evil. Third, Nietzsche acknowledges that his "going beyond" good and evil does not result in transcending morality, but rather in establishing a new morality that rests upon precisely that which former moralities concealed and precluded: a will to power that generates a creative, self-transforming, life-enhancing morality. Fourth, Nietzsche, again like Marx, holds that "going beyond" good and evil is not a philosophical or even hermeneutical issue, but rather a genealogical matter linked to a historical "countermovement" that contains a vision of the future. Going beyond good and evil will not result in finding new categories untainted by the double bind, but rather new distinctions of good and evil tied to building new communities or, for Nietzsche, building new "selves."

This building of new communities leads us directly to Jameson's misunderstanding of Hegel's critique of Kantian morality and Marx's rejection of bourgeois ethics. Jameson rightly notes that

one of the great themes of dialectical philosophy, the Hegelian denunciation of the ethical imperative, [is] taken up again by Lukács in his *Theory of the Novel*. On this diagnosis, the *Sollen*, the mesmerization of duty and ethical obligation, necessarily perpetuates a cult of failure and a fetishization of pure, unrealized intention. For moral obligation presupposes a gap between being and duty, and cannot be satisfied with the accomplishment of a single duty and the latter's consequent transformation into being. In order to retain its own characteristic satisfactions, ethics must constantly propose the unrealizable and the unattainable to itself. (*PU* 194)

But Jameson then problematically adds that dialectical philosophy addresses itself to the matter of "going beyond" good and evil and, in contrast to Nietzsche, "proposes a rather different stance (this time, outside the subject in the transindividual, or in other words in History) from which to transcend the double bind of the merely ethical" (*PU* 235).

The problem here is that Jameson reads Hegel through poststructuralist lenses in which "the double bind of the merely ethical" is a philosophical problem that demands categorical transcendence rather than through Marxist lenses in which "the double bind of the merely ethical" is an ideological activity to unmask and transform by collective praxis. This Marxist reading of Hegel is necessary in order to grasp the depths of Marx's rejection of bourgeois ethics. Hegel's disenchantment with Kant's morality was not simply because he believed that the categorical imperative was empty or that the moral ought was unattainable. But rather, more important, Hegel was disenchanted because the way in which Kant separates the real from the ideal requires a philosophical projection of an impossible ideal that both presupposed and concealed a particular social basis, namely, Kant's own specific time and place.[26] In other words, Hegel saw Kant's morality as a *Moralität*—a first-personal matter—that was derivative from a *Sittlichkeit*—a communal matter.

The Hegelian critique of Kantian morality opens the door to a Marxist viewpoint on ethics in two respects. First, it rejects the Kantian conception of what a theory about the nature of ethics must be. Second, it imposes severe limits on the role and function of ethical discourse (which is not reducible to moral convictions) in social change. As David Hoy rightly points out, "in giving up the Kantian metaphilosophical view about what theories of morality can and should do, Hegel is giving up the dream of ideal resolutions of moral conflicts. Conflicts are matters of weighing obligations, and moral obligations have no automatic priority."[27]

On this view, Marx's rejection of bourgeois ethics bears little resemblance to poststructuralist attempts to go beyond good and evil. Rather, Marx's rejection is based on giving up the Kantian dream of ideal resolutions of moral conflicts, giving up the Hegelian dream of philosophical reconciliation of the real and the ideal, and surrendering the poststructuralist dream of philosophical transcendence of metaphysical, epistemological, and ethical double binds.[28] The Marxist concern is with practically overcoming historical class conflicts. Therefore, the Marxist rejection of bourgeois ethics has less to do with attacks on binary oppositions such as good and evil and more to do with the Hegelian subordination of *Moralität* to *Sittlichkeit*. The Marxist aim is to discern an evolving and developing *Sittlichkeit* in the womb of capitalist society, a *Sittlichkeit* whose negative ideal is to resist all forms of reification and exploitation and whose positive ideals are social freedom and class equality.

The Marxist lesson here is that only if one has taken metaphysics, epistemology, and ethics seriously will one be attracted by Heideggerian rhetoric about going beyond metaphysics or Nietzschean rhetoric about going beyond good and evil. If one instead takes history seriously—as do Marx after 1844 and American pragmatism at its best—then metaphysics, epistemology, and ethics are not formidable foes against which to fight nor are the Ali-like shuffles of the deconstructions that "destroy" them impressive performances. On this view, deconstructionists become critically ingenious yet politically deluded ideologues, who rightly attack bourgeois humanism, yet who also become the ideological adornments of late-monopoly-capitalist academies.

Analogies and homologies, no matter how sophisticated and refined, between epistemology and ethics, metaphysics and morals, make sense as long as one clings to the notion that there are two such interrelated yet distinct spheres, disciplines, or discourses. One rejects this notion neither by enabling interdisciplinary moves nor by questing "beyond" both spheres, but rather by viewing the historical process outside the lenses of traditional or contemporary metaphysical, epistemological, and ethical discourses. That is, our history has not posed metaphysical, epistemological, and ethical problems that need to be solved or "gone beyond"; rather, it has left us these problems as imaginative ideological responses to once-pertinent but now defunct problematics.

To resurrect the dead, as bourgeois humanists try to do, is impossible. To attack the dead, as deconstructionists do, is redundant and, ironically, valorizes death. To "go beyond" the dead means either surreptitiously recuperating previous "contents" of life in new forms (Nietzsche) or else deceptively shrugging off the weight of the dead whether by promoting cults of passive, nostalgic "dwelling" (Heidegger) or by creative self-rebegetting and self-redescribing (Emerson, Harold Bloom, Richard Rorty).

What is distinctive about the Marxist project is that it neither resurrects, attacks, nor attempts to "go beyond" metaphysical, epistemological, and ethical discourses. It aims rather at transforming present practices—the remaining life—against the backdrop of previous discursive and political practices, against the "dead" past. Marxism admonishes us to "let the dead bury the dead"; acknowledges that this "dead" past weighs like an incubus upon prevailing practices; and accents our capacities to change these practices. Marx ignores, sidesteps, and avoids discussions of metaphysical, epistemological, and ethical issues not because he shuns his inescapable imprisonment in binary oppositions, remains insulated from metaphysical sedimentations, or hesitates to make knowledge claims and moral judgments, but rather because, for him, the bourgeois forms of discourse on such issues are "dead," rendered defunct by his particular moment in the historical process. The capitalist mode of production—with its own particular mystifying forms of social relations, technologies, and bureaucracies and its aim of world domination—requires forms of theoretical and practical activity, and modes of writing, acting, and organizing heretofore unknown to the "dead" past.

From this Marxist view, the deconstructionist disclosing and debunking of the binary oppositions in the Western philosophical tradition is neither a threat to European civilization nor a misplaced critique better enacted against the binary oppositions in ethics. Rather, deconstructions are, like the Left-Hegelian critiques of Marx's own day, interesting yet impotent bourgeois attacks on the forms of thought and categories of a "dead" tradition, a tradition that stipulates the lineage and sustains the very life of these deconstructions. My claim here is not simply that these attacks valorize textuality at the expense of power, but more important, that they are symbiotic with their very object of criticism: that is, they remain alive only as long as they give life to their enemy. In short, deconstructionist assaults must breathe life into metaphysical, epistemological, and ethical discourses if their critiques are to render these discourses lifeless.[29]

The major ideological task of the Marxist intervention in present philosophical and critical discussions becomes that of exposing the reactionary and conservative consequences of bourgeois humanism, the critical yet barren posture of poststructuralist skepticism and deconstructionist ironic criticism, and the utopian and ultimately escapist character of the Emersonian gnosticism of Bloom and the Emersonian pragmatism of Rorty. The negative moment of Jameson's Marxist hermeneutics initiates this urgent task. The basic problem with the positive moment in his project is precisely its utopianism, especially in linking the Nietzschean quest beyond good and evil to Marxist theory and praxis. In a crucial passage, Jameson writes,

> It is clear, indeed, that not merely Durkheim's notion of collective "consciousness," but also the notion of "class consciousness," as it is central in a certain Marxist tradition, rests on an unrigorous and figurative assimilation of the consciousness of the individual subject to the dynamics of groups. The Althusserian and post-structuralist critique of these and other versions of the notion of a "subject of history" may readily be admitted. The alternatives presented by the Althusserians, however . . . have a purely negative or second-degree critical function, and offer no new conceptual categories. What is wanted here—and it is one of the most urgent tasks for Marxist theory today—is a whole new logic of collective dynamics, with categories that escape the taint of some mere application of terms drawn from individual experience (in that sense, even the concept of praxis remains a suspect one). (*PU* 294)

It comes as little surprise that Jameson's plea for a "new logic" resembles Jacques Derrida's call for a "new reason," since Jameson enacts the deconstructionist strategy of going beyond binary oppositions. At this level of comparison, the major difference is that Jameson banks his positive hermeneutics on this "new logic," whereas Derrida merely invokes "new reason" in his rhetoric before returning to his negative anti-hermeneutical activity. Yet, from a Marxist perspective, Jameson's basis for a positive hermeneutics is utopian in the bad sense; for it is a utopianism that rests either on no specifiable historical forces potentially capable of actualizing it or on the notion that every conceivable historical force embodies it. Jameson clearly favors the latter formulation.

> The preceding analysis entitles us to conclude that all class consciousness of whatever type is Utopian insofar as it expresses the unity of a collectivity; yet it must be added that this proposition is an allegorical one. The achieved collectivity or organic group of whatever kind—oppressors fully as much as oppressed—is Utopian not in itself, but only insofar as all such collectivities are themselves *figures* for the ultimate concrete collective life of an achieved Utopian or classless society. Now we are in a better position to understand how even hegemonic or ruling-class culture and ideology are Utopian, not in spite of their instrumental function to secure and perpetuate class privilege and power, but rather precisely because that function is also in and of itself the affirmation of collective solidarity. (*PU* 290–91)

This exorbitant claim illustrates not only utopianism gone mad, but also a Marxism in deep desperation, as if any display of class solidarity keeps alive a discredited class analysis. Even more important, this claim, similar to the thin historicism and glib optimism of Bloom's Emersonian gnosticism and Rorty's Emersonian pragmatism, reflects the extent to which Jameson remains within the clutches of American culture. Given the barbarous atrocities and large-scale horrors inflicted by hegemonic ruling classes in Europe, Africa, Asia, and Latin America, only a Marxist thinker entrenched in the North American experience could even posit the possibility of ruling-class consciousness figuratively being "in its very nature Utopian" (*PU* 289). Benjamin's tempered utopianism or Bloch's doctrine of hope certainly do not support such Marxist flights of optimism or lead to such an American faith in the future.

Jameson's bad utopianism is but a symptom of the major political shortcoming of his work: his texts have little or no political consequences. On the one hand, his works have little or no political praxis as texts; that is, they speak, refer, or allude to no political movement or formation in process with which his texts have some connection.[30] They thus remain academic Marxist texts which, for the most part, are confined to specialists and antispecialists, Marxists and anti-Marxists, in the academy. On the other hand, his works have little or no political praxis in yet another sense: they provide little or no space for either highlighting issues of political praxis within its theoretical framework or addressing modes of political praxis in its own academic setting.[31]

Jameson's works are therefore too theoretical; his welcome call for a political hermeneutics is too far removed from the heat of political battles. By their failure sufficiently to reflect, and reflect on, the prevailing political strife, Jameson's works reenact the very process of reification that they condemn. Surely, the present fragmentation of the North American left, the marginalization of progressive micropolitical formations, and the rampant mystification of North American life and culture impose severe constraints on Jameson's textual practice; nonetheless, more substantive reflections on "practical" political strategies seem appropriate. My plea here is not anti-intellectual or antitheoretical, but rather a call for more sophisticated theory aware of and rooted in the present historical and political conjuncture in American capitalist civilization.

Of course, Jameson's own social positioning—an American professor of French writing Marxist hermeneutical works—solicits expectations of self-obsession, political isolation, and naive optimism. Yet Jameson's texts are not self-obsessed, though his style of elusive, elliptical sentences (which appear more contrapuntal than dialectical) borders on a Frenchifying of English prose. Jameson's texts are not isolated, monadic works, despite the consistent absence of any acknowledgments to fellow critics or colleagues in his prefaces, yet they direct us to look at France rather than at ourselves. Hence his critical treatments of Sartre, Lévi-Strauss, Althusser, Lacan, Bénichou, Deleuze, Guattari, and Lyotard are nearly hermetic and he is relatively silent on distinguished American critics such as his former Yale colleague, Paul de Man, or noteworthy historically minded critics like R. P. Blackmur, Philip Rahv, or Irving Howe. Jameson is not a naive optimist, but his sophisticated utopianism finally seems to be part and parcel of the American penchant for unquenchable faith in history and irresistible hope for romantic triumph.

My main point here is not simply that Jameson write less Frenchified, expand his fascinating Marxist discourse to include talented American friends and foes, and situate himself more clearly within the American Marxist tradition. Rather, Jameson's own historical predicament—his own conceptual tools, academic audience, utopian proclivities, and political praxis—should become more an object of his dialectical deliberations. Nevertheless, Jameson has done more than any other American hermeneutical thinker in achieving intellectual breakthroughs and accenting theoretical challenges of the Marxist tradition in our postmodern times. The path he has helped blaze now awaits those, including himself, who will carry on with the urgent tasks not simply of taking seriously history and politics, but more specifically, of taking seriously our intellectual, American, and socialist identities as writers of texts, shapers of attitudes, beneficiaries of imperialist fruits, inheritors of hegemonic sensibilities, and historical agents who envision a socialist future.

NOTES

Note: I would like to extend my gratitude to Jonathan Arac, Stanley Aronowitz, Paul Bové, Fredric Jameson, David Langston, Michael Sprinker, and Anders Stephanson for their incisive comments and criticisms of an earlier version of this essay.

1. Fredric Jameson, *Marxism and Form: Twentieth-Century Dialectical Theories of Literature*

(Princeton, N.J.: Princeton Univ. Press, 1971). Further references to this work will be given paren-thetically as *MF*. *The Prison-House of Language: A Critical Account of Structuralism and Russian Formalism* (Princeton, N.J.: Princeton Univ. Press, 1972). Further references to this text will be given parenthetically as *PHL*. *The Political Unconscious: Narrative as a Socially Symbolic Act* (Ithaca, N.Y.: Cornell Univ. Press, 1981). Further references to this book will be given parenthetically as *PU*. I shall include in this "trilogy" *Fables of Aggression: Wyndham Lewis, the Modernist as Fascist* (Berkeley: Univ. of California Press, 1979) since it was originally conceived to be a part of *The Political Unconscious* but was separated, enlarged, and published as an independent work.

2. In the preface to *PU*, Jameson refers to the "flawed yet monumental achievements . . . of the greatest Marxist philosopher of modern times, Georg Lukács" (13).

3. Fredric Jameson, *Sartre: The Origins of a Style* (New Haven, Conn.: Yale Univ. Press, 1961).

4. Jameson's treatment of Adorno in chapter 1 of *MF* is based on an earlier essay that appeared in *Salmagundi*, no. 5 (1967): 3–43.

5. For Jameson's view of Adorno's negative dialectics as an aesthetic ideal, see *PU*, 52, n. 29.

6. The major difference between Adorno and Derrida (or de Man), between a dialectical deconstructionist and a poststructural deconstructionist, is that the theoretical impasse the dialectician reaches is not viewed as an ontological, metaphysical, or epistemological aporia, but rather as a historical limitation owing to a determinate contradiction as yet unlodged because of an impotent social praxis or an absence of an effective historical revolutionary agent. For interesting comments on this matter, see Stanley Aronowitz, *The Crisis in Historical Materialism: Class, Politics and Culture in Marxist Theory* (New York: Praeger, 1981), 24–34.

7. See also *MF*, 373, where Jameson states that "we take a point of view not so much philosophical as hermeneutic."

8. Herbert Marcuse, *Eros and Civilization* (New York: Random House, 1955), 29, quoted in *MF*, 113.

9. This traditional hermeneutic strategy is enunciated in the following passage in *MF*: "Thus the process of criticism is not so much an interpretation of content as it is a revealing of it, a laying bare, a restoration of the original message, the original experience, beneath the distortions of the various kinds of censorship that have been at work upon it; and this revelation takes the form of an explanation of why the content was so distorted and is thus inseparable from a description of the mechanisms of this censorship itself." (404).

10. Note also his remark in *PU*: "That life is meaningless is not a proposition that need be inconsistent with Marxism, whose affirmation is the quite different one that History is meaningful, however absurd organic life may happen to be" (261).

11. For Jameson's interesting remarks on religion, see *MF*, 116–18 and *PU*, 70, 292.

12. Jameson is one of the few Marxists who explicitly rejects a realist epistemological position. See *MF*, 365–66. Note that he invokes the early work of the then American-style Marxist Sidney Hook at this point. For a persuasive treatment of the "textual idealism" of poststructuralists, see Richard Rorty, "Nineteenth-Century Idealism and Twentieth-Century Textualism," in *Consequences of Pragmatism* (Minneapolis: Univ. of Minnesota Press, 1982), 139–59.

13. *PU*, 139, 226.

14. *PU*, 97, 141. Bloch puts forward this complex notion in "Nonsynchronism and Dialectics," *New German Critique*, no. 11 (1977): 22–38. For Jameson's powerful critique of teleological and genetic forms of Marxism, see "Marxism and Historicism," *New Literary History* 11 (1979): 41–73.

15. *MF*, 402.

16. Fredric Jameson, "Criticism in History," in *The Weapons of Criticism*, ed. Norman Rudich (Palo Alto, Calif.: Ramparts Press, 1976), 31–50.

17. For the Lévi-Straussian language, see *PU*, 167 and for Frye's notion of literature, see *PU*, 70.

18. Yet I remain unconvinced that the cosmic body in Blake's anagogy is even roughly analogous to the individualistic bourgeois body. See Northrop Frye, *Anatomy of Criticism: Four Essays* (Princeton, N.J.: Princeton Univ. Press, 1957), 119f.

19. Geoffrey H. Hartman, "Ghostlier Demarcations: The Sweet Science of Northrop Frye," in *Beyond Formalism: Literary Essays 1958–1970* (New Haven, Conn.: Yale Univ. Press, 1970), 40.

20. Hartman, "Ghostlier Demarcations," 24–41. J. Hillis Miller, "Tradition and Difference," *Diacritics* 2 (Winter 1972): 6–13.

21. Note Jameson's remarks in *MF*: "This formal character of the concept of freedom is precisely what lends itself to the work of political hermeneutics. It encourages analogy: assimilating the material prisons to the psychic ones, it serves as a means of unifying all these separate levels of existence, functioning, indeed, as a kind of transformational equation whereby the data characteristic of one may be converted into the terms of other" (85).

22. Jameson explicitly states in *PU*: "I will argue that the critique [by poststructuralism] is misplaced" (21).

23. For the classic reply to Nietzsche on this matter, though not a thoroughly satisfactory one, see Max Scheler, *Ressentiment*, trans. William Holdheim, ed. Lewis A. Coser (New York: Free Press, 1961), 43–46, 79–89, 95–97, 103–11, 114.

24. Friedrich Nietzsche, *Beyond Good and Evil*, trans. Walter Kaufmann (New York: Vintage Books, 1966), 48.

25. Nietzsche remarks repeatedly that modern bourgeois European Culture is an amalgam of various traditions, only one of which is the Judeo-Christian tradition. Yet what Nietzsche stresses, and Jameson ignores, is that Christian morality is a weapon of the oppressed against the oppressor, not simply a symptom of impotence. On this point, Jameson follows not Nietzsche but Sartre. "The moral attitude appears when technical and social conditions render positive forms of conduct impossible. Ethics is a collection of idealistic tricks intended to enable us to live the life imposed on us by the poverty of our resources and the insufficiency of our techniques." This passage is an unpublished note of Sartre's quoted by Simone de Beauvoir, *Force of Circumstance*, trans. Richard Howard (New York: G. P. Putnam, 1965), 199.

26. This point is made most emphatically by Lucien Goldmann, *Immanuel Kant* (London: New Left Books, 1971), 170–79. Hegel puts forward this critique in *Philosophy of Right*, trans. T. M. Knox (Oxford: Oxford Univ. Press, 1967), 89–103 and *Philosophy of Mind, Part Three of the Encyclopedia of the Philosophical Sciences* (Oxford: Clarendon Press, 1971), 253–91. Jameson clearly grasps this point when he states, "as an ideological field, conceptions of ethics depend on a shared class or group homogeneity, and strike a suspicious compromise between the private experience of the individual and those values or functional needs of the collectivity which ethics rewrites or recodes in terms of interpersonal relationships." Yet, unlike Hegel and Marx, Jameson clings to the notion that the historicizing of ethics results in a "going beyond" good and evil. In the same paragraph quoted he continues, "In our time, ethics, wherever it makes its reappearance, may be taken as the sign of an intent to mystify, and in particular to replace the more complex and ambivalent judgements of a more properly political and dialectical perspective with the more comfortable simplifications of a binary myth." The basic point here is that Hegel, Marx, and Jameson agree that bourgeois ethics cannot do justice to the richness of moral experience without embarrassing equivocation. Yet Jameson believes that this has something to do with the binary oppositions of good and evil, whereas Hegel and Marx rightly hold that such poststructuralist itching does not require scratching but rather getting rid of the source of the itch. The passage quoted is from Jameson, *Fables of Aggression*, 56.

27. David Couzens Hoy, "Hegel's Morals," *Dialogue* 20.1 (1981): 99.

28. For a detailed examination of Marx's critique of Kant and Hegel on ethical approaches, see Cornel West, "Ethics, Historicism and the Marxist Tradition," Ph.D. diss., Princeton Univ., 1980, 28–74.

29. As Richard Rorty notes, "the non-Kantian *is* a parasite—flowers could not sprout from the dialectical vine unless there were an edifice into whose chinks it could insert its tendrils. No constructors, no deconstructors. No norms, no perversions. Derrida (like Heidegger) would have no writing to do unless there were a 'metaphysics of presence' to overcome. Without the fun of stamping out

parasites, on the other hand, no Kantian would bother to continue building.'' See "Philosophy as a Kind of Writing: An Essay on Derrida," *Consequences of Pragmatism*, 108. This is precisely the philosophical "game" Marx ignores, sidesteps, and avoids. For Rorty's brilliant historical situating of this modern "game," see *Philosophy and the Mirror of Nature* (Princeton, N.J.: Princeton Univ. Press, 1979); for a leftist critique of this text, see Cornel West, "The Politics of American Neopragmatism," in *Post-Analytic Philosophy*, ed. John Rajchman and Cornel West (New York: Columbia Univ. Press, 1985), 259–75.

30. For his brief characterization of the French and American left, see *PU*, 54, 31.

31. Jameson does address the role of the Marxist intellectual in the academy in his essay "Marxism and Teaching." *New Political Science*, no. 2/3. (Fall/Winter 1979/1980): 31–36.

Chapter 8
Feeling Global:
John Berger and Experience
Bruce Robbins

Don't start with the good old things, but
the bad new ones.—Bertolt Brecht

I

Much of John Berger's writing in the past decade has had to do with peasants.
What Berger calls "peasant experience" is the explicit subject of the short
fictions of *Pig Earth* (1979); it is the point of departure and social counterweight
of his essay on European migrant workers, *A Seventh Man* (1975); it provides
the privileged field of instances drawn upon by the art criticism of *About Looking*
(1980), the volume of and about photographic narration, *Another Way of Telling*
(1982)—like *A Seventh Man*, a collaboration with the photographer Jean Mohr—
and even the looser, less located reflections on time, love, and art in *And Our
Faces, My Heart, Brief as Photos* (1984).[1] Considering this choice of subject
matter in the light of Berger's own experience—for some years he has shared
in the labors of a peasant village of Haute-Savoie and he says he plans to remain
there—reviewers have wondered "whether his notion of peasants isn't an
idealized abstraction of rough-hewn nineteenth-century souls who aren't alienated
from their labor"[2] and have suggested that his "turning to the margins," whether
idealized or not, can hardly be anything other than "an attempt to escape the
hopelessness he finds in our culture by entering a world still heavy with the
density of Being."[3]

The first pages of *Pig Earth* offer evidence both for and against the charge of
pastoral simplification. They describe in unsettling detail the slaughter of a cow.
The abrupt unpleasantness of the scene seems intended as an initial guarantee
that unpleasant specifics will not, as in pastoral, be rounded out. On the other
hand, the animal's death might also be read as a bid to dissolve peasant specifics
in a "human" universal. Since it is a universal truth that homo sapiens kill

animals, the humanist can always use the killing of animals in order to slip the reader past the actual diversity of historical men and women to the putative species-being of a universal "Man." Berger's implicit argument, then, would be that the experience of peasants slaughtering a cow is representative of human experience itself. Although the fingers of the ordinary urban shopper are not permitted to touch the meat of life, the peasant alone can "experience" the universals of "Experience." And in so doing, Berger suggests, peasants also handle their own deaths: again and again the book parallels the deaths of animals and the deaths of those who care for them. But city dwellers, whose life is mediated through advertising and industrial abattoirs, cannot grasp its defining extremities: "Publicity, situated in a future continually deferred, excludes the present and so eliminates all becoming, all development. Experience is impossible within it" (*WS* 153). In their spontaneous present-tense fronting of the essentials of life, Berger's peasants preserve "experience" and thus form a pastoral refuge for the truly human.

Berger's work demystifies rural stereotypes, observes a scrupulous self-consciousness, experiments freshly with forms of narrative and authorship; it also commemorates the good old days, once again, in an uncorrupted countryside. So late a version of pastoral cannot expect to be greeted as the dernier cri. Nevertheless, I want to suggest here that what is most interesting about this writing is precisely its engagement with our impalpable postmodernity. Granted that peasant culture "is hardly an option" for us now,[4] the reader of the 1980s has more choices than merely to take or to leave the Frankfurt-schoolish pessimism about all things contemporary that trails in its wake. Almost half a century has gone by since Brecht told his friend Walter Benjamin to start with the bad new things, and the relation between this phrase and its opposite can be assumed to require reformulation. Whether or not we can usefully read Berger's peasants may depend on how well we can re-read our bad new things.

Literary modernism and academic departments of literature took shape in roughly the same period, and there are reasons for suspecting a complicity between them—between, say, the ejection of history from certain modernist texts and, simultaneously, from the New Critical apparatus that canonized them.[5] If this suspicion is justified, the awkward compound "post-modernism" can be understood both as the literary disturbance that produced Pynchon and Creeley and as a disturbance in the institutions of criticism. At least for those of us who study and teach the so-called humanities, postmodernity seems to present itself in large part as an unease with the humanistic principles that (so recently) brought our disciplines into being and (so powerfully) continue to shape our practice. One source of this unease may be the naturalization of Marxist thought, which has slowly passed (perhaps because it could free itself from the fortunes of "actually existing socialism") from the status of an exotic foreign dogma to an assured if limited place within humanist "common sense." On the other hand, this unease also seems to stem from the working vocabulary and operational procedures that Marxism and humanism have thus come to share. It is at this conjuncture that John Berger commands attention. He is both a "Permanent Red"—in 1979 he reissued this collection of twenty-five-year-old art criticism under the same defiant title—and a man of letters in the old Arnoldian sense. Writing outside the shelter of the university, he has tried for a quarter of a century to negotiate between a broadly Marxist view of the world and a broad nonacademic readership. He has as good a claim as anyone to have fought for and added to a new Marxist-humanist "common sense." And if he is thus implicated in its strains, compromises, and incoherences, by the same token his work is a valuable indicator of its latent powers and directions.

In the "Historical Afterword" to *Pig Earth*, Berger defends his interest in peasants as an effort to retrieve and preserve their neglected experience: "to dismiss peasant experience as belonging only to the past, as having no relevance to modern life, to imagine that the thousands of years of peasant culture leave no heritage for the future . . . to continue to maintain, as has been maintained for centuries, that peasant experience is marginal to civilisation, is to deny the value of too much history and too many lives" (*PE* 211-12). The issue here is the value of "experience." Adopting the vocabulary of humanism, Berger adopts along with it the assumption that writers like himself are enjoined by a sort of Hippocratic oath to "save lives"—to recover and protect the "heritage" of experience for its own sake, out of respect for life itself. The argument has immediate power: who cares to admit to disrespect for life? However, this view of humanist scholarship, in which a generous, democratic indiscriminateness seems to guarantee ideological neutrality, does not correspond to the inevitable selectivity of actual and potential practice. Worse, it sustains the mirage of a disinterested, nonideological tradition that would merely pay homage to what has happened—if not what the best have known and said, then what the rest have been through. Reverence for experience thus becomes a tool of mystification.

Berger also follows out a more convincing line of thought. The famous conservatism of the peasant is that of a culture of "survival," he suggests (*PE* 196), and therefore particularly suited to the 1980s, when hopes of revolutionary progress have (temporarily) given way to a scramble to avoid extinction. Commanding respect as the prime mover of twentieth-century revolutions, the peasant is now also a guide to conservationism and disarmament. This is a version of humanist practice in its most frequent Marxist inflection: the experience that needs to be salvaged, raised to canonical status, and propagated is assumed to be that of the proletariat, which is the locus of humanity's struggle to liberate itself and consequently of the creation of new values. But this position too is subject to the critique of "experience" and of its place in the human sciences that is one of the most important developments of recent years. "Experience, though noon auctoritee/Were in this world, is right ynogh for me," says the

Wife of Bath. But in a number of different fields, it has been noted that experience is no longer an opponent of authority: it has become authority itself. In ethnology, James Clifford has pointed out the powers and presupositions hidden away in the participant-observer's innocent "I was there."[6] In philosophy, when Althusser admonished Sartre that "Marxism is not a humanism," he was suggesting among other things that human experience (judged by the standard of his "science") is a history of errors and illusions. This proposition undermines a cornerstone of the humanities: the assumption that past experience is fraught with values that are worthy of being extracted and brought forward in canons and traditions to guide the present. A challenge to experience is a challenge to the fundamental practices of salvage and tradition building which, in disciplines like literary criticism and historiography, have allowed Marxists and humanists to come together. Long vulnerable to various theoretical attacks, experience now assumes a new importance as the center of debate about humanist practice.

The editor of History Workshop's *People's History and Socialist Theory* (1981)—one of the several places where, pace Berger, "peasant experience" is in no danger of neglect—devotes a preface to the defense of its project—"the recovery of subjective experience"—which concedes, however, that "the notion of 'real life experience' is certainly in need of critical scrutiny."[7] One full-scale scrutiny appears in Perry Anderson's *Arguments within English Marxism* (1980), where "experience" is taken as a crucial weakness of E. P. Thompson and of Marxist-humanist historiography in general. For Thompson, "experience is the privileged medium in which consciousness of reality awakens and creative response to it stirs." But this account "is irreconcilable with the blinkering from reality and the depth of disaster which such salient experiences as religious faith or national loyalty have brought upon those in their grip. Althusser wrongly identifies experience only with such illusions: Thompson inverts this error, identifying experience essentially with insight and learning."[8] The word appears in two senses: in the minimal, neutral sense of "subjective reaction . . . to objective events," and in the more loaded sense "of a *lesson*" that those who live through history learn from it—in other words, knowledge. Experience is both "mere" experience and the usable knowledge gained from it. Everyone has the first, but the second, especially with regard to "social relations," is rare. Anderson thus accuses Thompson's humanist rhetoric of "unconsciously transferring the virtues and powers of the (more restricted) second type to the (more general) first type of experience. The efficacy of the one is fused with the universality of the other"—the result being an exaggeration of the extent to which people are conscious, creative agents of history.[9]

In the field of literary criticism, Anderson's critique of Thompson is paralleled by Terry Eagleton's critique of Raymond Williams, in whose work "the insistence on experience, this passionate premium placed upon the 'lived' . . . supplies at once the formidable power and drastic limitation."[10] Eagleton traces this theme back to the humanist heritage of F. R. Leavis: "To combat 'ideology,' *Scrutiny* pointed to 'experience'—as though that, precisely, were not ideology's homeland." In what Eagleton calls the "Left Leavisism" of Williams, experience again draws a veil over ideological determinations, programmatically refusing the notion "that 'ordinary people' were not, after all, the true creators of 'meanings and values.'" [11] This is the vulnerable spot of the taken for granted (experience "must be the only word you use recurrently that is not given an entry in *Keywords*"—a gap filled in the 1983 revised edition) where Williams is also prodded by the interlocutors of *Politics and Letters*. They suggest to him that "the epistemological privilege of experience" in his work implies a "domain of direct truth," "a kind of pristine contact between the subject and the reality in which this subject is immersed." And Williams concedes both (in his words) "the impossibility of understanding contemporary society from experience" and the conclusions the interviewers draw concerning the limits of literary criticism: "It is not possible to work back from texts to structures of feeling to experiences to social structures. There is a deep disjunction between the literary text from which an experience can be reconstituted and the total historical process at the time." [12]

This concession disconnects literary criticism from the original source of power that has, for example, allowed a professor like Williams to become a national figure: the claim to serve as a repository safeguarding what is true and valuable in the national past. Without the authority of "experience," it is not clear where criticism can go but down. In a magisterial attempt to mediate between humanist and Althusserian attitudes, Richard Johnson concludes that critics of culture and ideology have arrived at an "impasse." If the humanist "move into the experiential" tends to ignore determining factors located "behind men's backs," it can at least speak about the troubles men and women see in front of them; and its critics, on the other hand, seem to achieve a more comprehensive view "at the cost of any real connection with a popular politics." [13] Somewhat less lucidly, Terry Eagleton's *Walter Benjamin, Or Towards a Revolutionary Criticism* (1981) leaves the reader in a similar bind. The book opens by discovering in Benjamin a protodeconstructionist whose version of the seventeenth century (in the *Origin of German Tragic Drama*) serves as antidote to the agrarian "unified sensibility" projected there by the humanism of Eliot and Leavis. However, the book also uses Benjamin—no less strangely—as the excuse for an enthusiastic critique of deconstruction, and in particular of its pretensions as a guide to revolutionary practice. Deconstruction, which helps purge the left of its residual Leavisite humanism, seems unable to duplicate or rival humanism's hold over feelings and actions. The bad new days start here: with the need to replace a humanist vocabulary that has been discredited along with the parties that have used it, and the equal need for a theoretical clarity that in interpreting the world would not renounce the drive to change it.

II

"Stranded between social democracy and Stalinism, his political options were narrow indeed. There was little left to him but 'experience.' . . . "[14] Eagleton's tactical unbending toward Benjamin's "idealism" might also be stretched to cover John Berger, who shares Benjamin's ambivalence about modernity and has borrowed freely both from the open nostalgia of "The Storyteller" and from the embrace of the media in "The Work of Art in the Age of Mechanical Reproduction." Benjamin can be forgiven because, in a time of limited political options, his retreat into "experience" also expanded and discriminated its categories. Does not Berger do the same? Clearly, the criticisms addressed to Williams and Thompson are pertinent to his work as well. He speaks both of and to ordinary experience: in something like the real language of men and women, neither academically exclusive nor carefully placed *sous rature*, his writing is shamelessly (if also strangely, as I will point out) empathetic, an effort to articulate how others construct the world. The ideological limits of "experience" are built into the literary form of this project. However, one must also say that the same writing reflects Berger's own experience, which has not been ordinary. In particular, it has been extraordinarily international—a key term in the "experience" discussion.

Referring to E. P. Thompson's *The Making of the English Working Class*, Perry Anderson argues that the absence of the international is one crippling consequence of the privileging of experience: "international dimensions of English working-class history" are missing, Anderson says, since "social revolutions abroad," for example, "cannot be entered as self-activity of the working class of England."[15] Pointing out a parallel lack of "foreign or overseas developments" in Raymond Williams's account of the 1840s, the interviewers of *Politics and Letters* suggest again that "the Parisian insurrections of 1848" could not be measured as an influence "because 1848 was not a national experience in the direct sense." Nor was the Irish famine: "if we consult the two maps of either the official ideology of the period or the recorded subjective experience of its novels, neither of them extended to include this catastrophe right on their doorstep, causally connected to socio-political processes in England." As Williams admits, we cannot expect that the (all-important) knowledge of how to act within "an integrated world economy" will turn up in the nets of literary criticism, for the movements of the world economy for the most part could not register in everyday consciousness, and thus—this is the rule that gives exceptions like Conrad and Pynchon their special interest—could not leave a literary record.[16]

But here, on the international border of the "experience" debate, it becomes interesting to listen to John Berger. In a number of ways, global movement has become an unusually large and unusually conscious part of his experience. For example, international ownership and exhibition of art objects and the existence of an international canon make an art critic like Berger *structurally* a cosmopolitan—unlike the literary critic, whose reproducible objects do not require the critic's change of place and who in any case is free to choose a respectable provinciality. In addition, the canonizing activities of the art critic are more directly exposed to pressure from the worldwide fluctuations of the market. Without prying any deeper into Berger's biography, it is safe to say that by profession alone he has had more direct experience of international determinants than is "ordinary." More to the point, this experience appears in the literature he has produced, whether as a central theme (as in *A Seventh Man*) or as a peculiar perturbation in the margins of the novels, the film scripts, even the art criticism. The same writing that can be read as a humanist's attempt to save the brand of experience he knows, endangered by the modern world, by finding refuge for it in the confines of a knowable (peasant) community, can also be read, more interestingly, as a series of preparatory inroads into the obscure, uniquely modern no-man's-land of global experience—not as a reduction but as an expansion of experience, in which sections of the impalpable but determining realm of the international begin to solidify and become sensuously present. Reading Berger, we can recognize that we have not yet learned how to "feel global."

To begin with, it is important to see how much of Berger's work does not simply retreat into the local. In a review of *Pig Earth*, Terry Eagleton complains of Berger's respectful fidelity to the "inevitably partial consciousness" of his peasant subjects—in other words, to the categories of their experience. But as Eagleton sees, this is a strange remark to make "to the author of *The Moment of Cubism.*"[17] As a champion of the cubists, Berger was of course celebrating paintings whose figures "when found . . . may have little connection with the sensuous experience of a body" (*SFP* 59). His description of cubism in terms of "interjacency" and "interaction" insists on the act of making visible a *relationship* that is not ordinarily available to the senses in the way an object is. In order to bridge the gap between cubism and "common sense," he repeatedly evokes the phrase "action at a distance"—the "traditional terms" in which Faraday posed the problem whose solution would be the "field of force" (*SFP* 67, 99). Challenging experience with the apparent anomaly of determination without visible agency, the phrase is worth pausing over: "action at a distance" might almost be the emblem of the international problematic Berger introduces into everyday national consciousness.

Behind the cosmopolitan best-seller that tries to milk exotic politics and international terrorism for every ounce of sterile sensation, there is at least one genuine problem of twentieth-century consciousness: how to measure the domestic weight of foreign revolution. This might be expressed as a problem of rhetoric: to what extent does each metaphor (the structurally similar event happening elsewhere) become a metonymy (effectively connected with processes underway here)?

152 □ BRUCE ROBBINS

Berger's writings, which are as cosmopolitan as those of Harold Robbins, are more useful in formulating such questions. Should his translation of Aimé Césaire's *Cahier d'un retour au pays natal* (*Return to My Native Land*—note that the detachment of "cahier" has been deleted and the idea of possession somewhat strengthened) and his fondness for Césaire's term "unique people" be understood as a wishful identification with a *négritude* he can never possess? Or, on the contrary—coming out at a time (1969) when the later history of the national-liberation movements was already beginning to reveal the impossibility of any "return" to traditional cultural identity—is his translation the bitter embrace of Césaire's knowledge that there are no "home" cultures, only "unique" ones? To the European or North American reader, Césaire's Martinique has more force in the latter reading.

In the novel *A Painter of Our Time* (1958), a suave, hateful art collector and diplomat named Sir Gerald Banks—as cosmopolitan as the finance capital his name suggests—is played off against the naive but positive provinciality of a neighborhood painter-butcher. The intended flow of sympathy is clear. At the same time, the reader is expected to feel as loyal to Lavin, the painter and exiled revolutionary of the title, as Lavin himself remains loyal to the political hopes of his distant homeland—and to its remembered organic life; characteristically, Berger conflates "revolution" and "experience." The local is celebrated both here and elsewhere: where is the reader supposed to be located? The celebration is also disrupted by Lavin's English wife. When he leaves eventless England at the end of the novel to return to where the action is (Hungary in 1956), he also leaves her. Poor in passionate political experience of her own (as Berger has made to seem inevitable in England), she has fallen in love with his, and both Lavin and Berger appear to despise this vicarious, secondhand fastening onto another's commitment. But of course the reader—like "John," the narrator—is precisely in the position of the wife: obliged to invest libidinal energies from afar in someone else's revolution.

Lavin is both a "native" and (for almost the entire novel) an exile, and in consequence the reader who shares his consciousness might be said to suffer an international dislocation. Is it possible that all Berger's natives are (also) exiles? If so, then readers are confronting not exotic Others whose difference might discourage their own activity but semblables who invite them to see all action in its new and difficult global terms. In this case, we could no longer describe Berger's literary project as "realist" in any simple sense. There is something elusive, for example, about even the most solid object of his supposed realism, "peasant experience." Discussing "Millet's ambition to paint previously unpainted experience," Berger uses "experience" as a synonym for "subject-matter" (*AL* 71). But when he explains "the writer's relationship with the place and the people he writes about" in *Pig Earth*, it is astonishingly hard to tell whether the "experience" he refers to is theirs or his own:

The act of writing is nothing except the act of approaching the experience written about. . . . To approach experience, however, is not like approaching a house. . . . Experience is indivisible and continuous, at least within a single lifetime and perhaps over many lifetimes. I never have the impression that my experience is entirely my own, and it often seems to me that it preceded me. In any case, experience folds upon itself, refers backwards and forwards to itself. . . . And so the act of approaching a given moment of experience involves both scrutiny (closeness) and the capacity to connect (distance). (*PE* 6)

When he says, a few lines later, "My writing about peasants separates me from them and brings me close to them" (*PE* 7), it seems that he has been speaking about "peasant experience" all along. But for most of the passage, "experience" belongs to anyone, or no one.

This vagueness as to the exact location of experience permits the odd inference that peasants do not in fact possess experience. And when Berger asserts that the "life" of the village is itself a fiction, like his own fictions, the ostensible object of his subjective naturalism dissolves into thin air. "What distinguishes the life of a village is that it is also a *a living portrait of itself* . . . constructed . . . out of opinions, stories, eye-witness reports, legends, comments and hearsay. . . . Without such a portrait . . . the village would have been forced to doubt its own existence" (*PE* 9). In allowing for the fictionality of peasant life, Berger stresses its vulnerability, the possibility of its nonexistence: "Should [this communal portrait] cease, the village would disintegrate" (*PE* 11). It is almost as if the threatened "historical elimination" of the peasantry (the last words of the book) had worked its way into "experience," signaling an internal dislocation. "Writing," Berger says, "has no territory of its own" (*PE* 6). Is this also the case, then, for peasant storytelling? The suggestion is made. Peasant experience, a "question of place," seems inseparable from spatial and temporal continuity, from the fact that the peasant "has no choice of locality": "it is very rare for a peasant to remain a peasant and be able to move" (*PE* 11). But there is a good deal of movement in *Pig Earth*. The last and longest story, which occupies almost half the volume, revolves elliptically around the foci of its two main characters' moves beyond the village. And yet it is this story, in Berger's opinion, that goes most "deeply in the subjectivity of the lives" it narrates (*PE* 13). Here, peasant experience has become that of emigration and displacement. Like "peasantry" itself in a time when the uneven and combined development of the world economy has forced us to use "underdevelop" as a transitive verb, the "life" of the peasant seems less a residual plenitude than a fragile modern construct.

Another Way of Telling in effect makes the same point when it asks the reader to participate in the process of construction. Like Benjamin, Berger senses a threat to "experience" in the free-floating polysignification of the photograph.

"It is because the photographs carry no certain meaning in themselves, because they are like images in the memory of a total stranger, that they lend themselves to any use" (*AL* 53). In the text of *Another Way of Telling*, this danger is embodied by journalism. "A journal sends photographer x to city y to bring back pictures. Many of the finest photographs taken belong to this category. But the story told is finally about what the photographer saw at y. It is not directly about the experience of those living the event in y" (*AWT* 279). The implication is that Berger and Mohr have avoided this surrender of experience to a "total stranger" by anchoring their photographs in the imaginary life history of an old peasant woman. But once again the text is strangely fuzzy on the point of *whose* experience the narrative is faithful to: "Photographs so placed are restored to a living context: not of course to the original temporal context from which they were taken—that is impossible—but to a context of experience. And there, their ambiguity at last becomes true" (*AWT* 289). Behind the screen of "true ambiguity," the reader, invited to use his or her "memory" to arrange and rearrange the captionless photographs from a number of different countries, has supplanted the experience of the peasants themselves, which is presumably no longer strong enough to hold the fragments together. What is left of peasant experience but, in Berger's powerful expression, "images in the memory of a total stranger"?

This striking metaphor for the *absence* of experience reappears in *A Seventh Man*, where it subverts one of the work's main premises. The subtitle, *A Book of Images and Words about the Experience of Migrant Workers in Europe*, places "experience" so as to parry the blow of analytic consciousness that falls on the peasant-workers and creates an equilibrium between their subjectivity and the global meaning of migration. This meaning "can only be fully recognized," Berger says, "if an objective economic system is related to the subjective experience of those trapped within it" (*ASM* 7). In fact he has tilted the balance still further in favor of experience: it is a paradigmatic individual experience ("Departure," "Work," "Return") of migration, rather than its historical roots, analogues, repercussions, or possibilities of development, that shapes the book and dictates crucial choices of emphasis. At the same time, however, the book begins by referring to its subject as a "dream/nightmare." "By what right," it goes on, "can we call the lived experience of others a dream/nightmare?" (*ASM* 7). The characteristic redundancy "lived experience" brings into existence the alternatives of unlived experience or lived inexperience, and these are precisely what Berger proceeds to evoke: "In a dream the dreamer wills, acts, reacts, speaks, and yet submits to the unfolding of a story which he scarcely influences. The dream happens to him." (*ASM* 7). The dreamer not only cannot influence his story, he also cannot understand it. Later in the book Berger uses the metaphor in a still more intense form:

his migration is like an event in a dream dreamt by another. As a figure in a dream dreamt by an unknown dreamer, he appears to act autonomously, at times unexpectedly; but everything he does—unless he revolts—is determined by the needs of the dreamer's mind. Abandon the metaphor. The migrant's intentionality is permeated by historical necessities of which neither he nor anybody he meets is aware. That is why he acts as if his life were being dreamt by another. (*ASM* 43)

Although Berger continues to insist that "the full measure of the violence being done to [the migrant] is revealed by what happens within him" (*ASM* 166), he has shown that the meaning of the phenomenon largely exceeds what appears in the migrant's consciousness. Like the photographs of *Another Way*, the peasant-migrant's "experience" now belongs to—makes sense in—the consciousness of another. At this remove, it is perhaps no longer accurate to speak of "experience" at all.

At the end of the book, the word seems to have begun its own emigration to the metropolis. Berger has been suggesting that migrant labor in the city abolishes experience, whether because it sacrifices the present to hopes for the future or because, in so doing, it is determined by forces it cannot comprehend, and that experience could only be restored by revolt or return: "To re-become a man (husband, father, citizen, patriot) a migrant has to return home" (*ASM* 58). But having returned to his native village, the migrant discovers that "an assured place for him no longer exists," that he is now "homeless," because "his different experience is not applicable" there, because he is "a man of different experience" (*ASM* 221). Is there, then, "experience" in and of the metropolis? Is this experience only in the minimal, universal sense of what one lives through, or does the restricted sense of valuable knowledge also apply? A great deal hangs on the word. To the extent that Berger has been obliged to allow the latter sense in reference to the urban destination, he avoids falling into the familiar total rejection of modernity, accepts the lived inexperience of emigration and global determination as a (new) norm, and begins assembling the materials out of which a new mode of "global feeling" can be constructed.

III

The planned metropolitan sequel to *Pig Earth* (the projected series is entitled "Into Their Labours") might be expected to resolve some of these questions. In the meantime, we can at least specify some of the elements of a hypothetical posthumanist "experience" toward which Berger might help to move us along. To what extent can he speak of the necessity for change without speaking in the name of a known state of affairs and of known values to which life cannot in fact return? Money, for example, is unlikely to disappear as a result of any presently conceivable revolution—other than that of U.S. computer technology. But Berger sometimes speaks as if a change that did not abolish it would be no change at all, as if it stood between humanity and the experiential ground zero of being, abstracting us forever from the sensuous, qualitative immediacy of use-value and thus causing a constant daily impoverishment of subjectivity. This attitude may or may not be attributable to Marx; the case has been made for a Marx who on the contrary saw money as one symbol in a universe of symbols where all action is symbolic.[18] But in any case, it is not too soon to remove from our "common sense" its fetishizing of Being and blindness to the inevitability of symbolic action. Does Berger only hinder or also help in this removal?

The celebration of a self-sufficient peasantry entails an equal hostility to emigration and to money, and Berger often brings the three elements together in a dense metaphoric cluster that shapes arguments on various subjects. *The Success and Failure of Picasso* (1965), for example, can be read as a parable of emigration as a fall from peasant plenitude to the abstract emptiness of money. Picasso's "success" is that of a "vertical invader" (*SFP* 40) from semifeudal Spain, where "the consciousness of the average Spanish peasant" still included the wish "to destroy all money" (*SFP* 19), and where life—even among Picasso's middle class—had not yet been "depersonalized and made anonymous by the power of money" (*SFP* 21). Picasso's "failure" is the consequence, on the one hand, of the emigration to France that cut him off from his premonetary society, and on the other, of his legendary "earning power and wealth" (*SFP* 4). "The truth has become a little like the fable of Midas. Whatever Midas touched, turned into gold. Whatever Picasso puts a line around, can become his. But the fable was a comic-tragic one; Midas nearly starved because he couldn't eat gold" (*SFP* 3–4). Money, like emigration, is opposed to experience, the synonym of subject matter. Exile has brought money but no new experience to digest: "What he has lacked are subjects" (*SFP* 140). As emigrant, the wealthy artist perishes of experiential inanition.

Does this mean that neither money nor emigration can be the source of new experience? An essay called "Hals and Bankruptcy" teases a different answer out of the same metaphors. Describing a portrait by Frans Hals, Berger finds a "metaphysic of money" that has released "a new energy" and has relativized "all traditional values." It is a portrait, in effect, of money: "What distinguishes this portrait from all earlier portraits of wealthy or powerful men is its instability. Nothing is secure in its place. You have the feeling of looking at a man in a ship's cabin in a gale. . . . At the same time the portrait in no way suggests decay or disintegration. There may be a gale but the ship is sailing fast and confidently" (*AL* 163–64). This portrait of money is once again a portrait of displacement. But here experience is its fruit (the German *Erfahrung* "experience" has "travel" in it) rather than its opposite.

When Berger maintains the opposition between experience on the one hand and emigration and money on the other, he is paradoxically obliged to deny experience precisely where his evidence tells us we would find it. The emigrant leaves and works, as the inhabitants of his place of destination complain, "in order to earn and save the maximum amount of money in the shortest time" (*ASM* 163). This is an initiative he takes—"the only initiative still open to the migrant"—"for the sake of a transformed future—or his attempt to transform his future" (*ASM* 164). Berger's point, here and elsewhere, is that this involves "negligence of the present." "To make present sacrifice for the sake of the future," he nonetheless concedes, "is an essentially human act." Is it possible that "experience" supports rather than condemns the migrant, that he alone escapes the devaluation of the present that results from the absence of a future? Backtracking, Berger insists only "that the value of his present sacrifice is denied" by the society around him (*ASM* 188). And if by some chance it were acknowledged? This is by no means inconceivable—could not capitalist society recognize its own entrepreneurial myth in foreign clothing?—and yet it would seem to deprive Berger of crucial humanist leverage against emigration. In order to keep the act of emigration, which vitalizes the present by adding to it a future, from becoming the very paradigm of human experience, Berger must refuse the contingency of the future. The "wager" cannot be allowed to succeed. As a result, his analysis omits at least one striking development of the past few years. After the expulsion of a large percentage of foreign workers, the ailing European economies have in some cases made it easier for the remainder to stay on and to be reunited with their families: high investment in the job training of a smaller, better-qualified work force encourages its stabilization. Of those emigrants who gambled on staying and won, or who at any rate—like himself—*will* stay, and of the lines of action open to the ethnic mix now discovering its permanence, Berger has little to say. Commenting on the paintings of Ralph Fasanella, he offers a view of New York that amputates the city of immigrants at the (past) point when they arrived, thereby cutting off their future and our present:

> Just as capital is compelled continually to reproduce itself, so its culture is one of unending anticipation. What-is-to-come, what-is-to-be-gained empties what-is. The immigrant proletariat, unable to return home, suffering from being who they were, yearned to become, or for their children to become, American. They saw no hope but to exchange themselves for the future. And although the desperation of the wager was specifically immigrant, the mechanism has become more and more typical of developed capitalism. (*AL* 101)

Ironically, here it is Berger who, fixated on what-has-been, creates the atmosphere of "bereavement" in which, as he explains, no new experience is possible (*ASM* 177–79).

After the saving of money, the migrant's major symbolic activity is the collection of photographs. In his exile, he—like Berger—arranges images. On his walls family snapshots coexist with nudes, icons, portraits of politicians, advertising, athletes—all amply documented in the photographs of *A Seventh Man*.

Cannot this promiscuous mosaic be seen as his construction, like the book's, of a new, exiled experience? If Berger acknowledges a parallel between his writing and the stories of the village, can he avoid seeing one here?

Berger's humanism reveals its outer limits in comparison with that of Susan Sontag, whose *On Photography* (1977), like Berger's writing on the subject, is largely inspired by Walter Benjamin.[19] For Sontag, photographs are another agent of capitalism's impoverishment of direct, spontaneous experience. "As a way of certifying experience, taking photographs is also a way of refusing it by converting experience into an image, a souvenir" (*OP* 9). Because it "is essentially an act of non-intervention" (*OP* 11), because "aesthetic distance seems built into" it (*OP* 21), photography tends "to subtract feeling from something we experience at first hand" (*OP* 168). The caption, which Benjamin hoped would make the wayward photograph politically responsible, "cannot prevent any argument or moral plea which a photograph (or a series of photographs) is intended to support from being undermined by the plurality of meanings that every photograph carries, or from being qualified by the acquisitive mentality implicit in all picture-taking—and picture-collecting—and by the aesthetic relation to their subject which all photographs inevitably propose" (*OP* 109).

Plurality of meaning, observation that is also a relation of power, action that is mediated and indirect—in convicting photography of these crimes, Sontag dismisses out of hand the ineluctable conditions of (modern) action in the world. Her naive technologism rejects the modern world in the name of a prephotographic world when action was direct, meaning singular, aesthetics innocent, and when experience was immediate because ideology had not already distorted the image of what was seen. Despite the glitter of avant-garde style and allusion, and despite the frontal assaults on "humanism," this is humanism of a particularly antique and despairing sort. Next to it, Berger's "experience" acquires hidden virtues.

Compare their comments, for example, on the famous "Family of Man" exhibition organized by Edward Steichen in 1955. Sontag takes Barthes's early critique of its "myth of the human 'community' " [20] and translates it into characteristic American terms, so that the exhibition's false universality, like photography for her in general, is now accused in particular of aiding and abetting U.S. imperialism's global reach. It is "the last sigh of the Whitmanesque erotic embrace of the nation, but universalized and stripped of all demands" (*OP* 31). Its "sentimental humanism" assumes "a human condition or a human nature shared by everybody," suppressing "historically embedded differences, injustices, and conflicts" in order to make its international viewers into "citizens of World Photography all" (*OP* 32–33). Berger, who also rejects the word "humanism," takes much the same position, though with a nuance of difference that seems significant both of what he has kept of the humanist legacy and of the eventual possibilities for a posthumanist discourse. He cannot entirely dismiss the idea of "treating the existing class-divided world as if it were a family" (*AL* 5). "Steichen's intuition was absolutely correct: the private use of photographs can be exemplary for their public use." In the arrangement of photographs "as though they formed a universal family album," Berger finds both sentimental complacency and, equally important, "an alternative photographic practice":

> Photographs are relics of the past, traces of what has happened. If the living take that past upon themselves, if the past becomes an integral part of the process of people making their own history, then all photographs would reacquire a living context, they would continue to exist in time, instead of being arrested moments. It is just possible that photography is the prophecy of a human memory yet to be socially and politically achieved. Such a memory would encompass any image of the past, however tragic, however guilty, within its own continuity. The distinction between the private and the public uses of photography would be transcended. The Family of Man would exist (*AL* 57).

Although it has the frailty of prophetic abstraction, this statement is also a source of practical strength. For Sontag, experience is a past plenitude from which we have been sundered by the proliferation of photographic images, and there is little to do now but "apply the conservationist remedy" (*OP* 180), that is, allow as few as possible of them. For Berger, however, these images also invite the new practice that would in turn give them a "living context." In the mind of the "total stranger" in today's "class-divided world," they induce familiarity and make possible a new, global experience.

In Berger's humanism, experience is always also (to stay within the realm of agrarian metaphor) a field where alternative practices, like weeds, feed on the same ideological fertilizers intended to nourish the crops of hegemony. For this reason it is clearly inadequate to see the treatment of subjectivity in Berger's novels as naively realistic. If he does not routinely lay bare the workings of ideology in individual experience, it is in part because he does not *record* experience at all. The much-remarked violence of his metaphors, which never submissively bend to the subjectivity of the characters but hang awkwardly outside it, is a sign that subjectivity is being wrenched out of its normal channels, that the weeds, not the crops, are being harvested. By this violence (which can of course be read as indecorous authorial intrusion or simply as bad prose) "ordinary" experience is cultivated and made to yield up moments of apocalyptic disturbance; sex, sports, work become "exemplary" of messianic truth. Reading experience against itself without sacrificing its authority, Berger manages to politicize it. As a program for literary criticism that avoids some of the limits of a populist "Left Leavisism," this is perhaps a provisional compromise, while the discipline rethinks itself, between humanism and whatever will succeed it.

Berger himself would probably not see his attitude to experience in this Nietzschean way. With regard to photography, he prefers to view the furnishing of an "adequate context" as a move *back*—"back into the context of experience" (*AL* 61)—rather than forward. "Logically," he says, the boards to which people pin personal snapshots "should replace museums" (*WS* 30). But this logic does not carry him to the recognition that other exiles can collect photographs, as he does, in an effort to seize and hold the new world of events that occur, as he often repeats, "on a global scale." The eyes of the migrant can only be trained on his lost home. Thus the photographs of *A Seventh Man* are said to work "in the opposite way" from those of the migrants they display: "seen in this book when reading it, the image conjures up the vivid presence of the unknown boy. To his father it would define the boy's absence" (*ASM* 17). Migrants must be assumed not to require fresh information, for they are assumed not to be able to act any differently if they had it.

Like Sontag, Berger has difficulty imagining a public, international context of experience—that is, of action. When Sontag attacks photography's "false sense of ubiquity" and connects its "overview" to "our very notion of the world—the capitalist twentieth century's 'one world'" (*OP* 174), she assumes that action on a global scale is the prerogative of cosmopolitan capital. Foucault's paradigmatic suspicion of the "universal intellectual" would seem to take the same set of facts into consideration.[21] It would be possible to make a case for Berger's peasants as a Foucaldian strategic retreat to local margins: he is literally, as Paul Bové recommends, cultivating his own garden.[22] For Berger, too, all total and universal images are tainted by the powers that operate at their level. The globes that fill the paintings of the Renaissance are icons of conquest and possession, and even the photographs of worldwide atrocity to which we have become accustomed work, for the moment at least, against rather than for experience. Since there is nothing adequate to do about what one sees, Berger argues, it would be better not to see at all; the supposed stimulation of human concern in fact wears it down, turns it inward, squanders it:

> The most extreme examples . . . show moments of agony in order to extort the maximum concern. Such moments, whether photographed or not, are discontinuous with all other moments. But the reader who has been arrested by the photograph may tend to feel this discontinuity as his own personal moral inadequacy. *And as soon as this happens even his sense of shock is dispersed:* his own moral inadequacy may now shock him as much as the crimes being committed in the war. (*AL* 39–40)

Hence "the issue of the war which has caused that moment is effectively depoliticized" (*AL* 39–40). Berger wishes to curtail atrocity photos, as Matthew Arnold said he suppressed "Empedocles on Etna" from *Poems* (1853), because they find "no vent in action," because "there is everything to be suffered, nothing to be done." But this argument could also be taken as a plea for the "vent in action," the global contextualizing that would use these images and thus make "global feeling" possible. If Berger cannot provide, and does not promise, such a new "experience," he at least makes us desire it. And to say this is to say something for his humanist heritage.

NOTES

1. References to Berger's works will be given in the text. The editions and abbreviations cited are the following: *About Looking (AL)* (London: Writers and Readers, 1980); *And Our Faces, My Heart, Brief as Photos (AOF)* (New York: Pantheon, 1984); *A Painter of Our Time (APT)* (London: Writers and Readers, 1958); *A Seventh Man: Migrant Workers in Europe* (Harmondsworth: Penguin, 1975); *Permanent Red (PR)* (London: Writers and Readers, 1960); *Pig Earth (PE)* (London: Writers and Readers, 1979); *Return to My Native Land* (with Anya Bostock) (Harmondsworth: Penguin, 1969); *The Success and Failure of Picasso (SFP)* (Harmondsworth: Penguin, 1965); *Another Way of Telling (AWT)* (with Jean Mohr) (New York: Pantheon, 1982); *Ways of Seeing (WS)* Harmondsworth: Penguin, 1972).

2. Carrie Rickey, "John Berger Is a Big Deal," *Village Voice* 25.35 (1980): 31.

3. Fred Pfeil, Review of *Pig Earth* and *About Looking*, *Minnesota Review*, n.s. 15 (Fall 1980): 124. For an eloquent reminder that Berger's earlier writings do not refer exclusively to the rural past, see David E. James, "Cubism as Revolutionary Realism: John Berger and *G.,*" *Minnesota Review* n.s. 21 (Fall 1983): 92–109.

4. Pfeil, Review, 125.

5. See, for example, Edward Said, "Reflections on Recent American 'Left' Criticism," *boundary 2* 8.1 (1979): 11–30.

6. "On Ethnographic Authority," *Representations* 1.2 (1983): 118–46.

7. Raphael Samuels, ed., *People's History and Socialist Theory* (London: Routledge and Kegan Paul, 1981), xviii–xix, xxx.

8. Perry Anderson, *Arguments within English Marxism* (London: Verso, 1980): 57–58.

9. Anderson, *Arguments*, 26–28.

10. Terry Eagleton, *Criticism and Ideology* (London: New Left Books, 1976), 22. Like Anderson, Eagleton refers to but does not make central use of the distinction between *Erlebnis* and *Erfahrung* developed by Walter Benjamin. See, for example, "On Some Motifs in Baudelaire" in *Illuminations*, trans. Harry Zohn, ed. Hannah Arendt (New York: Schocken, 1969). Eagleton's own treatment of "experience" is criticized, and the concept is defended, in Ian Craib's *"Criticism and Ideology*: Theory and Experience," *Contemporary Literature* 22 (1981): 489–509.

11. Eagleton, *Criticism and Ideology*, 15, 28.

12. Raymond Williams, *Politics and Letters: Interviews with New Left Review* (London: Verso, 1979), 170.

13. Richard Johnson, "Histories of Culture/Theories of Ideology: Notes on an Impasse," *Ideology and Cultural Production*, ed. Michèle Barrett (London: Croom Helm, 1979), 51–55.

14. Terry Eagleton, *Walter Benjamin, Or Towards a Revolutionary Criticism* (London: Verso, 1981), 177.

15. Anderson, *Arguments*, 36.

16. Williams, *Politics and Letters*, 165, 170–71.

17. Terry Eagleton, "A Sort of Fiction," *New Statesman* 97 (1979): 876.

18. See Marc Shell, *The Economy of Literature* (Baltimore: Johns Hopkins Univ. Press, 1978), 39–42 and Hayden White, *Metahistory* (Baltimore: Johns Hopkins Univ. Press, 1973), 296.

19. Susan Sontag, *On Photography* (New York: Delta, 1977); hereafter cited as *OP*.

20. Roland Barthes, *Mythologies*, trans. Annette Lavers (New York: Hill and Wang, 1972), 100.

21. Michel Foucault, *Power/Knowledge: Selected Interviews and Other Writings, 1972–77*, ed. Colin Gordon (New York: Pantheon, 1980), 78–92.

22. Paul Bové, "The End of Humanism," *Humanities in Society* 3 (1980): 34–35.

Contributors

Jonathan Arac is the author of *Commissioned Spirits* (1979) and *Critical Genealogies*, forthcoming from Columbia University Press. He is Professor of English, University of Illinois at Chicago.

Paul A. Bové is Professor of English at the University of Pittsburgh. He is the author of *Destructive Poetics* (1980) and *Intellectuals in Power* (1986), both from Columbia University Press.

John Higgins has taught in the English Department of the University of Geneva (Switzerland) and now teaches at the University of Cape Town. He is completing a book on Raymond Williams to be published by Croom Helm.

Rainer Nägele, Professor of German at The Johns Hopkins University, has published books in German on Böll, Handke, and Hölderlin and has written *Reading after Freud*, forthcoming from Columbia University Press.

Andrew Parker, who teaches English literature and critical theory at Amherst College, is finishing *Re-Marx: Studies in Marxist Theory and Criticism "After Derrida."*

Dana B. Polan teaches Film and English at the University of Pittsburgh. He is the author of *The Politics of Film and the Avant-Garde* (1984) and *Power and Paranoia*, forthcoming from Columbia University Press.

Mary Louise Pratt is the author of *Toward a Speech Act Theory of Literary Discourse* (1977) and coauthor of *Linguistics for Students of Literature* (1980). She teaches in the Department of Spanish and Portuguese and the Program in Comparative Literature at Stanford University.

Bruce Robbins teaches in the Department of English at the New Brunswick campus of Rutgers University. He is the author of *The Servant's Hand* (1986) and is currently writing a historical study of the relations between rhetoric and literary criticism.

Cornel West is the author of *Prophesy Deliverance!* (1982) and coeditor of *Post-Analytic Philosophy* (1985). He is Associate Professor of Philosophy of Religion in the Divinity School, Yale University.

Index

Index

Prepared by Ruth Ross

165